ARCHAEOLOGY AND ANCIENT HISTORY

Some classicists deal with the ancient world as if archaeological evidence other than art and architecture is of little relevance to their work. This can mean that territories or subjects for which there is little textual evidence can be marginalized or not studied at all. Similarly, many historical archaeologists, dissatisfied with their ancillary role, assert that material evidence for the ancient world can and should be studied independently.

Though efforts are being made in some quarters to erode these disciplinary boundaries, in others they have become increasingly fossilized, and rifts within subjects are leading to the development of ever more isolated new sub-disciplines. While representatives of each different specialism may believe they have found the path to historical truth, the real truth is that the straitjackets of these divisions – whether generations old or fashionably novel – are stifling innovation, creativity and the possibility of illuminating the past with all the knowledge at our disposal.

This collection of pieces from a wide range of contributors explores in detail the separation of the human past into history, archaeology and their related sub-disciplines. Each piece challenges the validity of this separation and asks how we can move to a more holistic approach. While the focus is on the ancient world, particularly Greece and Rome, the lessons that emerge are significant for the study of any time and place.

Eberhard W. Sauer is lecturer in classical archaeology at the School of History and Classics, University of Edinburgh. He is also an honorary lecturer at the School of Archaeology and Ancient History, University of Leicester. Previously he was a British Academy Postdoctoral Fellow at Keble College and the Institute of Archaeology, University of Oxford.

ARCHAEOLOGY AND ANCIENT HISTORY

Breaking down the boundaries

Edited by
Eberhard W. Sauer

LONDON AND NEW YORK

First published 2004
by Routledge
11 New Fetter Lane, London EC4P 4EE

Simultaneously published in the USA and Canada
by Routledge
29 West 35th Street, New York, NY 10001

Routledge is an imprint of the Taylor & Francis Group

© 2004 selection and editorial matter, Eberhard W. Sauer;
individual chapters, the contributors

Typeset in Garamond by
Florence Production Ltd, Stoodleigh, Devon

Printed and bound in Great Britain by
The Cromwell Press, Trowbridge, Wiltshire

British Library Cataloguing in Publication Data
A catalogue record for this book is available from the British Library

Library of Congress Cataloging in Publication Data
Archaeology and ancient history: breaking down the boundaries/edited by
Eberhard W. Sauer.
Includes bibliographic references and index.
1. Archaeology and history.   2. Classical antiquities.   3. Mediterranean
Region – Antiquities.   I. Sauer, Eberhard W., 1970–
CC77.H5A685 2004
930.1–dc21   2003013490

ISBN 0–415–30199–8 (hbk)
ISBN 0–415–30201–3 (pbk)

CONTENTS

CONTENTS

FIGURES

CONTRIBUTORS

Alkis Dialismas studied at the University of Athens and is now a doctoral research student at Jesus College and the Department of Archaeology of the University of Cambridge.

Lin Foxhall was educated at Bryn Mawr College, University of Pennsylvania and the University of Liverpool. She taught at Oxford University and University College London. She is now Professor of Greek Archaeology and History at the School of Archaeology and Ancient History, University of Leicester.

Martin Henig studied at the universities of Cambridge, London and Oxford. He taught at Queen's University, Belfast, the University of East Anglia and the University of Wales, Newport. Currently he is a fellow of Wolfson College and a visiting lecturer in Roman Art at the Institute of Archaeology, University of Oxford.

Birgitta Hoffmann went to the universities of Freiburg i.Br. and Durham. She taught at the University of Manchester and University College Dublin before moving to her current post as a research fellow at the University of Liverpool's School of Archaeology, Classics and Oriental Studies.

Raimund Karl was educated at the University of Vienna. He has taught at the University of Wales at Aberystwyth where he also held a post at the Centre for Advanced Welsh and Celtic Studies. Currently he is a lecturer in Archaeology and Heritage in the Department of History and Welsh History, University of Wales, Bangor, as well as external lecturer in Celtic Studies at the University of Vienna's Department of Ancient History.

Ray Laurence studied at the universities of Wales (Lampeter) and Newcastle. He has taught at the universities of Durham, Lancaster, Manchester and Newcastle. He held a Rome Scholarship at the British School at Rome and later a British Academy Postdoctoral Research Fellowship at Reading. He is now a senior lecturer at the University of Reading's Department of Classics.

Janett Morgan is a doctoral research student in the Ancient History Division of Cardiff University's School of History and Archaeology.

Eileen M. Murphy was educated at the University of Sheffield, the University of Bradford and Queen's University, Belfast. She is now a lecturer in Osteoarchaeology and Palaeopathology at the School of Archaeology and Palaeoecology, Queen's University, Belfast.

Boris Rankov was educated at the University of Oxford, where he also held a research fellowship, and has taught at the University of Western Australia, Perth. He is currently a senior lecturer in Ancient History at Royal Holloway, University of London.

Eberhard W. Sauer studied at the universities of Tübingen, Freiburg i.Br. and Oxford. He has taught at the University of Leicester and edited this volume while holding a British Academy Postdoctoral Research Fellowship at Oxford. He is currently a lecturer in classical archaeology at the University of Edinburgh's School of History and Classics as well as an honorary lecturer at the University of Leicester's School of Archaeology and Ancient History.

ACKNOWLEDGEMENTS

This volume is based on a session on 'Breaking down boundaries: the artificial archaeology–ancient history divide' held at the Theoretical Archaeology Group Conference at Dublin on 15 December 2001. I am indebted to all contributors who travelled to Ireland for the occasion, to those who attended the session and to Dr Joanna Brück who organized the conference. Various colleagues at Leicester, where I was based when I conceived the idea for the session, provided important advice and encouragement, notably Dr Neil Christie, Professor Lin Foxhall, Dr Mark Gillings, Professor David Mattingly and Dr Rob Young. The volume was edited, and my own contributions written or substantially revised, during my tenure of a British Academy Postdoctoral Fellowship at Oxford, and I am most grateful to the British Academy for its support. Several scholars read and commented on individual papers and their help is acknowledged there. Figure 3.1, a photo by Alexandra Guest, has been reproduced with the permission of the Dr Boris Rankov (Trireme Trust). Figure 9.1 has been kindly provided by Grahame Soffe, the photographer. Figures 9.2a, 9.2b, 9.3 and 9.4 appear by permission of Oxford University's Institute of Archaeology. Figure 11.3 has been reproduced from H. Schedel, *Registrum huius operis libri cronicarum . . .* (1493): XII [Douce 304], with kind permission of the Bodleian Library, University of Oxford. We are grateful to Susan Harris for help with the latter. Figures 2.1, 4.1, 11.1 and 11.2 are those of the authors. We would like to thank Richard Stoneman, Catherine Bousfield, Oliver Escritt, Alan Fidler, Linda Paulus and Celia Tedd for all their essential encouragement, help and editorial efforts in seeing the book through to press.

Part I

GENERAL

1

INTRODUCTION

Eberhard W. Sauer[1]

Are the archaeology and history of the ancient world two disciplines that can be studied genuinely in isolation from each other – one based on the investigation of material culture, the other on texts? If so, do all data, questions and phenomena neatly fall into the competence of one or the other? If not, where precisely do we draw the line? Or, if there is no sharp division, how far may either group incorporate the other's data or results (and the grey zone in between) while still maintaining a clear, separate identity? Are archaeology and history of equal status or is one a source-studying discipline that provides data for wider synthesis by the other – and, in the latter case, how can this attribution of roles be justified logically? What are the differences in the quality of the data they provide in terms of geographical and thematic coverage, accessibility, veracity or distortion, and to what extent can they therefore be understood in isolation from each other? Is the separation of the two an ideal to be sought and to be defended – and, if so, why? Or is it based on mere pragmatism? In the latter case, is this separation necessary to achieve a perfect methodology or merely an excuse for laziness allowing the scholar to avoid studying a substantial proportion of the relevant evidence? If, however, it is indeed considered necessary to divide the study of the human past into separate disciplines because of the sheer quantity of information, should method be our first criterion for defining those disciplines? Are not other ordering principles (such as geography, chronology and subject matter, or a combination of these) just as valid? Is there one right and one wrong way at all or would it be more fruitful to employ a multiplicity of approaches rather than, mainly, the traditional ones?

Is more interdisciplinary dialogue the way to overcome divisions, or is this a mere 'red herring' to distract us from the real problem – namely, that in order to have an '*inter*disciplinary' dialogue in the first place we have to take sides and thus need to maintain our division into different opposing camps? In other words: do we have to decide whether we are historians who tell archaeologists what they can learn from textual sources, *or* archaeologists who tell historians what they can learn from material culture, in this *inter*disciplinary dialogue – while none of us must ever learn the lesson and pay equal attention to both types of evidence? Or, if we do, what are we, and how can we logically justify preserving separate identities while we ourselves no longer neatly fall into one category or the other? Should we not rather ask whether or not there is any intrinsically logical reason for our institutional separation in the first place?

It is astonishing how seldom these crucial questions are asked. Instead, implicit assumptions about what does and does not form part of a specific discipline frequently become the basis of subject definitions at university level, while the endeavour is seldom made to provide a logical explanation. Of course, it might be objected that every field of knowledge is somehow related to other fields and that in order to create disciplines of manageable size some arbitrary decisions have to be taken. There is no attempt here to deny that a discipline is defined according to our own criteria and not natural law, yet it is equally clear that definitions can vary according to the coherence of what is grouped together and to the quality of the answers the disciplines so created are likely to provide. On the premise that archaeology and history are trying to answer the same questions and are separated merely by method, the question indeed must be allowed whether the exclusion of a part of the evidence available for a specific research problem is likely to produce more accurate, reliable and complete answers.

It was to explore whether or not the very existence of history and archaeology as separate disciplines could be justified that a session was organized at the Theoretical Archaeology Group Conference in Dublin in 2001 under the deliberately provocative title: 'Breaking down boundaries: the artificial archaeology–ancient history divide'. This monograph contains exclusively contributions based on papers delivered at this session and is complete except for John Moreland's paper on 'Archaeology and text', which went far beyond his recent synonymous book (2001). We greatly regret that, because of other urgent commitments, he decided early on not to submit a written version of this splendid paper.

The contributors to this volume vary in their background and training: at the moment three of us are nominally attached to archaeology departments, four to history, ancient history or classics departments, two to the ancient history division of joint schools and one to an undivided joint school. Some of us read classical texts in the original language, some do not; some carry out archaeological fieldwork, some do not; some, indeed, do both. While we are all currently based in the British Isles, there are five different nationalities represented amongst us and some of us have studied or taught in more than one country. We thus bring a range of different experiences to bear on a multi-faceted problem and thus offer different perspectives.

It is inevitable that in choosing whom to invite, there was a preference for those who had expressed opinions on the subject before (though, unfortunately, several of them were unable to come and contribute). Even though participation was open and not dependent on subscription to any particular ideology, it can also come as no surprise that those who were attracted to offer papers independently after having read the abstract for the session on the web, were again those who had some sympathy for the proposition rather than being fiercely opposed to it or apathetic. (The former group, incidentally, accounts for five, the latter for four of the contributors, John Moreland and myself excluded.) There is thus no claim here that the contributors form a statistically representative sample of views on the matter within the academic community, nor was it ever intended to achieve this. Equally it would be wrong, however, to assume that we are all just 'singing from the same hymn sheet'. Indeed, while no hard-line advocate of the *status quo* offered to contribute, the differences between us are quite substantial. There is no agreement amongst us, for example, as to how far we should go in integrating archaeological and textual evidence. Rankov argues that separate disciplinary identities should be maintained to safeguard standards and to allow us to test the independently achieved results against each other. At the same time he urges us to have the humility to recognize that other disciplines may force us to overrule the perceived wisdom in our own discipline. Several other contributors, by contrast, would go much further towards integration; indeed, I myself make no secret of my view that in an ideal world such divisions would be abolished. Dialismas shares Rankov's scepticism that a single scholar can be in control of archaeological and textual evidence and argues in favour of analysing archaeological and historical data independently and only bringing them together at the level of synthesis.

Yet there are also important points on which we all agree, notably that it would be beneficial to integrate archaeological and historical evidence more fully and that it is important to pursue the question of how this can be achieved rather than just carrying on as before in our small worlds. We also all favour a multiplicity of approaches rather than 'defending' the wisdom of one disciplinary approach passed down over generations and accepted as unquestioned truth. None of us would doubt that some specialization is necessary, yet several of us express concerns about the tendency of only specializing within traditional units, rather than transcending them, thus further cementing conventional views as to what is and what is not relevant and related to each other. Henig, for example, makes a powerful case that the art and archaeology of the north-west of the *united* Roman Empire has been sidetracked and ignored by many Mediterranean-centred art historians and archaeologists for no reasons other than prejudice. This is so indefensible on a rational basis that those responsible for this omission scarcely acknowledge it, let alone even try to find a logical justification. It is certainly not the fact that scholars specialize in a particular geographic area *per se* that Henig and I would object to; if they pretend, however, that it can be understood in isolation, show little interest for closely related phenomena elsewhere or make an arbitrarily defined area, be it Britain, Germany, Italy or the Mediterranean, stand for something much grander, such as the whole of the Roman Empire, they should be asked to think again.

All of us would agree that archaeologists and historians can learn from one another rather than just one side from the other. Even if our examples vary in the emphasis they place on the neglect of either textual or material evidence, it is not possible to identify two distinctive groups who advocate either at the exclusion of the other (and we would have failed our target if there had been two such groups). Indeed, our views are complex and cannot easily be subdivided into those supporting or opposing any one proposition. For this reason a conventional chronological and geographical structure has been adopted. My general paper is followed by those which deal with the Greek world, which in turn are followed by those concerned with the Roman world. The final section deals with neighbouring cultures, not because we consider these marginal or less relevant, but because they, and the Celts in particular, cannot neatly be fitted into either the Greek or the Roman world.

Our emphasis on the ancient western world (broadly defined) here should not imply that we consider developments elsewhere (in Han China, for example) or in other periods of history and historical archaeology (such as the Middle Ages) to be less relevant. Yet, in keeping to the above principle that it is sometimes necessary to specialize, as long as the definition of the study area is as coherent as can reasonably be achieved, it was felt that the western world in Graeco-Roman antiquity, including some of its neighbours as well as the transition to the Middle Ages and relevant comparative evidence from other periods, fulfils this criterion (though there would, of course, have been infinite possibilities to shift the chronological and geographical parameters to define a different, but similarly coherent area).

My general paper explores (with negative results) whether coherent definitions of archaeology and history as separate subjects that provide full answers to the questions under examination and are yet sufficiently different from each other are possible. It tries to place the subject in a global perspective and is not confined to any particular period of history. It advocates on a deliberately idealistic level that the boundaries between the 'two disciplines' and those between their respective sub-disciplines should be broken down and that areas of specialization should be as varied as possible without any institutional pressure to stay on either side of the fence.

The ten papers with a specific chronological and geographic focus explore related questions:

- if and how the divide between history and archaeology and related disciplinary boundaries within them have affected research in these specific subjects in the past and present;
- how these boundaries came into being or how they became 'fossilized';

6

- whether or not there is any logical justification for these boundaries, and
  (a) if so, what (and what risks, if any, might their dissolution involve),
  (b) if not, what could be gained from overcoming them with concrete examples from the period under examination; and
- what would be the most suitable way forward: closer co-operation (and, if so, how and at what level) or adoption of the methods of the 'other' discipline by archaeologists and historians themselves?

Not all papers deal with every one of the above questions; Henig, for example, places considerable emphasis on the history of disciplinary separatism while most other contributions are concerned mainly with the recent past (and future) of the phenomenon. All, however, focus on several of these central questions, and there is no contribution which merely includes textual and material evidence without discussing the relationship of history and archaeology. Neither is any paper confined to generalities, but each places the discussion in the specific context of the period under examination and provides one or more concrete case studies.

The Greek section is introduced by Boris Rankov's chapter on the *Olympias* project, a perfect example of a highly complex interdisciplinary project which is by no means just restricted to the relationship between history and archaeology. A wide range of experts in different fields contributed to this reconstruction of an ancient warship. Unlike in normal academic debate between representatives of different disciplines, in such a project it was impossible simply to agree to disagree where separate categories of evidence seemed to suggest different solutions if one ever wanted to see the ship afloat. Decisions on every constructional detail had to be reached, forcing the experts to be as open-minded as possible towards the contributions of other specialists in order to reach a workable consensus. Where they remained at loggerheads, the organizers had to take sides as to who was more likely to be right or wrong. The very complexity of the task leads Rankov to conclude that disciplinary identities should be maintained rather than broken down. In his view this allows an individual to master a discipline and thus to check the results reached independently against each other. However, it was also important that the key participants were experts in more than just one field, or at least had an exceptionally broad expertise so that they could develop a mindset open to question the received wisdom in their own discipline. This is a crucial observation; indeed, Rankov points out that the greatest obstacle to interdisciplinarity is subject pride, the belief in the received wisdom of one's own discipline, allowing others merely to fill in the gaps but never to compete on an equal level and challenge opinions formed on the basis of one's 'own' sources. Laurence, incidentally, equally sees such pride as a major hurdle for integration and key reason for academic isolationism; it is perpetuated through training in competitive university departments too proud to concede that another discipline can make valuable contributions to solving one's 'own' questions.

Rankov thus argues that while the methodological vigour of a discipline should not be watered down, it is indeed possible to be an expert in more than one discipline and that academics should be sufficiently familiar with neighbouring disciplines, and open-minded towards them, to recognize where their contribution may overrule conclusions drawn on the basis of the evidence provided by their own. Rankov's strategy may well have a greater chance of leading to the dissolution of the boundaries in the short term than the idealistic and more radical demand, advocated by myself, of abolishing the history–archaeology divide altogether – whether or not the latter is our long-term goal.

Rankov's view that some division of labour between the disciplines is necessary because of the sheer quantity and complexity of the different sources of information is shared by Alkis Dialismas. He argues for a separate analysis of the data, but for an integration of all evidence at the level of wider inter-pretation and synthesis. Indeed, explosion of information is no excuse for ignoring archaeological or historical evidence at this level. If both historians and archaeologists are capable of making borrowings and of being inspired by influences from a range of other disciplines, why is it fashionable just to stress the differences between these two uniquely close subjects? Dialismas covers the transition between the Late Bronze Age and the Early Iron Age in the Aegean. Not only is this the earliest period included in this volume, but the coverage by written sources is sporadic and problematic, there are gaps of several centuries and the Homeric poems were written down long after the period under consideration and represent an amalgam of real and imagined elements from different epochs. It is thus, he argues, very much a period at the transition between prehistory and history. He postulates that written testimonies are useful as analogies even for prehistorians. This is particularly true if the culture under examination is in close geographical and chronological proximity to that covered by the sources, which are thus more likely to reflect circumstances at the time than the average ethnological analogy (a case also powerfully supported by Karl in his contribution on Celtoscepticism). Incidentally, Dialismas points out that ethnologists do not produce separate descriptions of a culture under examination, one solely based on material evidence, the other on written or oral sources. Should archaeol-ogists and historians not follow their example?

Yet, are the fundamental aims of archaeology and history really the same? This is one of the central questions Lin Foxhall explores in her paper. Foxhall's chronological focus is later than that of Dialismas and her period is gener-ally much more extensively and reliably covered by written sources. Nevertheless, she demonstrates that it is not easy, often indeed impossible, to link rural sites, for example, identified through survey or excavation with information on ownership patterns provided by literary texts. The latter are

not specific enough, tend to lack any topographical precision and are sometimes no more than general *topoi*. This is in sharp contrast, for instance, to
vernacular housing in sixteenth- and seventeenth-century rural Suffolk
where it has been possible to link specific types of houses with individuals
of known profession and social status. Thus in principle the aims of archaeological and historical research are the same; only in classical Greece (and in
antiquity in general) the questions which the material and textual evidence
allows us to answer are often not identical. Is this an argument for maintaining the current division between archaeology and history? Quite on the
contrary, an awareness of both types of evidence is essential to avoid using
the evidence provided by the 'other' discipline in a much more uncritical
manner than that of the 'own' (a conclusion similar to the one reached by
Hoffmann on the basis of her case study in Roman Britain). Crucially, Foxhall
concludes that we need to 'develop our awareness of the full range of evidence
for the Greek past' and, as she demonstrates amply, neither material culture
nor texts have the capacity to furnish us with anything like the complete
picture in this period.

Janett Morgan provides another survey of the relationship between history
and archaeology in Greek antiquity, yet with a very different focus. Morgan
scrutinizes the implicit assumptions and political agendas which underlie
ideologies about the greater importance either of the literary wisdom versus
material culture, or of idealized works of art divorced from their contexts versus ordinary objects, or of the objective 'science' of archaeology
versus distorted elitist, if not fictional, texts. This results in the mutually
exclusive claims of the disciplines about the primacy of their evidence.
Morgan exposes the hollowness of such assumptions and stresses that all
types of evidence require interpretation; none provides the undistorted truth.
'A divided discipline', she warns us, 'is more vulnerable to the academic
agendas of individuals with strong beliefs about the past.' Interestingly, the
same conclusion is, once again, reached independently by a second contrib-
utor: Karl points out that politically correct Celtoscepticism could only
develop once archaeology had 'freed' itself from textual evidence, proclaimed
'irrelevant', which would have made it much more difficult to shape the past
in ways that suited the political agendas of the present. The theories stressing
alleged high levels of resistance against imperial rule throughout Roman
history, and discussed in my contribution, equally have to be seen in the
context of modern views on imperialism. Failure or unwillingness to differentiate between the levels of discontent in different empires and their colonies
or provinces as a result of our general dislike of imperialism in any shape
or form has again been facilitated by an exclusion of parts of the evidence
(e.g. by looking at the north-west of the Empire in isolation). Whether the
past is used to support morally reprehensible political ideals (Morgan refers
to cases of modern nationalism and military aggression) or to educate us
about the dangers of nationalism (the good intention of Celtosceptics in

Karl's view), they both draw our attention to the dangers of consciously or unconsciously distorting the past to propagate our own political views (and to the fact that the history–archaeology division leaves more room for pushing the evidence in the direction we like). Even if our political mission is benign and beyond reproach, are we not sawing off the branch on which we sit if we do not do the utmost to make sure that our 'supporting evidence' stands up to scrutiny? Yet there is a positive as well as a negative side to the multiplicity of approaches, including interdisciplinary ones, in Morgan's view. They not only keep the past relevant but also prevent the dominance of any single dogma. This is an important point: perhaps we need not be too worried about researchers using the past to promote their own political agendas (if these do not go beyond accepted norms), as long as we find ways to ensure that they are not allowed to silence those who disagree.

The Roman section starts as the Greek ends with a 'celebration of . . . pluralism'. Ray Laurence, like Morgan, argues that there is not just one right way to approach the past. This does not mean, of course, that either of them proposes an unreserved celebration of all approaches. Indeed, in his general overview of Roman archaeology and ancient history Laurence draws our attention to the dangers inherent in the ideology that separate single-disciplinary approaches to the past should be adopted. No subject, he argues persuasively, can afford to shut itself off from related evidence or inspirations and stimuli for its interpretation provided by other disciplines. Laurence pays particular attention to the way the division is influenced by the current power structure of higher education in the UK, and he shows how this cements disciplinary separatism, despite a popular demand for joint approaches. The public is often blissfully unaware of the fact that there are two factions of researchers who study the same past in such institutionalized different ways. Such public incomprehension may reflect the illogicality of the division rather than ignorance. Indeed, while there is not necessarily a need to interact in the most basic study of the primary evidence (e.g. fieldwork and textual analysis), the very idea that it is possible to analyse archaeological and historical evidence in total separation and then somehow to compare the results is based on ideology rather than on any coherent argument. The impossibility of a clear separation of these two categories of evidence is also discussed in my general contribution. While many would disagree with Laurence and myself that it is both undesirable and illusory in practice to study the evidence at any level independently, those who wish to prove us wrong should attempt to write a book on the archaeology of the Roman Empire devoid of all textual evidence or any conclusions derived from textual sources, however indirectly; such a book would, incidentally, already have to omit the words 'Roman' and 'Empire' from the title, and the very concepts of imperial rule and of being Roman in all its multiple meanings from the discussion. If it is stifling progress even to attempt to keep the 'disciplines' apart, and if we follow Foxhall's advice that it is often impossible to ask the same questions of different types of evidence, how can a successful integration be achieved? Laurence advocates that focusing attention on new questions which make it easier to join up archaeology and history is one way of bridging the disciplinary divide and that models derived from recent research in sociology can help in formulating such questions (e.g. by refocusing attention away from how people lived and towards what the conception of dwelling meant).

Laurence and Foxhall certainly have a very strong case that in many instances it is not possible to link the archaeological and historical evidence directly, that one needs to be aware of the limitations, and that new ways of bridging the divide can be highly productive. Nevertheless, it is worth adding that in many other cases archaeological and historical evidence indeed perfectly complement each other and that a combination of the two allows us to answer some very specific questions or to paint the wider picture. This observation, of course, in no way contradicts Foxhall and Laurence, but provides merely a change in emphasis. One of the examples examined in my paper on the Roman period is the question of where Rome suffered its most momentous military defeat in Germany – the famous Varian disaster. Only a combination of discoveries on the ground and the archaeological and statistical interpretations of (historically datable) coins against the background of the literary sources provides the answer. The first to provide a correct interpretation was Mommsen on the basis of his open-mindedness towards, and familiarity with, a wide range of different categories of evidence. By choosing a nineteenth-century obsession, namely the search for the location of a specific battlefield as an example, I am sticking my neck out in a way that is bound to earn me the reputation of being 'old-fashioned'. Yet, as pointed out in my introductory contribution, the current dislike of narrative elements in history is in my view (and that of Anthony Giddens, incidentally) misguided and, more importantly, near suicidal if we want to do everything possible to capture the fascination of the public who, after all, is providing the finances for research. Disciplinary separatism, incidentally, is not a phenomenon in any way related to current fashion and is equally found amongst traditionalists and modernizers in 'different' disciplines and across the world. Besides arguing against a division of scholars on the basis of methodological criteria, I equally oppose the arbitrary division of territories which formed political units in the ancient world into separate study regions which are examined as if they had nothing to do with each other. The fragmentation of the Roman Empire in modern research can lead to misinterpretation and makes it more difficult to grasp and to convey to the public why the Roman period still matters to us today.

The theme of territorial division of the Roman Empire is further developed by Martin Henig. Henig's study is particularly powerful as it draws on extensive personal experience and challenges fundamental concepts about the definition of university disciplines. Why is it that the art and archaeology

11

of the Mediterranean are often taught as if it was a world of its own (with many sub-worlds within it) and with no relation whatever with what happened at the same time and within the same empire in Britain? We should not 'privilege one part of the ancient world as opposed to another, even if the productions of one area please an average viewer more than those of another', he urges us. 'An "art historian" is, after all, a historian and not an aesthete.' The very fact that Henig often has to argue on an anecdotal level is due to the fact that those who follow this ideology have not normally been brave enough to try to find a rational explanation for this solely arbitrary subdivision of the ancient world and to put it in print – if they are conscious of it at all. Romano-British archaeologists, perhaps partially because they resent their study area being sidetracked by those who have no time to spare for its 'inferior' art and architecture, have largely abandoned any interest in art, whether Mediterranean or 'peripheral'. This leaves Romano-British art as a field virtually nobody feels responsible for and at the very margins of all disciplines. Henig explores the history of this divide: a chapter full of insights that makes depressing reading.

Britain is also the focus of the second geographic case study within the Roman section. Roman Britain cannot boast excessive coverage by written sources; there are fewer passages in literature and fewer inscriptions on stone than are available for most other parts of the Empire of similar size and similar estimated population. The recent discoveries of significant numbers of wooden writing and leaden curse tablets have gone some way to redress the balance, but written coverage is still sketchy, with major geographic, chronological and thematic gaps – probably the main reason why many literature-centred classicists pay little, if any, attention to the island (following the example set by Roman art historians, even if for different reasons). All the more has Tacitus' *Agricola*, the longest surviving literary source for Roman Britain, been 'milked', by archaeologists more than ancient historians, for any scrap of information it might provide. And it is this central text which is the subject of Birgitta Hoffmann's study. Hoffmann observes that in recent decades the gulf between classical philologists (who are mostly uninterested in Romano-British archaeology) and archaeologists (who increasingly lack training in classical languages or in-depth knowledge of the political history of the centre of the Empire) has widened. Nowadays most archaeologists read the *Agricola* exclusively in translation. All contributors to this volume would probably agree that this in itself is commendable, or at least preferable to ignoring it altogether as some single-disciplinary purists would have us do. Yet Hoffmann is able to demonstrate that a sophisticated understanding of the structural details of this work of literature is a considerable advantage in assessing the reliability of individual passages. She points in particular to the dangers in relying on Tacitus' work to provide us with a 'hyper-exact chronological framework' for individual sites. Tree-ring dates, assemblages of small finds and multiple phases of occupation point to a much more complex military history of northern Britain, with some major advances pre-dating Agricola's arrival. Hoffmann does not advocate that Roman archaeologists should acquire the skills needed for an in-depth study of Latin literature (even though she herself is a living example of the ability of an individual to provide a sophisticated interpretation of classical texts and of practical fieldwork). Yet there should be a closer collaboration with classics to overcome the current rift between the disciplines. Despite her criticism of an over-reliance on this structurally elaborate work of literature in reconstructing the details of the history of the military occupation of northern Britain, Hoffmann considers the *Agricola* by no means to be irrelevant. Amongst other insights, Tacitus' *Germania* and *Agricola* 'add substantially to our understanding of the Roman aristocracy's view of the outlying, exotic Roman provinces . . .'

Should we be equally sceptical about all information provided by ancient literary sources about 'exotic' areas and cultures? Such a 'one-size-fits-all approach' may well suit the agendas of those archaeologists who would like to ignore textual evidence, be it for reasons of convenience or to be 'freer' in their interpretations – and, similarly, the agendas of classicists who would rather avoid exploring whether or not there might be any material evidence for pieces of information that seem implausible or uninteresting to them. It is, however, precisely because of the complexity of written sources that we need to be open-minded. Hoffmann and Foxhall rightly warn us that we should not uncritically take every detail as a factual account and, in particular, that we should be cautious in applying such information to different contexts.

Neither, however, should we discount the possibility out of hand that seemingly invented passages in ancient literary texts could have a core of truth, or that cultural practices or the social structure of communities could have been very similar in neighbouring societies and might have changed little for a very long time. Eileen Murphy and Raimund Karl examine the Scythians, related groups and their neighbours, and the Celts who lived at the periphery of the world known to classical authors – though the Celts, more than the Scythians, were known to some of them through travel and personal observation. If we should be so sceptical to what is, on the surface, a plausible and coherent account by Tacitus, how much more should we be wary of Herodotus' reports on goat-footed and one-eyed peoples living beyond the main group of the Scythians which, at first sight, appear to be the products of fairy tales without any conceivable foundation in fact? Eileen Murphy, however, makes the attractive suggestion that specific 'malformations' (in these instances clubfoot deformity and cases of an enlarged and protruding eyeball or a reduced or absent eye) observed amongst the skeletal remains of burials in relevant parts of Eurasia could have sparked such rumours. One is tempted to agree with Murphy that it is indeed more plausible to assume Herodotus based these accounts on rumours which contained a factual core rather than on pure inventions. Indeed, Murphy makes a powerful case that humans with 'malformations' have always attracted exceptional attention amongst their contemporaries, especially if the observer came from an environment where there were no such individuals. It is well known that infanticide was widespread in classical antiquity, and Murphy suggests that in Greece such unfortunate human beings would have been eliminated at birth. All the more must the sight have left a lasting impression on those who had not previously seen adults with such bodily 'deformities', and probably not even babies whose lives would have been ended before there was an opportunity for the public to see them. As such Murphy's account is much more important than merely helping to explain the odd passage in the work of a single classical author. It confronts us directly with the brutal reality as to how disability was probably dealt with in Greece and with the differences between the classical Greek world and the 'uncivilized'(?) inhabitants of northern Eurasia. No classicist should ignore such research merely because it is based on human remains rather than on adored works of literature or masterpieces of art.

Some of the skeletal remains examined by Murphy, however, date to the centuries after Herodotus and some might ask whether this constitutes yet another case of literary evidence being applied out of context. Not all, but many customs, however, have a remarkable longevity and, as long as there is no evidence to the contrary, it seems perfectly possible that some of the cultural practices amongst the Scythians and their neighbours reported by Herodotus are likely to have continued for some time beyond the compilation of his work; the attitude to disability may well have been one of them. Equally, considering the ease of movement and the absence of significant natural barriers between eastern Europe and central Asia, there is no strong reason to rule out the possibility that many customs were practised over extensive territories.

That archaeologists have been over-cautious in claiming that it would be wrong to apply any piece of information to a different period or geographic area than the one described is a theme which Raimund Karl takes up in his chapter criticizing Celtoscepticism. Can it really be coincidence that druids and bards are described in classical Roman sources and again in medieval Irish and Welsh texts with almost identical terms and with very similar functions, while we are meant to believe that there cannot possibly be any element of continuity? Karl is, of course, fully aware that there was no such thing as a monolithic Celtic bloc, but that there were many shared elements in social and political structures and language with neighbouring communities as there were variations within what has traditionally been considered to be the Celtic world.

It has always struck me (without meaning to impose this view on Karl) that trying to deconstruct the 'Celts' is similar to any attempt today to deny that the 'Arabs' exist. Surely they form no monolithic bloc in terms of their culture, ethnicity, political and social structure and not even language and religion; but what, if anything, would be gained by abolishing the term? Celtosceptics might counter that in one case there is incontrovertible evidence for self-definition and in the other there is not. Yet, since there are no ancient written documents in which members of the communities in question elaborate on their ethnic identity we simply cannot know how they would have defined themselves. If we followed similar arguments we would have to abolish the ancient Germans, Scythians and, indeed, the vast majority of ancient ethnonyms applied to the members of illiterate, or largely illiterate, societies. It seems more useful to me to raise awareness of the limitations of ancient terminology rather than to embark upon the Sisyphean task of 'purifying' it.

Karl, however, is able to demonstrate that far more is at stake than simple terminology. He exposes blatant errors in the treatment of textual evidence by John Collis: Collis considers Caesar's *Gallic War* to be so irrelevant that it is not even necessary for him to read and examine it in translation to prove that it is indeed as irrelevant as he claims it to be: a classic case of a circular argument. That this gives Collis the authority to postulate that a classical author's knowledge of how societies functioned is limited in comparison with our own is highly questionable, as Karl points out, especially in the case of Caesar who spent almost a decade, albeit with interruptions, in Gaul. Caesar had, of course, a political agenda, but this is a different matter and cannot be attributed to his limited understanding. Celtoscepticism, Karl argues, is no more than a convenient excuse for ignoring non-archaeological evidence. It does not lead to a more sophisticated understanding of the societies under examination but to one that is more one-sided and obscures or fails to take into account many essential elements for reasons of convenience and political correctness (as discussed above). There is a tendency that new approaches are thought to be superior to the ones they supersede, or try to supersede, for no reason other than novelty. Yet, as the contributors to this volume have repeatedly shown, new, modern and 'fashionable' approaches are neither inherently more nor less likely to lead to correct interpretations than old, traditional and 'old-fashioned' ones. The difference lies in the range of evidence which is considered and the open-mindedness towards it. Narrow approaches (new or old) are less likely to provide accurate and complete answers than those which fully take into account all testimonies and their real, but not merely postulated, limitations.

We hope that the diversity of our thoughts will stimulate debate, at least amongst the open-minded or sympathetic, more than would a single-authored monograph containing just one opinion and perspective. There is certainly agreement amongst contributors that the problems need to be discussed – enough to justify the risk that those who prefer the *status quo* will selectively quote statements which stress some advantages in pursuing separate approaches or which point to disagreements amongst ourselves. The argument is often provocative and deliberately so: it is our intention not to offend, but to challenge those who disagree or who have not previously seen the fragmentation of the study of the human past as a major issue to come up with counterarguments or to change their minds. We hope that even if not all readers would go as far as some of us, they may still reconsider their position and go a step further towards integration as opposed to further separation. A few discrete and bland hints between the lines would have served no purpose and would have had no effect. Yet, in daring to tackle delicate issues related to subject pride and even individual pride in a candid manner, one faces an unenviable choice. Failure to provide specific examples for an alleged shortcoming exposes one to the charge of breaking down an open door (i.e. criticizing something nobody does or advocates anyway), while providing specific examples can be seen as offensive. Indeed, questioning established research traditions, especially by anybody less than the Nestor of the respective discipline, can easily expose oneself to the accusation of arrogance. Yet, given the alternatives of being considered arrogant or making unsubstantiated claims, we really have no choice other than to be 'arrogant'. We hope that those who disagree, and are not won over by our arguments, will at least agree that it is an issue worth airing and discussing rather leaving the definition of the disciplines to be based on implicit assumptions. In the spirit of a joint search for the right way forward, they will hopefully forgive us wherever they feel that any one of us has overstepped the mark in our criticism of current practice.

Note

1   This chapter has considerably benefited from valuable improvements and suggestions made by Dr Peter Haarer and Dr Martin Henig, who both read and commented on it.
2   The abbreviations for classical authors used in this volume are those listed in Hornblower, S. and Spawforth, A. (eds) (1996) *The Oxford Classical Dictionary* (3rd edn), Oxford and New York: Oxford University Press: xxix–liv.

Bibliography

Moreland, J. (2001) *Archaeology and Text*, London: Duckworth.

2

THE DISUNITED SUBJECT

Human history's split into 'history' and 'archaeology'

Eberhard W. Sauer[1]

'History' and 'archaeology', and many specialist subjects within these (two disciplines), are taught at most universities all over the world as if they were subjects in their own right. And, indeed, there are many who firmly believe that they are: 'The fact it co-operates with history makes archaeology no more a kind of history . . . than contacts with men make horses human, or vice versa. Archaeology is archaeology, is archaeology' (Klejn 2001: 39).

The same author reiterates this credo as the first of his twenty-five 'commandments [*sic*!] . . . to the members of L. S. Klejn's seminars':

> Archaeology is not history armed with a spade, but a detective story in which the investigator has arrived at the scene a thousand years late. History is pronounced later by judges. So you must decide: to go in for one or for the other.
>
> (Klejn 2001: 132)

Yet the question must be allowed as to *why* researchers into the past are subdivided into two distinct factions – those who deal with the written sources and those who focus on the material evidence for human history. The fundamental questions asked by both are identical; it could be argued that the sole difference lies in the sources of information that are neglected in attempting to answer them. This may appear to be self-evident to some scholars (but by no means all) who do indeed try to take all the evidence into consideration. Then, however, the question arises for what purpose the boundary between the 'two disciplines' is maintained (or, indeed, the boundaries between specialist subjects within them).

This chapter is not focused on any one particular country, but tries to adopt a global perspective. It is undeniable, of course, that there are differences between countries, since it is not easy to break away from established research traditions (cf. Dyson 1998: 284–5). But the tendencies I am arguing against do not all cluster in any particular part of the world; some are stronger in one country, some in another; indeed, the differences within one country between approaches within various specialist subjects and between individual scholars are often greater than national differences.

Equally, a second possible misunderstanding has to be pointed out from the start. Disciplinary separatism can be driven by pragmatism (cf. Carver 2002: 489–90), quite irrespective of whether or not there is a genuine belief that division will produce better research, as Ian Hodder, for example, states quite explicitly:

> as archaeology has expanded over recent decades it has increasingly been able to define itself as a discipline independent of history and Classical studies. In order to establish a professional institute or a university department of archaeology it is important to be able to demonstrate distinctive methods, bodies of data and bodies of theory.
>
> (Hodder 1991: 7)

This chapter, by contrast, is about breaking down boundaries at an ideal-istic level, not about preventing expansion, let alone providing justification for downsizing. In largely state-funded university systems there is a risk that melding disciplines together could be misused as an excuse for cutting jobs or funding in what is 'only' a single (but a much wider) subject. At a time when the monuments and old traditions of our past are disappearing faster than ever (while only a fraction can be recorded), this is a risk which must be avoided at all costs. It is certainly not a price worth paying for the unifi-cation of historical and archaeological disciplines which is advocated here. Unification, we should note, must be distinguished from subordination of one discipline to another, which is even less desirable than division.

What is archaeology?

Archaeology is today normally defined as the exclusive investigation of material culture. Symptomatic, for example, is the definition provided by Renfrew and Bahn in their recent introduction to the subject:

> *Archaeology* is the 'past tense of cultural anthropology.' Whereas cultural anthropologists will often base their conclusions on the experience of actually living within contemporary communities, archaeologists study past societies primarily through their material remains – the buildings, tools, and other artifacts that constitute what is known as the *material culture* left over from former societies.
>
> (Renfrew and Bahn 1996: 11)

18

Whether the first part of the definition is correct is open to debate since, unlike cultural anthropologists, archaeologists of historic periods who adhere to the second part of the definition (i.e. focus on material culture, but not on textual sources) deny themselves an important part of the evidence available for their field of study. This is further explored by Dialismas below. The second part of the above statement, namely that archaeologists examine primarily or exclusively 'material remains . . . left over from former societies', is much more widely used to define the subject matter of archaeology.

Many are unconscious of the fact that this is not the original sense of the term. The meaning of the Greek word *archaiología* (ἀρχαιολογία) is 'ancient history' (from the perspective of the classical world), and can refer both to legends and to facts (Stephanus 1831–56: 2095–6, with references; cf. Liddell and Scott 1996: 251). The Greek word *historía* (ἱστορία) is used to describe an inquiry or scientific observation, as well as the history of past events (the result of such investigations), occasionally again including those of a mythical nature (Liddell and Scott 1996: 842, with references). There is thus a greater emphasis on the general scholarly method in *historía*, and a more specific description of subject matter in *archaiología*. As far as the period of interest is concerned *historía* could be employed for a narrative account of the past irrespective of chronological distance. It is worth noting, however, that some literary figures used both the Greek word and its Latin equivalent, *historia* or the plural *historiae* (as opposed to annals, *annales*), specifically for contemporary history or for accounts of a period the writer (Tacitus for example) had consciously experienced during his own lifetime (Gell., *NA* 5.18.1–6; Hose 1998).

There is no space here to discuss the origins and development of historiography, the attention and neglect of different aspects of history and the methods used to gather data; the latter were, from Greek antiquity to the Middle Ages, mainly restricted to the study of written documents, to oral accounts and personal observation. Historians, of course, frequently referred to extant monuments and objects created by past generations or societies which they or their sources had seen, read or heard about, even if they conducted no excavations or surveys to recover additional remains of this nature. Notwithstanding a multiplicity of approaches, they did not conceive the concept that those who included such evidence should do so at the exclusion of written and oral sources. While the study and interpretation of material evidence in antiquity and the Middle Ages was very much based on intuition rather than following any systematic methodology and thus can in no way serve as a model for our time, it is still worth stressing that the factional division of research into humanity's past on the basis of method is of very recent origin. For most of historiography's long history there has been no such split.

This is borne out by the terminology, as we have seen, and there was naturally no appropriate classical Greek term for the investigation of the material record, a discipline created in post-medieval times (notwithstanding sporadic fieldwork with similar objectives as early as the Neo-Babylonian Empire [Daniel 1981: 14]). Words can, of course, be redefined, but it is, nevertheless, worth remembering that the original meanings of both 'history' and 'archaeology' are very similar, the main difference being the emphasis on the ancient in archaeology, not the research methods employed. Literally, and in the original sense of the word, archaeologists are historians of ancient times.

Despite the modern redefinition of 'archaeology' as the study of material evidence for the human past, recent as well as ancient, and of 'history' (in one sense of the word) as the discipline devoted to text-based studies of the same object, the original definition of 'archaeology' is, of course, still valid insofar as material traces reach back much further than written sources. Indeed, the entire history of humanity before the introduction of writing in the later fourth millennium BC, the so-called 'prehistory' (some 99.8 per cent in terms of its length), is the domain solely of archaeologists. 'History' deals only with a maximum of 0.2 per cent of human history (and with far less for most parts of the world) and excludes the origins of the human species, agriculture, permanent settlements and urbanism.

Even within the last five millennia only archaeologists have the competence to deal comprehensively with the history of any culture for which there is no documentary evidence. Once, however, the first texts give a partial insight into a culture, the term 'historian' is claimed by those who attempt a historical interpretation of these documents. This terminology gives a false impression: do archaeologists cease to be interested in historical questions once written sources are available, no matter how sparse they are or how selective the information they provide? Are archaeologists of a historical period only interested in objects and are they merely engaged in preparatory work for historians? This is a widespread misconception about archaeology. In common perception archaeology is indeed normally thought of as 'digging up things', and this attitude is exemplified by the occasion when the author was once asked whether he would then go to the historian to ask what these discoveries tell us about history (while he has long lost count of how often he has been asked whether he is an archaeologist or a historian, implying that the separation is clear-cut and that every researcher of the past falls into one category or the other). Yet the view that archaeologists are incapable, or at least less capable, of understanding and reconstructing history than historians is held not only by lay people and historians but even amongst archaeologists themselves. Paul Courbin is quite clear about this:

> And just as historians and anthropologists try to do without archaeologists to gather their archaeological documentation themselves, often with great success, in the same way archaeologists can become historians, epigraphists, or anthropologists: but as happens every

time one leaves one's speciality, the result will perhaps – or probably – not be as good as if the work were done by a historian or an
anthropologist. It would no doubt be better to use a specialist.

(Courbin 1988: 154)

If, however, an archaeologist can indeed not be dissuaded from playing 'at
being a historian' then he or she at least ought to be aware that he or she
'is no longer doing "archaeology," but something else' (Courbin 1988: 155,
cf. 148–9).

Courbin's view is based on two implicit premises: (1) that virtually nobody
is capable of developing expertise in more than one discipline that matches
that of the average single-subject expert, and (2) that archaeology and history
are two totally separate monolithic blocs. Since it seems likely that every
reader can think of examples to disprove the first premise, I shall discuss
here only the second: are we indeed dealing with two separate monolithic
entities? This seems highly questionable to me. Nobody is an expert in all
archaeological remains, structural, artefactual and environmental, in all countries from the earliest hominids to modern times, all conventional and
scientific methods available to record and explore them and all theoretical
models ever suggested to interpret them. Equally, no historian can claim
mastery in the study of all documents ever composed in all ancient and
modern languages illuminating the history of all parts of the world, all theoretical approaches, etc. As it is thus inevitable that both archaeologists and
historians will have to specialize within their respective fields, there is no
logical reason why they should have to concentrate most of their energies
on one or the other, nor why devoting 50 per cent to one and 50 per cent
to the other may not produce just as good (or, indeed, better) research.

To take a concrete example, had I taken my doctorate in Germany I would
have faced the choice of doing so either in a sub-discipline of archaeology
(e.g. 'provincial' Roman archaeology) or in ancient history. For most topics
in provincial Roman archaeology I would have been expected to acquire
expert knowledge on all types of small finds likely to be found on a Roman
site (especially all types of pottery), all possible parallels, etc. Building up
such an expertise on a multitude of relevant categories of small finds alone
can easily take years. In ancient history, by contrast, I would have been
expected to become an expert on classical Greece as well as on Republican
and Imperial Rome. Does my eventual choice of specializing in Roman
studies and trying to use all sources available automatically make me an
amateur in one field or the other? Conversely, would I escape classification
as an amateur if instead I had attempted to master ancient history from the
early Aegean to Late Antiquity (let alone all epochs and territories covered
by written documents from ancient Egypt and Mesopotamia to 2003), or
even archaeology in a global context from the earliest evidence for the use
of stone tools some 2.5 million years ago to world war archaeology or beyond?

It seems quite clear that Courbin's insistence that one cannot be a historian and archaeologist at the same time is driven by the desire (perhaps subject pride) to define archaeology as something separate. In the first paragraph of the chapter 'What is Archaeology?' in Courbin's synonymous book we find the following statement: 'Finally, it is out of the question to "reduce" archaeology to another discipline, history or anthropology' (Courbin 1988: 110). While Courbin's book is essentially a critique of new or processual archaeology, he shares with Lewis Binford (1983: 20–2), the most influential representative of this branch of theoretical archaeology, at least the belief that archaeology and history are quite separate and independent disciplines. Having excluded the possibility that archaeology can be 'reduced' to history, Courbin seeks to define it by investigating 'What Archaeology Alone Can Do' (Courbin 1988: 111), concluding 'that the establishment of facts is the archaeologist's proper role and mission' (Courbin 1988: 132); the context makes it clear that Courbin thinks here of the correct interpretation of material evidence comprising sub-fields as diverse as interpreting stratigraphy, identification of animal bones and classifying black- and red-figure Greek vases and *not* of the establishment of facts as a result of examining works of literature, inscriptions and papyri: 'if the archaeologist extends his research into history or anthropology he ceases to act as an archaeologist proper and becomes, with greater or lesser success, a historian or an anthropologist' (ibid.) It is obvious that Courbin presents us here with a circular argument: he claims it is out of the question that a certain range of methodologies can be grouped together with a certain other range. No reasons are given as to why it is out of the question. Instead of showing why the boundary has to be drawn precisely where Courbin thinks it ought to be drawn, or why there needs to be a boundary at all, he simply states that archaeologists are better in research activities A, B and C than in D, E and F, because A, B and C constitute archaeology while D, E and F do not, without realizing that this line of separation is an artefact of our own making. Anybody who crosses Courbin's arbitrarily defined line (dealing with C and D, for example) is doing something different which he or she is not really competent to do, while anybody who stays on either side of it, even if ranging more widely than the person crossing it, remains within his or her field or expertise. Martin Carver (2002: 486; cf. Andrén 1998: 146–7), without referring to Courbin, has recognized the weakness of such an argument when pointing out that 'an awareness of the prodigious variety of information types within both material culture and text' ranging from a bus timetable to the Bible and from a refuse pit to a cathedral is largely missing from discussions on such 'artificial "dualities"'.

Courbin is not alone in basing his definition of archaeology on the unproven postulate that it is 'not history' (besides also being different from other subjects, like anthropology). We have seen above that Klejn metaphorically equates the archaeology–history relationship with that between horses and 'men' (or humans); had apes and humans been selected as examples, he would have implied that the 'two disciplines' are uniquely close; horses and humans, by contrast, are no more closely related to each other than to many other mammal species and, by implication, the same is true for the 'two disciplines'. While his sentence is slightly ambiguous, its structure even seems to imply that archaeology is represented by horses and history by 'men', and the 'vice versa' suggests that 'men'/historians do not become horses/archaeologists through contact with the other species or discipline rather than that historians could be represented by horses and archaeologists by 'men'. Even if this equation should have been unconscious rather than deliberate in Klejn's endeavour to create a catchphrase, it is nevertheless worth noting that the role of the master is reserved for history, that of the subservient working animal for archaeology. The suspicion that this formulation reflects, consciously or unconsciously, Klejn's belief in the relative hierarchy of the 'two disciplines' is confirmed not only by the above-cited equation of archaeology with the investigator and history with the judge, but also by a second catchphrase: 'Let us render what is Caesar's to the Caesar of archaeology and what is God's to the God of history' (Klejn 2001: 18).

Again there is no ambiguity here about the implied power relationship between the 'Caesar of archaeology' and the 'God of history'. Other passages eradicate any remaining doubts that Klejn really means this rather than being unlucky in his choice of examples: 'Meanwhile culture as a whole cannot become the subject matter of archaeology because an adequate study of it in statics and dynamics demands a huge involvement and application of other methods' (Klejn 2001: 17). Here and elsewhere he defines what falls and does not fall within the subject matter of archaeology: 'Yet not causal explanations of the historical events and processes – they are the business of history, while archaeology is a source-studying discipline' (Klejn 2001: 127, cf. 17). Historians, we are meant to believe, have the 'God-of-history'-given(?) capacity to apply a wide range of other methods while archaeologists have not – no logical explanations provided.

We should be grateful to Klejn; he had the courage to express his views clearly in print and to offer a useful overview of scholarly opinion on the role of archaeology, while many others, despite adopting a similar approach in their research, have not put their cards on the table. Instead, as Stephen Driscoll (1988: 166) has observed, 'unstated and thus unexamined assumptions' underlie the conventional position on the relationship between history and archaeology. 'The validity or usefulness of the separate disciplines is never questioned by conventional practitioners because the distinction between document and artefact is believed to be so fundamental' (Driscoll 1988: 165). While it is indeed very difficult to examine unstated assumptions, Klejn offers us the opportunity to follow his argument. His above-quoted view seems to be based on a classification of archaeology as a 'source-studying discipline' like philology – 'narrower' than 'disciplines synthetic by "nature"' like history (Klejn 2001: 17). Yet he fails to recognize that the division of text-based studies into a 'source-studying discipline' (philology) and a 'discipline synthetic "by nature"' (history) is no more than an artificial product of tradition. While one could argue that some field archaeologists fall into a category similar to the former and some theoretical archaeologists into one similar to the latter, there are many transitional positions (as there are between philologists and historians); however, unlike in text-based studies, the subdivision of archaeology into a 'source-studying discipline' and a 'discipline synthetic "by nature"' has never been formalized. No more than an accident of tradition thus provides the justification for Klejn to reduce archaeology to a 'source-studying discipline' and to leave the synthesis exclusively to a subgroup of text-users.

This has already been recognized by David Austin and Julian Thomas (1990: 49–50) who rightly stress that the word 'history' has two senses which have often been conflated: (1) 'history' as 'an academic discipline which concerns itself with the interpretation of written texts', and (2) 'history' as 'the process of social life'. Klejn's mistake is to assume that the representatives of category (1) have the sole competence for a comprehensive interpretation of the latter. Austin and Thomas (1990: 50), by contrast, point out that, while in their judgement 'a complete understanding of any event is a practical impossibility, a closer approach to completeness will come from the consideration of both written and material text'. In the words of Neil Christie and Robert Young (1996: 181) 'both sets of data form pieces from the *same* reconstructional jigsaw . . .' This is a strikingly clear comparison: the best strategy by which to complete the jigsaw is not to divide the pieces into two heaps and try to reassemble them independently. Many connections will only become apparent when the pieces from both heaps are fitted together, and the same is true for material and textual evidence. Logically there is no reason to share Klejn's and Courbin's view, even if we also accepted their implicit assumption that 'historians' (of Austin and Julian's category [1]) always have the intention and ability to include all evidence, written and non-written, that 'archaeologists' are not equally capable of doing that. Yet, frequently, the intention to include all the evidence is lacking on both sides, as observed by Christie and Young (1996: 170): 'Often, indeed, there is no debate at all – *an historian's got to do what an historian's got to do and it doesn't always include talking to archaeologists* (or vice versa).' This is mirrored in David Austin's (1990: 13) similar assessment of the current state of affairs: 'the debate between documentary and archaeological history is more a monologue than a dialogue'. The necessity to look at both types of evidence does not concern the prehistorian or the contemporary historian (except in order to provide analogies, to establish the wider context and to reconstruct long-term developments). Yet only in very recent times do written documents and other, more modern forms of documentation, together with the testimony of living eyewitnesses, provide comprehensive coverage of all aspects of history (but even then one must exclude forensic science and, more importantly, the buildings, structures and portable objects all around us; even if we learn about contemporary material culture mainly by oral communication and the broadcast and printed media, the visual experience is still important). This is largely the domain of the 'historian', as prehistory is that of the 'archaeologist'. For any time, however, for which both written and non-written evidence is available and in which one of them can give information of essential importance which the other does not give, there are two factions amongst researchers who have equally justified claims to be called historians concerned with the process of social life; the most reliable and complete accounts are likely to be produced by those who do not stay on either side of the fence, no matter from which side they are coming.

The relationship between archaeology, history, sociology and other disciplines

'Archaeologists' and 'historians' have exactly the same field of interests, involving all aspects of human life in the past, all its economic, social and spiritual components and all factors that have an impact on life and culture, including the whole environment in (or in the reach of) habitable regions. Given this all-embracing nature of the discipline(s), almost every other discipline can make a contribution to research into cultural history. This is true both for the interpretation or understanding of facts and, on a more fundamental level, for the decipherment and decoding of texts and of non-written evidence. Research methods developed in the natural sciences, for example, are essential, as they allow the dating or analysis of relevant objects or elements of structures. Nevertheless, it is problematic to claim that 'archaeology' and 'history' are not more closely related to each other than is 'archaeology', for example, to geology or botany. Though the methods applied by such disciplines and the research results achieved can be of funda-mental importance, there is only a partial overlap in the questions, whereas the overlap between 'history' and 'archaeology' is total. There are no differ-ences whatsoever in the questions that 'both disciplines' would like to answer, only the different nature of the evidence does not allow either 'archaeolo-gists' or 'historians' to explore certain questions or periods. This is apparent from the fact that modern history is certainly concerned with topics insuffi-ciently covered, and therefore largely neglected, by ancient historians, such as the lives and working conditions of ordinary people. Obviously, the connection between human history and ethnology is closer than with the sciences as this discipline equally deals exclusively with human societies; yet it does not furnish any primary evidence about the distant past, even though it provides models for interpretation and analogies. As far as the rela-tionship with sociology is concerned, I would agree with Anthony Giddens who answers the question 'what distinguishes social science from history?' as follows:

> I think we have to reply, as Durkheim did (albeit having followed a different line of reasoning to arrive at this result): nothing – nothing, that is, which is conceptually coherent or intellectually defensible. If there are divisions between social science and history, they are substantive divisions of labour; there is no logical or methodological schism. Historians who specialize in particular types of textual materials, languages or 'periods' are not freed from involvement with the concepts of, and the dilemmas inherent in, social theory. But, equally, social scientists whose concerns are the most abstract and general theories about social life, are not freed from the hermeneutic demands of the interpretation of texts and other cultural objects. Historical research is cultural research and vice versa.
>
> (Giddens 1984: 357–8)

This is a crucial point: Giddens argues that there is no difference between social science and history. Historians in his definition also include those who specialize in particular types of textual materials (which must include philologists, papyrologists and epigraphists) and, notably, he makes no distinction between the study of texts and of 'cultural objects'. If Giddens's definition is accepted that there is no difference between social science and the study of historical texts, and no difference between social science and the study of cultural objects, then it follows logically that there equally can be no difference between the study of historical texts and that of cultural objects, i.e. between 'history' and 'archaeology' (cf. Giddens 1984: 357). It is also worth noting in the light of the current fashion for labelling history with a narrative element as 'old-fashioned', if not primitive, that Giddens (1984: 359–60) rightly points out that good history contains an analytical as well as a narrative element.[2]

The dangers of one-sided approaches

While it is permissible to choose to study questions and periods for which a favoured research method is of paramount importance, it is hardly justifiable to deal with more complex topics while ignoring a significant part of the available evidence. There are, indeed, subjects one could classify as mainly 'historical' or mainly 'archaeological'. Ancient philosophy forms an example of the former; even depictions of philosophers and excavated places of teaching are only identifiable as such against the background of historical texts. If one is dealing with living conditions in fourth-century Britain, however, one cannot base a study on direct written sources, because – to my knowledge – there are none that shed any direct light on this phenomenon.

But even in these examples, it seems questionable whether it is wise entirely to ignore the non-written evidence in the first case and the written evidence in the second. For the ancient historian who is dealing with a philosopher it is important to get a visual idea of the specific environment. Archaeology is essential for that – as it is probably in the understanding of examples and images used by the philosopher. While direct written evidence for living conditions in fourth-century Britain is lacking, there are analogies. Furthermore, one needs to have substantial background knowledge about the ancient culture, society and economy. It is not always easy to say to what extent one can apply knowledge about the culture in one part of the Roman Empire at a certain time to another part at a different time, but without any knowledge of Roman culture one could come to the most absurd inter-pretations of the material evidence.

Even methodological purists who advocate that one should look at archaeo-logical and historical evidence independently do not, and cannot do so consistently in practice, as they will always consciously or unconsciously be influenced to some extent by their literature-based knowledge of history. For example, nobody, to my knowledge, has questioned the premise that Britain and Egypt formed part of the same state during the High Empire, while it could be argued that in terms of their material culture they were as different then as they are today when they are not part of the same political unity. Neither am I aware of anybody who has dismissed coins as dating evidence only because their precise chronology relies in many instances exclu-sively on written sources. Equally, the dating of other categories of finds, such as pottery, has frequently been calibrated on the basis of their associa-tion with coins or their presence or absence from sites whose foundation or abandonment is recorded in textual sources (e.g. the towns and villas buried under the ashes and lapilli or the lava from the eruption of Mount Vesuvius in AD 79). Clearly, the idea that it is possible to study written and material evidence independently and then to compare the results is only possible when testing very specific hypotheses; it is a mere illusion when trying to build up the larger picture. Even the most critical minds have to adopt some infor-mation derived from texts without questioning it or assuming it did not exist. Greg Woolf (2002: 52) has pointed out that 'we cannot begin every paper from first principles', and that in his view it would not be 'helpful to reinstate the old dichotomy between "historical approaches based on textual evidence" and "archaeological approaches based on material culture"'.

That it is indeed impossible to look at archaeological evidence in isola-tion is very obvious; for example, take the case of the Ostrogothic kingdom between the conquest of Italy (AD 489–93) by Theoderic and the Gothic War (AD 535–62) under Justinian. It is well known that Italy had already been under the control of a Germanic ruler, Odoacer, since AD 476. Further-more, even before the forced abdication of the last western Roman emperor in AD 476, Germanic generals, whose power was based upon Germanic tribesmen who served as soldiers in Italy, had gradually taken over the power in the state. We would not have the faintest idea of these developments without written sources. Archaeology would allow us to trace population movements from central and eastern Europe to western Europe and the western half of the Mediterranean in the fifth and sixth centuries. That even holds true if we focus on territories where the immigrants made up only a very small percentage of the overall population, such as in Italy. I am not aware, however, of any material evidence that would suggest that Italy was under Germanic rule for 60–80 years before the reconquest under Justinian. I exclude coins, since they bear legends and are not material evidence in a narrow definition. Many of them, especially of the pre-war issues, depict, in any case, either the late Roman/Byzantine emperors or the personification of Roma (Arslan 1994; Grierson and Blackburn 1986: 24–38), since the Ostrogothic kingdom nominally remained part of the Empire. If all this had happened in a prehistoric context we would have concluded that there was an influx of small groups of settlers, possibly farmers or traders from the north, bringing with them (and retaining) their distinctive types of brooches, buckles and other artefacts. We would never have guessed that these people ruled the country. The absence of weapon graves (Bierbrauer 1974: 63, 68–9; 1994: 172), which are frequent at the same period in central and north-western Europe, would have confirmed our opinion that we were not dealing with invaders who had wide territories under military control. We would rightly have concluded that there was no major disruption in cultural development. One cannot claim that the long process of decline of public installations in Late Antiquity accelerated during this period of foreign rule. Such a link, by the way, is also unproven for Vandalic northern Africa (Christie 1995; Potter 1995: 17, 19, 79, 103–8; Sjöström 1993: 35–9); and decline would not prove foreign rule anyway. Church building in Ravenna continued right through the migration period, and the architecture gives no clue to the origin of the rulers of the country (Deichmann 1969–89). The mausoleum of Theoderic (Figure 2.1) is of distinctive architectural form, but if sixth-century Italy had been a prehistoric culture, nobody would have guessed that this monument, with its monolithic ceiling weighing over 230 metric tonnes (Deichmann 2.1, 1974: 211–39, esp. 218), was built for a king whose ancestors had lived on the Baltic Sea, subsequently for a long time north of the Black Sea and later in the central Danubian region, and who had been unfamiliar with monumental stone architecture (Deichmann 1, 1969: 216–17). Even the 'Zangenfries' ('frieze of tongs') on the mausoleum, a Germanic element (Heidenreich and Johannes 1971: 152–9; Deichmann 2.1, 1974: 233), would fail to demonstrate that this was a period of foreign rule – again on the theoretical assumption of a prehistoric context.

Likewise, the pyramid of Cestius in Augustan Rome would not prove a phase of Egyptian rule then, and neither would strong Egyptian influences on contemporary art, the popularity of Egyptian cult objects or the massive

Figure 2.1 Theodoric's mausoleum at Ravenna (photo E. Sauer)

output of Augustan coinage with the depiction of a crocodile chained to a palm tree at Nîmes (Nemausus) in southern Gaul.

Even if we had known that the distinctive brooches had been introduced by a conquering tribe, we could not have established correctly the extension of the area under control: the Ostrogothic kingdom stretched from Sicily to the middle Danube and, for about twenty-five years, to the mouth of the Rhône (Wolfram 1990), and yet no graves or hoards containing specific artefacts have been detected in southern Italy or on Sicily (Bierbrauer 1974: 38–41, 209–15; 1994: 172, 174–5). To sum up: archaeology would tell us that a smaller number of foreigners were present in some parts of Italy, but we would not know that this was a period of foreign rule if we had to rely on material evidence. This example clearly shows the limitations of archaeology. However, to assess where these limitations are we need historical analogies. Archaeologists who are unaware of such analogies are in no position to express an informed opinion as to whether or not Iron Age Britain was affected by invasions or to assess or even question the reliability of written sources on how the Anglo-Saxons gained control over south-east Britain.

The reality: clear division in principle and unavoidable inconsistency in practice

I do not wish to imply that any archaeologist would investigate a culture for which written evidence is available in the manner described above for the Ostrogothic kingdom. However, this is the way we would have to do research if we were consistent. No classical or medieval archaeologist, and no historian of these periods, ignores written or, alternatively, non-written sources completely. Some historians and some archaeologists, but by no means all, consider all evidence that is related to the topics they are investigating. But then the absurdity of the division becomes apparent. If scholars of both groups are using all the evidence which is available for certain periods of history, why do some describe themselves as 'historians' and others as 'archaeologists'? A restriction of the latter term to field archaeologists would not solve the problem, because the results of fieldwork are of fundamental historical importance, which, however, can only be recognized once the discovery is put into a wider context. Consequently, it is equally important for both (the majority of) archaeologists involved in fieldwork and those limiting themselves purely to theory or interpretation to be familiar with material evidence and written sources alike. If we intend neither to ignore one category of evidence entirely nor to pay equal attention to both, where do we draw the line? Should the archaeologist consider all the archaeological evidence and just include written sources when it is impossible to avoid them? And should the historian dealing with the same subject take the opposite approach? Would it not be much more sensible to produce just one interpretation and to take each piece of evidence on its merits?

That there are very few 'text-free zones' in historical archaeology, notwithstanding the fact that ancient written sources tend to pay less attention to the lower classes in society or basic technical processes, has been rightly stressed by Moreland (2001: 13–15, 94–5) and Woolf (2002: 52), so there is no need to repeat their argument here. Neither is it possible to study the elite while ignoring the material manifestations of its power and wealth nor to understand the roles of the poor and the rich and powerful in isolation from each other. One might still be able to think of a justification for the division in the case of the chosen examples of ancient philosophy or houses and living conditions in fourth-century Britain, but in many other cases it is indisputable that the division just does not make sense. In cases such as maritime trade in the Indian Ocean in antiquity, the frontier policy of the

Roman Empire, human sacrifices in the late Iron Age in western and central Europe or in numerous other examples, both written and non-written testimonies are of essential importance. If one ignores either category of evidence, the chances of coming to the wrong conclusions or to no conclusions at all are far higher. And an exclusive study of the written or of the material evidence is just preparatory work. It is unlikely to produce meaningful results whose reliability is evident without further research. Therefore, either archaeologists and historians with an interest in the same literate cultures who are only familiar with their own subject (narrowly defined) have to co-operate closely all the time, or they have to include the research methods and results of the 'other' discipline, if possible without bias for or against a certain category of evidence.

Co-operation is undoubtedly essential and of growing importance, but this does not mean that 'archaeologists' and 'historians', co-operating in a wide field, have to subdivide it according to established and rigid research traditions. The current university system at the majority of higher education institutions (and here I am not referring to the university system of any particular country) keeps artificially alive this division of researchers with an identical field of interest – human history – into two distinct factions, not to mention the sub-disciplines. If students today are indoctrinated with the ideology that written evidence is far more important than material evidence (or the other way round), or that it is possible to study either in isolation, they are likely to pass this doctrine of narrowness on to future generations, especially since they would otherwise have to admit as future university lecturers that there are essential fields of research in which they have no training. Not even the most brilliant scholars can have expertise in every field, but that is no justification for not being open-minded towards the potential of those areas.

The risks of a necessity: specialization

I have already stressed that no single individual will be able to deal with the history of humanity in its entirety and use all research methods at his or her disposal – unless in a superficial way. This chapter argues against blindly following the rigid definitions of disciplines created in the past; it does not argue against specialization. The work of specialists who devote themselves entirely to the study of an extremely narrowly defined topic is of fundamental importance, but it would be of none whatsoever if everybody followed their lead. If we devoted ourselves, for example, entirely to certain wares of pottery in a specific culture we would probably know as little about this culture as we would know about our own if we knew everything about the shapes of contemporary plastic packaging for food but nothing else. That is not to say that research on pottery is unimportant, but it gains significance only once this information is linked with other fields. Pottery typology can help to date buildings and traces of human activities. It can reveal the geographic spread of cultures and patterns of trade. It may illuminate technical know-how, conditions of production and eating habits. The study of the typology of a particular group of objects is like the foundation of a building: it is the essential basis for further research but it is useless if one stops at this stage. While this observation will strike many as no more than a truism, it is not difficult to find 'typology for the typology's-sake' studies which do not consider wider interpretation worth the additional space.

In a time of an ever-increasing flood of publications it is tempting to confine oneself to an ever more narrowly defined subject. I am not referring here to special projects, theses or publications, many of which by their nature always have been, and always will be, focused on a very narrow topic. I doubt, however, that it would be an advantage if all researchers devoted their entire academic lives to the investigation of a single, very specialized topic. Nobody could deny that the contributions of specialists in certain categories of objects or research methods are of an ever-increasing importance, but this is true only if one puts them into a wider context. This can only be done by generalists who have to strike a sensible compromise between knowing everything about next to nothing or next to nothing about everything; they need to have as much factual knowledge as specialists, only spread over much wider areas of interest. The ideology that everybody should have a very small area of expertise is dangerous. The motivation behind subdividing archaeological and historical research into smaller and smaller independent subjects which isolate themselves may be perfectionism, fear of criticism, or the desire to be an expert without being a workaholic. The increasing depth in knowledge is sadly often paid for with a lack of sense for the wider context and with a loss in creativity in research and in interpretation. In extreme cases specialists may have difficulties in explaining to a non-expert the sense of what they are doing. This could be a fatal tendency, considering that without public interest it is unlikely that funding for research can be maintained, let alone increased.

In a world which is changing at a speed which has no parallel in history, people have an enormous potential interest in their roots and in their identity. History, historical places and monuments provide this identity. As modern technology is more and more dominating our lives, pre-industrial cultures have a strange fascination, since they seem to preserve something which we have lost, such as a much closer contact with nature. History is like a form of time travel, which can bring us to the most exotic places. This provides us with a different perspective on our own culture and its position in history. We learn to understand our own world. Why do certain religions dominate certain parts of the world? What is the background of contemporary conflicts and wars? What is the origin of specific customs? There is no reason to worry about the future of research into cultural history if we manage to present a colourful picture of the past in ways that are attractive and interesting for today's audience. If we do not present the whole mosaic, if we split it up into individual *tesserae*, we may ourselves forget the sense of our work, and we will not be able to convey it to anybody else.

The emancipation of archaeology?

While some archaeologists (and many historians) are content with archaeology playing the role of the proverbial 'handmaiden of history', others strive towards equality. Austin (1990: 10) laments that school textbooks 'are based almost solely on documentary evidence, although they may incidentally include pictures of material things such as castles or coins'. Similarly, many university classics departments offer modules in art and architecture (sometimes confined to a few Mediterranean centres) as little more than an illustrative background to the 'great' works of literature. John Moreland (2001) has produced one of the most powerful studies of this kind of interrelation between archaeology and text, exploring the historical origins of our 'logocentric world' where it is taken to be 'common sense' that 'written sources from the past are more informative than those recovered archaeologically' (Moreland 2001: 33; cf. Carver 2002). Yet it appears that he almost comes to the opposite conclusions when criticizing demands that archaeology should recover ancient texts, be it in Mesopotamia, the Mediterranean, China, Vindolanda in Roman Britain or on Maya sites in central America:

> Subservience to the demands of history is even more evident in those cases where the practice of archaeology is explicitly directed at the recovery of ancient written material. Here archaeology ceases to be a discipline in its own right and serves merely as a producer of texts to be consumed by historians and philologists.
>
> (Moreland 2001: 18)

Does Moreland deny that texts offer a different perspective and dimension to the mute material traces of human activity, and does he imply that they are less relevant than virtually any non-inscribed object or structure? Or does he imply that archaeologists are so separate and should be so disinterested in historical sources that they should excavate anything else and let writing tablets rot in the ground rather than recover them? (At some sites at least the very survival of texts written on organic materials is at risk as a result of fluctuations in the water table.) This view seems out of place in Moreland's otherwise balanced study which stresses repeatedly that in historical periods both texts and artefacts have to be taken into consideration, and indeed have to be approached in a similar manner, as they are both products of human creativity (e.g. Moreland 2001: 30–1). One wonders whether this paragraph reflects Moreland's desire that archaeology should exert its influence and should emancipate itself. Here, I feel that it is important not to confuse two unrelated questions: first, is archaeological evidence of the same importance as textual evidence; second, should these two bodies of data be studied in isolation from each other?

Since the latter question has already been discussed above, this chapter is primarily concerned with the first, though this will ultimately lead us to pose the question as to whether archaeology should strive towards 'emancipation' in the sense of asserting equal status and importance or in the sense of striving towards even fuller independence. Notwithstanding the frequent neglect of archaeology in education, I would argue that archaeologists have no reason to develop an inferiority complex in terms of the relative value of the contribution of their preferred research methods to the reconstruction of human history. There is no need or justification to go as far as to argue that historical texts are necessarily less objective than our own interpretation of the material evidence, a claim voiced occasionally and rightly rejected by Carver (2002: 474–5) and Jones (1999: 222), amongst others. The sheer chronological and geographical omnipresence of archaeological evidence and its dynamic growth, as opposed to the much more limited availability and more static nature of the documentary evidence, is sufficient to reject any claims that it is of secondary importance. Indeed, as has been stressed above, only for the last 0.2 per cent of human history is written evidence available at all, and for most parts of the world the percentage is even far lower than that (Andrén 1998: 5, fig. 1). The stress placed on the 0.2 per cent time period should, of course, not imply that this low percentage reflects the historical importance of the last five millennia. The relevance of phases of human history, in my personal view, does not depend on their length. Nobody would claim, for example, that knowledge of the six years of the Second World War and a period of the same length in the palaeolithic have equal importance for us today, even if we could date traces of activity in the early Stone Age to a precise year. And in case of a potential future nuclear world war between existing or emerging superpowers, the events of a few hours could potentially result in more radical historical changes than those of hundreds of thousands of years of cultural development. I would argue that the attention we should pay to a period of history (apart from the quantity of information available) is related to the speed of change – not in the sense that slowly evolving cultures are of little interest, but that very short phases of history which saw decisive developments can be regarded as being of comparable importance.

Yet this must not form an excuse to look at such phases in isolation. In human history, like in a chain reaction, every development depends on earlier developments. As in a long mathematical calculation one cannot afford to neglect any part, otherwise the equation of cultural evolution and present state of development will not balance. It would be futile to discuss whether, for example, the Stone Age or the Middle Ages are of greater historical interest for us today. It is impossible to understand a culture without having a clear idea of its position in world history. The geographical dimension is as important as the chronological framework: it is desirable to know not only its immediate neighbours but also more distant peoples with whom it had contacts. As it is hardly possible to trace any changes in the basic psychology of human behaviour throughout history, even completely isolated cultural developments can provide fascinating analogies.

No one with a genuine interest in history can be exclusively interested in a single culture. Those who have 'discovered' the beauty of Greek art or of Latin poetry, and consider cultures without such 'achievements' to be far inferior and not worth dealing with, take a subjective aesthetic rather than a historical approach (cf. Andrén 1998: 10–12, 107–13, 138; Bietti Sestieri *et al.* 2002: 430). Why the elites in a few cultural centres developed a deep interest in certain forms of literature or art, culminating in often short-lived 'golden ages', can only be understood in comparison with cultures (or periods) where (or when) there was no desire or ability to engage in such non-utilitarian activities in a similar way. If it is accepted that even well-documented periods which saw decisive changes in geographically narrowly confined cultural centres cannot be understood in isolation, then the virtual omnipresent archaeological evidence is of major importance even for the best-documented episodes in ancient and medieval history. And creative phases in literature cannot be understood anyway in isolation from similar devel-opments in art and architecture as the underlying driving forces (namely sponsorship, competition, and exposure and openness to a wide range of influences) were often the same.

To summarize: I would argue that the historical importance of a culture is related to the speed of change and the significance of traceable develop-ments and cannot be gauged by temporal duration, not even if multiplied with geographic size or estimated population. On this premise the second above-mentioned criterion for assessing the relative importance of archaeo-logical evidence – namely its dynamic growth – becomes as relevant as, if not more relevant than, its chronological and geographical omnipresence. Indeed, while the amount of archaeological documentation and the number of finds has multiplied over recent decades (one of the main reasons for the tendency to a general increase in the level of specialization), ancient historians are facing the opposite problem: the quantity of primary written sources available about the ancient world is growing only very slowly. The bulk of new texts (inscriptions, *papyri*, writing tablets and coin legends), however, has been yielded by archaeology and are 'archaeological' as much as 'historical' evidence. There are many fields of research for which there has been hardly any new textual evidence for more than a century. Since there have been many excellent scholars in the past, the speed of progress in ancient history is not as rapid as in archaeology. If today one writes a conventional solely literature-based biography of a well-known figure in the ancient world, of Julius Caesar for example, it is increasingly less likely to contain interpretations which revolutionize our perception of history and which nobody has ever thought about. By contrast a study of the culture in Gaul at the time which can draw on Caesar's report as well as on a vast body of new archaeological data would differ much more from a book on the same subject written a century ago. In a general biography that excludes such new material evidence for the environment Caesar was operating in during his war of conquest in Gaul (which has shaped north-western European history to the present day), or for specific key events such as the siege of Alésia (Reddé and Schnurbein 2001), there will probably only be some nuances to add to earlier work about Caesar. It is certainly important to preserve a level of knowledge acquired in the past and to present it to a modern audience in today's language and with a focus on issues related to our own time, but in many fields of research ancient history is confined to the role of preserving knowledge rather than adding new information. And while the application of new theoretical approaches or models allows new insights and a deeper understanding of some aspects (though this is not the subject of this chapter), even there disciplines with a stagnant and widely studied source-base will, in terms of the relative increase of our knowledge, lag behind disciplines where those approaches can be applied to a growing body of data.

This is not to deny that there is real progress in ancient history, but it lies mainly in fields for which there is new evidence or which have been neglected in the past. Genuinely new approaches and the compilation of the evidence for phenomena which have never been systematically investigated before are also very useful. And the most fruitful areas are precisely those which transcend the borderlines of traditional subjects. There are more rewarding tasks than to reinvestigate the same questions, based on the same testimonies and without redefining the subject area again and again.

It would be equally wrong, however, to study the new archaeological evidence independently – as if there was nothing else. Material evidence on its own will always give us a selective insight into history. (But written sources for most historical periods give a selected insight as well – though a different one.) Archaeology (if we neglect the fact that most new texts are yielded by excavations) allows us to reconstruct merely the material culture. This enables us to trace developments in technology, art and architecture, settlement patterns and so on with a high degree of reliability, provided that the chosen materials and landscape developments have allowed objects and structures to survive. The limits become obvious if we try to investigate social structures, individual biographies or the spiritual culture. If there are traces, they mostly allow more than one interpretation.

This is most obvious in prehistory. It is worth stressing how little we know in concrete terms for example about religion, let alone mythology, in the palaeolithic period. Despite the discovery of burials, elaborate cave paintings and female figurines, all conclusions remain extremely superficial in comparison with well-documented historical periods. We learn that concern for food, procreation and probably the thought of an afterlife of some form manifested itself in religion. We have an idea of some of the rituals that were performed, and it is possible to establish a chronology of the physical traces. Often even the physical traces are ambiguous, such as in cases of ritual cannibalism, the extent or scarcity of which is subject to intense academic debate (e.g. Peter-Röcher 1994) in contrast, for example, to the almost world-wide proven cult of human head trophies. A comprehensive study of the archaeological, historiographic and ethnographic evidence is necessary to understand the spread, extent and ritual background of such practices. The origins of religion are as fascinating as they are nebulous. To gain a deeper insight into an ancient religion we need written testimonies (where available), or at least analogies. The study of the existing documentary evidence for historical periods will remain essential. We need written evidence to understand archaeological discoveries, and archaeological discoveries often help us to understand the literary sources. No specialist discipline within the field of cultural history has a future in isolation.

Even though Hawkes's ladder of inference (1954: 161–2) which summa-rized similar observations has been criticized (Moreland 2001: 13–15), it is undeniable that archaeological evidence taken on its own tends to allow more definite interpretations of technological processes or the material traces of subsistence economy than of social structure or religion. While the former tend to follow a pragmatic and thus reconstructable logic, social status can manifest itself in an unlimited variety of expressions without any being firmly linked to a specific position in all societies; similarly, religious ritual is by its very nature irrational. At Jordan Hill, on the site of a Romano-Celtic temple on the British south coast, for example, ravens, crows, buzzards and starlings were buried in a late Roman votive pit 'sandwiched' individually together with coins between stone roof slabs; spear-heads, swords and other objects were also found in the same pit (Warne 1872: 226; Drew 1932: 267–8, 270). As we can establish how a pottery kiln functioned, we can reconstruct the technical aspects, e.g. the burial process; we can also draw parallels with coin and weapons offerings elsewhere to trace to some extent foreign influences and indigenous elements, yet we are unable to reconstruct the underlying belief system which led to this peculiar form of bird burials. Of course, archaeology can make essential contributions to social and reli-gious history, yet it is clear that we need textual information (where available) to gain in-depth insights into pagan theology.

Many ancient historians include the classical art and architecture of their period and area of interest in their studies, but the potential of other archaeo-logical research methods is often underestimated or completely ignored. This is not meant to be a general condemnation, since more and more ancient historians are becoming fully aware of the importance of such evidence, but it is an appeal to those historians who still limit themselves to traditional ways of studying the classical world. One cannot deal with wider aspects of the ancient world and ignore the results of modern scientific techniques. The study of human remains has told us at least as much about ancient demography as inscriptions and *papyri*, and the future potential is immeasurably higher. It also gives a fascinating insight into the spread of diseases, into injuries caused by accident or fighting, into surgery, living conditions and nutrition. All that is of interest for anybody who tries to understand an ancient culture. That one 'is not an archaeologist' should no longer be an acceptable excuse for disregarding such essential research. Admittedly, there is more than one side to blame; specialization has led to many detailed studies of human remains of individual sites, but there is a need for more up-to-date compilations of data which make the research results accessible to non-experts.

Similarly the development of dating techniques over recent decades has been groundbreaking. The establishment of absolute oak chronologies in central and north-western Europe back to prehistory (Becker 1993: back to the late ninth millennium BC in southern Germany), besides chronologies for other sorts of timber, opens up entirely new possibilities. Only for parts of the ancient world is there yet an absolute chronology, but there is rapid progress. Tree-rings are formed in climatic zones where seasonal climatic factors impede the growth of trees, such as cold winters, dry summers or annual floods (Schweingruber 1993: 33–5). Dendrochronology is therefore geographically widely applicable, and many more local chronologies will be established (Kuniholm 1996, 2002). Given the frequency of preserved timber in buildings in wet (or in arid) environments, this dating technique is leading to the establishment of an absolute chronology of many historical developments which could not previously be dated. In the near future archaeology will have yielded more absolute data than all textual evidence for the ancient world taken together, inscriptions included, and without bias towards periods when the epigraphic habit was at its peak, or when historiography was flourishing. While tree-ring dates illuminate, of course, in part different aspects of the past than historiography, such as the intensity of construction works, they are certainly of major significance for economic and military history. These and other modern research techniques push back the frontiers of our knowledge; nobody who ignores them has a valid claim of being able to develop a comprehensive understanding of any ancient culture.

Such precision dating renders it, incidentally, also highly questionable whether David Clarke is right in arguing that

> We fully appreciate that these entities [i.e. archaeological entities] and processes were once historical and social entities but the nature of the archaeological record is such that there is no simple way of equating our archaeological percepta with these lost events.
>
> (Clarke 1978: 11)

It is even more difficult to agree with Klejn (2001: 35), who not only endorses Clarke's statement but considers it 'worth adding that archaeology and history have different inspirations of knowledge; history strives to understand unique events and heroes, whereas archaeology is obsessed with generalisation, typification, and its central concept is "type"'. Quite apart from the fact that many historians would have problems with the concept that they are not interested in general developments and are only interested in unique events (let alone 'heroes'), and that also a large number of archaeologists (though not all) would find the idea uncomfortable that typification is one of just two key areas of their work, is it really true that it is virtually impossible to link archaeological findings with historically recorded unique events? To quote just two examples to the contrary: archaeology has been able to verify and refine the partially recorded chronology of the speed of the Roman advance during the first phase of the Augustan wars in Germany (Kühlborn 1992) and during the conquest of southern Britain (Sauer 2002) on the basis of construction timbers datable to a precise year or even season. These findings have, of course, implications far beyond simple chronology, such as in terms of military strategy, policy objectives, the impact on native communities, etc. which there is no space here to discuss.

The foundations for progress are primarily laid by those who provide or are able to study a growing body of new evidence: field archaeologists, natural scientists analysing objects, papyrologists, epigraphists, numismatists, etc. Knowledge of as many fundamental research methods as possible is a precondition for the wider interpretation. Not all ancient or medieval historians have to become field archaeologists, but they need to include the results if they want to be historians in the sense of the word and not philologists with historical interests. Equally not all historical archaeologists have to acquire the skills required for translation, let alone sophisticated scrutiny, of classical texts in the original language. Reading the translation of ancient sources or secondary literature summarizing the written evidence for a period or phenomenon should, however, be a minimum standard and is in any case far preferable to ignoring it. The same should be true for the attitude of historians towards complicated archaeological reports and synthetic studies which compile and discuss the evidence for specific cultures or phenomena. Mutual understanding and interest could overcome the one-sided approaches altogether. Nobody should act like a detective who is unaware either of the importance of witness accounts or of the forensic evidence, or, to use an image created by Carver (2002: 489), like a GP who either does not listen to the patient's report on his or her medical history or fails to carry out any analysis of the physical symptoms. There is not necessarily a need to decide whether one wants to focus on ancient languages or on archaeological research methods. If one knows both the relevant ancient languages and the archaeological fieldwork, one is more likely to appreciate all aspects of a culture and less likely to reduce it to poetry or pottery.

I would thus argue that both historians and archaeologists of historical periods should not misdirect their energy into arguing that their pile of pieces of the *same* jigsaw (to use Christie and Young's analogy cited on p. 24) is more relevant than the other pile or is important enough to be studied in its own right (an absurd strategy if we want to make progress in completing the jigsaw), but that they should try to outdo each other by excelling themselves to be better synthetic scholars. Such synergy would provide a challenge to both factions to strive towards a common goal and might ideally lead to full integration of a fragmented subject.

The future of historical research: fixed approaches or flexibility?

The necessity remains, however, that one has to specialize somehow, and it is essential to ask how a breaking through of old barriers can be achieved without replacing them with new ones. Areas of specialization are normally defined by a combination of various factors: geography, chronology, specific research methods, objects and phenomena. All specialization increases the awareness of certain contexts at the expense of others. Therefore the approaches should be as varied as possible, and research areas should overlap. One should freely combine the methods of various disciplines. There should be no separate blocs of scholars specializing only within these blocs and without attempting to look at their evidence from a different viewpoint. Great ideas are only born in a climate of diversity, flexibility and stimulating influences. In this I am in full agreement with Klejn (2001: 90): 'As a rule, the more a school upholds its uniqueness, its monopoly on the right to be held as a science (or scholarship), the more it is isolated and the more it falls into decay.'

The most persuasive argument for this observation is provided by history itself. The following examples will demonstrate that the unrestricted flow of influences and ideas has always and everywhere been one of the most powerful stimuli for technological and scientific advance, not only for individual researchers but for entire cultures. Giddens (1984: 242, cf. 232) warns us of the 'danger . . . to identify superior power, economic, political or military, with moral superiority on an evolutionary scale', and it is worth stressing that I will use the terms 'advance' and 'progress' here only to describe increasing sophistication of technology and science without meaning to imply that this had any positive effects on moral standards or the general level of happiness etc. within the societies concerned. Many of the 'advanced' civilizations in antiquity, in the Mediterranean, the Near East and southern and eastern Asia, formed states of vast territorial extension, and even the smaller ones (such as the Greek city-states) had geographically far-reaching direct contacts. It was within these civilizations that the major developments in natural and social sciences, in architecture and technology took place. More isolated regions did not become the centres of technical or scientific evolution, even if there was some population pressure. Indeed, it is difficult to find any examples of largely isolated societies confined to smaller territories that were world leaders in any field of the arts or science at their time. It can hardly be coincidence that restrictions in personal freedom and economic flexibility in Late Antiquity and the subdivision of the western half of the Roman Empire into smaller states resulted in a loss of theoretical knowledge and technological know-how (for example in stone architecture and water supply). The Church remained to be an international organization in the Middle Ages and consequently a guardian of cultural achievements (not only because of the essential importance of the ability to read and write for the representatives of a codified religion). A comparison between medieval Europe and more cosmopolitan and, in many respects, more 'advanced' cultures in the Islamic world and in eastern Asia is also revealing.

Europe and the west achieved the lead in military technology and the sciences only after its seafarers had gained dominance on the oceans, and once the horizon of western and southern Europeans had become wider than that of societies in any other part of the world. Contacts with new cultures could, of course, only stimulate 'progress' if there was at least some degree of open-mindedness towards them. Fanatics solely interested in exploiting others and stamping out anything foreign to them did not enjoy these benefits. Competition between states was another important reason for 'advance'. Industrialization started in Britain at a time when it was, perhaps more than any other country, exposed to new and stimulating influences from all over the world. From the neolithic to the early post-medieval period civilizations of a comparably high state of development have always existed contemporaneously in more than one continent (and now this is again the case). Only the intervening period (from the seventeenth century to the nineteenth) was clearly dominated by some European and western states alone. Never before or after was any part of the world technologically so far ahead of the rest, and never had any part of the world so much more geographically wide-ranging contacts than any other part.

This is not meant to be a simplistic reduction of all reasons for 'advance' in history to one factor; there is no doubt that a multitude of causes are involved in every change. It is undeniable, however, even if some might label such conclusions 'politically incorrect', that there is a connection between isolation and slow progress, stagnation or regression. Whether there were geographic barriers or whether a cultural group deliberately cut itself off from foreign influences, all over the world and throughout history it can be observed that the degree of isolation is in inverse proportion to the speed of 'progress'. A wide range of contacts not only allows an early adoption of useful inventions and ideas but is also one of the main conditions of creativeness in building upon the world's past 'achievements'. Only the combination of the two main driving forces behind 'progress' – competition (the struggle

41

for economic and military power over a longer period of time) and a wide range of influences – has led to the revolutionary advances in technology and science in post-medieval times. (In most periods of history one of these factors had not been strong enough to set such groundbreaking developments going.)

To sum up: the cultural historian can learn from history that any factor preventing the widest possible exchange of ideas slows down the pace of 'progress' in human history as well as in research. And the breaking down of boundaries between isolated entities who take little notice of each other's work would at the same time also create more competition between individual scholars, the second main stimulus for advance.

When I gave an earlier version of this chapter in December 1996 in the ancient history and classical archaeology graduate work-in-progress seminar in Oxford, I expected fierce opposition. I was thus all the more surprised to learn that the audience by and large seemed to share my basic opinions. Nobody argued that one particular research method or one culture was of superior importance. The criticism largely focused on practical issues: while some agreed entirely, there were different opinions on how many research methods one person could possibly master without becoming too superficial or without increasing the risk of misinterpretation. I was also asked whether my aim was not unrealistic, since it required a revolution at universities, and whether it would not be more useful to take small steps, such as organizing more interdisciplinary colloquia. While I agree that this would be a step in the right direction, I do not share the view that one should not formulate radical ideas. Far more revolutionary changes, which had been unthinkable for a long time, took place in history, and only provocative argument stimulates discussion.

The last decade has been characterized by revolutionary changes in the economy. Only highly flexible and creative businesses survive in a time of growing internationalism and accelerated technological progress. In such a rapidly changing world scientific separatism and persistence in unquestioned ideologies regarding the methods and aims of research no longer have a place. It would be the right time to abolish the division between 'history' and 'archaeology' and all the rigid subdivisions within these disciplines. If all 'historians' and 'archaeologists' (and 'sociologists' as well) united in their joint pursuit of studying humanity's past, everybody would still have to specialize, but there would be boundless possibilities and encouragement to be open-minded, and in any case not to be a slave to antiquated and unquestioned traditions.

Notes

1 I would like to thank Professor Barry Cunliffe, Dr Peter Haarer, Dr Martin Henig and Ross Samson for reading and commenting on various versions of this chapter.

To Dr Haarer and Dr Henig I am particularly grateful for various significant improvements, suggestions and critical comments; those of Dr Haarer made me rethink and substantially revise several controversial passages. Needless to say, it should not be assumed that the views of any of these scholars necessarily coincide with those expressed in this chapter or any of my other contributions to this volume. I would also like to mention the stimulating criticism of all those who attended my talk in Oxford in 1996. An earlier version of this chapter, based on the lecture given in December 1996 to the classical archaeology graduate work-in-progress seminar in Oxford, was submitted to the *Scottish Archaeological Review* and accepted for publication in 1997. Unfortunately it was decided in 2000 to discontinue this journal prior to the publication of volume 11 which would have contained this article. Despite this long delay I feel the issues raised are no less relevant in 2003 than they were in 1996/7. While the original paper has been updated, taking into account some recently expressed scholarly opinions on the roles of history and archaeology, it is not intended to be a review of the academic debate on all aspects of disciplinary boundaries in historical and archaeological research. A conventional treatise on such a wide subject would distract from its central aim, which is to raise awareness of the widespread, yet widely unnoticed or unlamented, fragmentation of research into human history.

2   I am unconvinced, incidentally, that the abstract and complicated language used by some sociologists, sociology-inspired archaeologists or historians (though not by Giddens) allows us to convey insights which could not be expressed in plainer language and that what are, in my view, unnecessarily complicated terms and formulations, as advocated by Egon Flaig (1992: 14–37), are anything more than a hindrance in getting our message across to a wide audience; this, though, is a different subject.

Bibliography

Andrén, A. (1998) *Between Artifacts and Text. Historical archaeology in global perspective*, New York and London: Plenum Press.

Arslan, E.A. (1994) 'La moneta dei Goti in Italia', in Bierbrauer *et al.* (1994): 252–65.

Austin, D. (1990) 'The "proper study" of medieval archaeology', in Austin and Alcock (1990): 9–42.

Austin, D. and Alcock, L. (eds) (1990) *From the Baltic to the Black Sea: Studies in medieval archaeology*, London: Unwin Hyman.

Austin, D. and Thomas, J. (1990) 'The "proper study" of medieval archaeology: a case study', in Austin and Alcock (1990): 43–78.

Becker, B. (1993) 'An 11,000-year German oak and pine dendrochronology for radiocarbon calibration', *Radiocarbon*, 35.1: 201–13.

Bierbrauer, V. (1974) *Die ostgotischen Grab- und Schatzfunde in Italien*, Biblioteca degli Studi Medievali, 7, Spoleto: Centro Italiano di studi sull'alto Medioevo.

—— (1994) 'Archeologia degli Ostrogoti in Italia', in Bierbrauer *et al.* (1994): 170–213.

Bierbrauer, V., von Hessen, O. and Arslan, E.A. (eds) (1994) *I Goti. Palazzo Reale 28.1.–8.5.1994*, Milan: Electa Lombardia.

Bietti Sestieri, A.M., Cazzella, A. and Schnapp, A. (2002) 'The Mediterranean', in Cunliffe *et al.* (2002): 411–38.

Binford, L.R. (1983) *In Pursuit of the Past: Decoding the archaeological record*, New York: Thames and Hudson.

Carver, M. (2002) 'Marriages of true minds: archaeology with texts', in Cunliffe *et al.* (2002): 465–96.

Christie, N. (1995) 'Italy and the Roman to medieval transition', in J. Bintliff and H. Hamerow (eds) *Europe Between Late Antiquity and the Middle Ages. Recent archaeological and historical research in Western and Southern Europe*, Oxford: BAR Int. Ser., 617: 99–110.

Christie, N. and Young, R. (1996) 'Reflections on the old and sterile debate: archaeology and history. What relationship?' *Medieval History*, 4: 170–86.

Clarke, D.L. (1978) *Analytical Archaeology* (2nd edn), London: Methuen & Co.

Courbin, P. (1988) *What is Archaeology? An essay on the nature of archaeological research*, Chicago and London: University of Chicago Press.

Cunliffe, B., Davies, W. and Renfrew, C. (eds) (2002) *Archaeology. The widening debate*, Oxford: Oxford University Press and the British Academy.

Daniel, G. (1981) *A Short History of Archaeology*, London: Thames and Hudson.

Deichmann, F.W. (1969–89) *Ravenna. Hauptstadt des spätantiken Abendlandes*, 1-2.3, Wiesbaden and Stuttgart: Steiner. (Individual volumes quoted by volume no. and date.)

Drew, C.D. (1932) 'The excavations at Jordan Hill, 1931', *Proceedings of the Dorset Natural History and Archaeological Society*, 53: 265–76.

Driscoll, S.T. (1988) 'The relationship between history and archaeology: artefacts, documents and power', in S.T Driscoll and M.R. Nieke (eds) *Power and Politics in Early Medieval Britain and Ireland*, Edinburgh: Edinburgh University Press, 162–87.

Dyson, S.L. (1998) *Ancient Marbles to American Shores: Classical archaeology in the United States*, Philadelphia: University of Pennsylvania Press.

Flaig, E. (1992) *Den Kaiser herausfordern. Die Usurpation im Römischen Reich*, Frankfurt am Main and New York: Campus.

Giddens, A. (1984) *The Constitution of Society: Outline of the theory of structuration*, Cambridge: Polity Press.

Grierson, P. and Blackburn, M. (1986) *Medieval European Coinage I. The early Middle Ages (5th–10th centuries)*, Cambridge: Cambridge University Press.

Hawkes, C. (1954) 'Archaeological theory and method: some suggestions from the Old World', *American Anthropologist*, 56: 155–68.

Heidenreich, R. and Johannes, H. (1971) *Das Grabmal Theoderichs zu Ravenna*, Wiesbaden: Steiner.

Hodder, I. (1991) 'Archaeological theory in contemporary European societies: the emergence of competing traditions', in I. Hodder (ed.) *Archaeological Theory in Europe. The last three decades*, London and New York: Routledge, 1–24.

Hose, M. (1998) 'Historia', in *Der Neue Pauly*, 5, Stuttgart and Weimar: Metzler, 634.

Jones, S. (1999) 'Historical categories and the praxis of identity: the interpretation of ethnicity in historical texts', in P.P.A. Funari, M. Hall and S. Jones (eds) *Historical Archaeology: Back from the edge*, London and New York: Routledge, 219–32.

Klejn, L.S. (2001) *Metaarchaeology*, Acta Archaeologica, 72.1, Suppl. 3, Copenhagen: Blackwell–Munksgaard.

Kühlborn, J.-S., with Schnurbein, S. von (1992) *Das Römerlager Oberaden III. Die Ausgrabungen im nordwestlichen Lagerbereich und weitere Baustellenuntersuchungen der Jahre 1962–1988*, Bodenaltertümer Westfalens, 27, Münster: Aschendorff.

Kuniholm, P.I. (1996) 'Long tree-ring chronologies for the Eastern Mediterranean', in Ş. Demirci, A.M. Özer and G.D. Summers (eds) *Archaeometry 94. The Proceedings of the*

29th International Symposium on Archaeometry, Ankara 9–14 May 1994, Ankara: Tübitak, 401–9.

—— (2002) 'Dendrochronological investigations at Herculaneum and Pompeii', in W.F. Jashemski and F.G. Meyer (eds) *The Natural History of Pompeii*, Cambridge: Cambridge University Press, 235–9.

Liddell, H.G. and Scott, R. (1996) *A Greek-English Lexicon* (9th edn, with a revised suppl.), Oxford: Clarendon Press.

Moreland, J. (2001) *Archaeology and Text*, London: Duckworth.

Peter-Röcher, H. (1994) *Kannibalismus in der prähistorischen Forschung*, Universitätsforschungen zur prähistorischen Archäologie, 20, Bonn: Habelt.

Potter, T.W. (1995) *Towns in Late Antiquity: Iol Caesarea and its context*, Sheffield: Ian Sanders Memorial Fund Occasional Publication, 2.

Reddé, M. and Schnurbein, S. von (eds) (2001) *Alésia 1 – Les fouilles & 2 – Le matériel*, Mémoires de l'Académie des inscriptions et belles-lettres, 22, Paris: De Boccard.

Renfrew, C. and Bahn, P. (1996) *Archaeology. Theories, methods and practice* (2nd edn), London: Thames and Hudson.

Sauer, E. (2002) 'Alchester and the earliest tree-ring dates from Roman Britain', *Bulletin of the Association for Roman Archaeology*, 13: 3–5.

Schweingruber, F.H. (1993) *Jahrringe und Umwelt – Dendroökologie*, Birmensdorf: Eidgenössische Forschungsanstalt für Wald, Schnee und Landschaft.

Sjöström, I. (1993) *Tripolitania in Transition: late Roman to early Islamic settlement*, Aldershot: Avebury.

Stephanus, H., with Hase, C.B., Dindorfius, G. and Dindorfius, L. (1831–56) *Thesaurus Graecae Linguae*, 1.2 (3rd edn), Paris: Ambrosius Firmin Didot.

Warne, C. (1872) *Ancient Dorset, The Celtic, Roman, Saxon, and Danish Antiquities of the County*, Bournemouth: D. Sydenham.

Wolfram, H. (1990) *Die Goten. Von den Anfängen bis zur Mitte des sechsten Jahrhunderts. Entwurf einer historischen Ethnographie* (3rd edn), Munich: Beck.

Woolf, G. (2002) 'Making the most of historical Roman archaeology', *Archaeological Dialogues*, 9.1: 51–5.

Part II

GREECE

3

BREAKING DOWN BOUNDARIES

The experience of the multidisciplinary
Olympias project

Boris Rankov

The *Olympias* project, which began some twenty-three years ago in 1981, involved the investigation of the design of the most important warship type of the ancient world, the trireme or *trieres*, the building of a ship to that reconstructed design, and the sea trials of the reconstructed ship, which was named *Olympias* (Figure 3.1). What distinguished this from almost all other ship reconstruction projects was that no trireme wrecks have been discovered to date. This state of affairs is likely to continue, since ancient warships were almost certainly unballasted (the rowing crew acted as ballast), and therefore, being built of wood, had an inherent positive buoyancy (Landels 2000: 148–9; Morrison *et al.* 2000: 127–8). Several literary texts indicate that when warships are spoken of as sunk, this really means only that they were holed and swamped, and could, as recorded, be collected together and towed away after a battle (e.g. Thuc. 1.50.1; 2.90.6; 7.34.6; Xen. *Hell.* 1.7.32). Unless we have an extraordinary stroke of luck, no triremes are ever likely to be found on the seabed.

Consequently, the reconstruction had to be based instead on a very wide range of ancient evidence – iconographical, archaeological, literary and epigraphic – combined with the basic principles of physics, naval architecture and rowing. Both the design and the experimentation on the ship have involved the skills of historians and archaeologists, naval architects and ship-builders, rowers and sailors, and physicists and physiologists. The *Olympias* reconstruction thus offers an extreme example of a multidisciplinary project, which involved the breaking down of very many and disparate disciplinary and indeed mental barriers. The experience gained in breaking down those barriers may, therefore, be of value in identifying the potential problems of an interdisciplinary approach, by throwing them into high relief.

The design of *Olympias* relied on the use, by a trained and highly experienced naval architect, of a variety of key data from the ancient (fifth/fourth

49

Figure 3.1 The *Olympias* (photo Alexandra Guest)

century BC) evidence as a basic ship specification.[1] The remains of the fourth-century trireme sheds at Zea harbour in the Piraeus determined that the vessel should be less than 5.9 metres across at its widest point and less than about 40 metres long (Dragatzes 1886; Blackman 1968: 181–6; Morrison *et al.* 2000: 4–5, 128, 132–4, 157, 192–5, 272). The hull had to conform to the standard Mediterranean mortise-and-tenon type of construction, as found in countless merchant wrecks, such as the fourth-century Kyrenia wreck (Swiny and Katzev 1973; Steffy 1985, 1994: 37–78, esp. 42–59; Morrison *et al.* 2000: method of construction 182–4, 201–4, Kyrenia wreck 128, 180, 197, 201) (the use of which in warships is confirmed by the planking found inside the early second-century Athlit ram: Linder and Ramon 1981; Steffy 1983; Casson and Steffy 1991; Morrison *et al.* 2000: 129, 167, 193, 204, 222). This form of construction and the overall dimensions determined by the ship-sheds helped to confirm that the hull should have a wine-glass cross-section, similar to that of the third-century Punic oared ships found off Marsala in Sicily (Frost 1972, 1973, 1974a, 1974b, 1981; Basch and Frost 1975; Crumlin-Pedersen 1993; Morrison *et al.* 2000: 129, 197, 200–1).

The three-level oar-system, requiring the use of an outrigger at the top level, was based not just on the name of the ship-type but also on the fifth-century Lenormant relief found on the Acropolis in Athens, and on a painting on an early fourth-century Attic red-figure vase (the Talos vase) found at Ruvo in southern Italy (Morrison 1941; Morrison and Williams 1968: 170–6; Morrison *et al.* 2000: Lenormant relief 15–24, 138–48, 158–60, 171, 198–9, 273; 280–3, Talos vase 146–8, 158, 168). The number of oars, their length, and their distribution within the ship (62 at the top level, 54 in the middle, and 54 on the bottom – 170 in total) were all indicated by detailed fourth-century ship inventories inscribed on stone and found in the Piraeus (*IG* 2².1615–18; see Morrison *et al.* 2000: 135–6). That the oars were single-manned is revealed by various literary passages, indicating that a trireme crew numbered some 200 men in total (Hdt. 3.13.1–2; 7.184.1; 8.17; Thuc. 6.8.1; 8.29.2; Dem. 4.28; see Morrison *et al.* 2000: 107–8), together with a passage of Thucydides describing the members of such a crew crossing the Isthmus of Corinth on foot, each carrying his own oar, cushion and thole-strap (Thuc. 2.93.2; see Morrison *et al.* 2000: 20, 111).

The crucial element in the reconstruction was that the naval architect then had to design a ship which would both conform to these data in terms of length, breadth, hull-type, and arrangement of oars and oarsmen, as well as float, be stable enough to sail and row, and be capable of being rowed by oarsmen distributed as described. It was the extraordinarily tight para-meters produced by all these requirements acting upon each other which made it worth while to turn the design into a real ship for further experimentation.

The first observation to be made about the interdisciplinary nature of this project is that it necessitated much more than a simple sharing of material between the classical scholar who collected the data, John Morrison, and the naval architect who designed the ship, John Coates. The two of them had to engage in a continuous dialogue over several months so that Coates could understand the ancient material and Morrison the physical constraints. They also had to consult more widely to interpret the evidence, with archaeolo-gists such as David Blackman on the ship-sheds, with nautical archaeologists such as Richard Steffy and Honor Frost on hull construction, and with experts on boat building such as Eric McKee, on ancient sail rigs such as Owain Roberts, and on rowing and modern oar rigs such as Timothy Shaw. An Advisory Discussion was hosted at Greenwich in 1983 at which a variety of participants suggested design modifications. Some of these were eventually adopted: e.g. the need was recognized for a hogging truss to support the long, narrow hull; the lines of the stern, originally based on the Marsala ships, were modified for speed; and the depth of the keel was increased for better handling under sail. Some were rejected: e.g. the use of a tension tourniquet (Spanish windlass) for tensioning the hogging truss was shown by experiment to be impracticable, and it was decided that a rockered (i.e. continuously curved) keel would have caused problems both with hauling ashore and with the arrangement of the oars. And some were rejected for *Olympias* but have been reinstated in the light of her sea trials: e.g. there now appears to be no good reason why the oars at different levels should have had differing blade shapes; and the advantages of canting the rowing seats outwards instead of aligning them fore-and-aft have been recognized (Coates and McGrail 1984: hogging truss 89–90, 134, modification of Marsala ship stern 131–2, modification of keel 133, Spanish windlass 90, 124–5, rockered keel 85–7, 101, 114–29, 132, differing blade shapes 105, canting of seats 105, 111–13).

It was thus essential to the project that there existed a variety of specialists who understood (relatively) narrow fields extremely well – naval architecture, the archaeology of shipwrecks, the rigging and geometry of oar systems – and that these specialists were consulted throughout. On the other hand, it was equally essential that the expertise of these individuals could be questioned, tested in the light of other disciplines and expertise, and, if appropriate, rejected. This is in some ways easier to do when there are many disciplines involved, and many specialists within each discipline rather than just two, and it is arguably much easier than when any one individual attempts to straddle more than one discipline alone. This is an argument, in effect, for the maintenance of disciplinary identities, both as a practical measure to enable individuals to master a discipline and for the sake of preserving rigorously independent modes of thinking which can be used as a check upon each other.

Nevertheless, one of the common characteristics of those most closely involved in the *Olympias* project was that either they had some expertise in at least two separate areas of the project or they had developed a very broad expertise within their own discipline that extended well beyond the usual boundaries of the individual scholar. John Morrison, for example, began his academic career as a tutor in Greek literature, specializing in ancient philosophy. It was his attempt to understand a passage in the tenth book of Plato's *Republic* (616B–C), which described the universe as being held together by a shaft of light 'like the *hypozomata* of *triereis*', which led him to investigate the nature of these ships and the multifarious evidence for them (Morrison and Williams 1968: 1, 297–8; Morrison *et al.* 2000: 169–71). John Coates was Deputy Director of Ship-Design for the Ministry of Defence and for several years oversaw the construction of the Royal Navy's warships, but throughout this period investigated the history of ship construction from the earliest times, became expert in the design of wooden ships, and acted as a consultant on several important archaeological projects, including the Ferriby boats and the raising of the *Mary Rose*. Much of the work on the mechanics of the oar system was done by Timothy Shaw, a rowing coach who was a physicist and chemist by training. Two of the rowing masters who ran the sea trials were experienced oarsmen and professional academic classicists, and one of them had also trained as a (terrestrial) architect.

In practice, each of them took the lead in only one area of the project. But each individual's in-depth knowledge of more than one discipline created a mindset within the team which encouraged not only a willingness to attempt to understand other disciplines but also, crucially, a willingness to accept that these might overturn the received wisdom of their own discipline.

This last observation is not self-evident or trivial. The greatest barrier to interdisciplinarity is the subject pride of the disciplinary expert, who may be prepared to allow evidence from another discipline to fill in the gaps in his own, or to lend some of his own expertise to fill in the gaps in somebody else's, but retains a firm belief in the received wisdom of his or her own discipline. It has been observed that all disciplines are necessarily based on such received wisdom, which often consists in reality of 'factoids' – ideas which began as scholarly suggestions but which have been repeated so often that they have become accepted as undisputed facts.[2] And woe betide the scholar from outside a discipline who questions one of these sacred factoids. When John Morrison, then a young don at Cambridge, first demonstrated in 1941 that a three-level oar system was practicable, Dr (later Sir) William Woodthorpe Tarn, the author of several chapters of the *Cambridge Ancient History*, an acknowledged expert on ancient warships, and a firm believer in the single-level *trieres*,[3] told him that he would be better off sticking to philosophy.

The value for researchers of expanding their current expertise beyond the boundary of one discipline into another is not that it enables them to make direct use of more than one discipline or to conflate the two into a single discipline. Rather, its value is that it enables them – gives them the humility – to question the received wisdom of both. That, in turn, can make them receptive to questioning by yet other disciplines in which they have no expertise. Furthermore, when the insights of two disciplines are brought to bear on a problem, it is essential that this is not simply a process where one discipline gives way or is temporarily given ascendancy over another. On each occasion, the assumptions of *both* sides must be investigated, even at their most fundamental. It may then be necessary to discard one or the other, or reach a compromise, or even accept that both are essentially flawed.

This process had to be gone through very many times in developing and testing the design of *Olympias*. For instance, Morrison's original solution to the nature of the mysterious *hypozomata* – 'undergirdings' – in Plato was to see them as ropes wrapped lengthways around the ship's hull to keep the timbers together (Morrison 1955; Morrison and Williams 1968: 294–8). The vertical rope shown round the stern of the vessel in the early second-century Lindos relief on Rhodes was interpreted as the end fastening for this sort of device, which ran along the hull beneath the outrigger and was therefore not visible on the relief (e.g. Casson 1971: 91–2; for the Lindos relief see Basch 1987a: 363–5). This corresponds, moreover, with a known practice for supporting a wooden hull under stress, which even has its own technical term, 'frapping'. This is described as being applied to St Paul's ship in the Acts of the Apostles (27.17), when it was caught in a storm off Malta and subsequently wrecked. John Coates initially accepted this interpretation, until his calculations showed that while longitudinal frapping might be effective for a short, round merchant ship it could not be tightened sufficiently to have any effect on a long, narrow hull.

On the other hand, such a hull had an absolute need for a device to prevent excess hogging from drastically shortening the life of the vessel and making it even more vulnerable to rough seas. Morrison and Coates therefore reinterpreted the *hypozomata* as hogging trusses – ropes stretched within the hull from bow to stern, like a bowstring, at a sufficient height to counter the tendency of a hull to arch or hog at sea. Hogging trusses are known from their depiction on Egyptian vessels of the second millennium BC (see Casson 1971: 17, 20). Since these could be rigged beneath the cross-beams of the ship, such an interpretation still conformed to the basic meaning of *hypozomata* as 'undergirdings'. Such trusses require daily tensioning because hempen fibres under tension will gradually relax, and Coates followed Morrison's suggestion, based on the same Plato passage and another in the *Argonautica* of Apollonius of Rhodes (1.367–70; see Morrison *et al.* 2000: 169–71), that the tensioning was done by passing a bar through the ropes and twisting them tight, a device known as a tension tourniquet or Spanish windlass. Experiment, however, has shown that this is impracticable because the twisting required would strain the rope fibres too close to their breaking point. He has now suggested the use of deadeyes and tackle (certainly known from the Roman period at least) which would allow tensioning by manual hauling on rope tackles (Coates 1987; Coates and Shaw 1993; Morrison *et al.* 2000: 196–9, 204–5, 211, 220–1). There has thus been a constant reconsideration and testing of the literary and iconographical evidence on the one side and the mechanical requirements and possibilities on the other. This is, in fact, one of the details of the reconstruction that has not been finally resolved: the hogging stresses in *Olympias* have been countered by a fixed steel cable (Morrison *et al.* 2000: 234). But the continuous dialogue between the different areas of expertise has carried the debate much further than would have been possible either with a single-discipline approach or a simple acceptance of a solution from one side or the other.

Another bone of contention has been the rigging of the oars. Should they be rigged forward of the thole-pin, with the oar being worked against a leather strap or rope looped around the pin (as remains the practice in Mediterranean fishing boats today), or aft of the pin and working against it (as in the northern shipbuilding tradition and modern sport rowing)? The evidence – iconographical and archaeological – is predominantly (but not exclusively) in favour of the oar being placed forward of the pin.[4] Virtually all those who rowed the ship felt that the oars would have been better rigged aft of the pin (as they themselves were used to). The sea trials in fact demonstrated that the oars could be worked perfectly well and efficiently forward of the pin, as long as the straps could be kept tight; this in turn suggested that it was necessary to fit straps or ropes which could be easily tightened (Morrison *et al.* 2000: 241–3). This is an instance in which, it can be argued, the rowing experts have been shown (probably) to be wrong in their interpretation of something which they saw as within their domain. It must equally be admitted that most of them have remained steadfastly unconvinced.

The breaking down of disciplinary boundaries thus needs to be an active process which entails vigorous self-questioning on both (or all) sides. It requires considerable effort, and the humility to accept that one can be wrong about something on which one thought one was an expert. The experience of *Olympias*, however, suggests that the struggle does not end there. One of the great advantages of breaking down boundaries is that in the process of doing it the researcher becomes sensitized to the uncertainties which lie behind his or her conclusions and generally to the assumptions and factoids of his or her own discipline. This has been especially true of the *Olympias* project, and all those who have worked on it are aware that the ship is only a hypothetical reconstruction, or rather, as Seán McGrail has called it, a floating hypothesis (McGrail 1992). They *know* that it can be questioned both as a whole and in detail, although they *believe* that it is essentially accurate.

The multidisciplinary approach, however, has made it harder for non-specialists to question the project, and the current vogue which sees interdisciplinarity as something positive and desirable in itself also makes the results of interdisciplinary research inherently more persuasive. It has been all too easy to convince non-specialists, and certainly the general public, that *Olympias* really does represent the form of an ancient trireme. Both popular and academic texts, as well as television, now invariably make use of either photographs or drawings of *Olympias* whenever there is a need to illustrate a trireme. Moreover, although *Olympias* is an archaeological experiment, and it is a fundamental requirement of any scientific experiment that it can be replicated, the extraordinary circumstances which allowed the experiment to take place together with the actual cost – £750,000 at 1987 prices – mean that it will in fact be very difficult to replicate. There is thus a real danger that *Olympias* will become *the* trireme, that the floating hypothesis will turn into a factoid.

Conversely, it has proved almost impossible to convince some subject specialists that the *Olympias* design has any validity at all. The project has met with particularly vehement criticism from many nautical archaeologists who simply will not accept that one can make a reconstruction of a ship without basing it on physical remains (e.g. Basch 1987b; Westerdahl 1992, 1993; Crumlin-Pedersen 1995; Bill 1996; Ward 2001). This attitude undoubtedly betrays a failure to understand, or rather a refusal to accept, the argumentation behind *Olympias*, but the root cause of that failure and refusal is the subject pride which has already been noted. The shades of Sir William Tarn are living yet. An early published review of the project concluded:

'But so far, well done boys! But please don't repeat it with other ghost ships before having found the real thing' (Westerdahl 1992: 85). Another, published more recently in a highly respected journal, notes that 'Reconstructing *Olympias* has been an intellectually appealing and challenging premise, but removed from primary archaeological evidence . . . we can but hope for one of the hundreds of *triereis* reported built and sunk in battles 2,500 years ago to be recovered and studied by nautical archaeologists' (Ward 2001: 556).

Perhaps even more significantly, the multidisciplinary approach has made the project very difficult to explain as a whole, even to open-minded scholars who view it favourably. Another recent review, in the *Transactions of the Newcomen Society*, the journal of a scientific organization itself much concerned with the philosophy of reconstruction and replication (in this case mainly of railway locomotives) as an experimental tool, shows a good grasp of the naval architectural issues, but questions the viability of an oar system that required eighty-five rowers per side at three levels in so narrow a hull, because the crew were so tightly packed together and had difficulties in learning to row together: 'Curiously, the whole issue seems to have become a challenge for determined enthusiasts to overcome, rather than being seen as possibly a very poor system for rowing a boat' (Smith 2001: 150). This ignores not just the ancient evidence presented, but the fact that, as every oarsman knows, rowing well (even in an eight) is quite a skilful business and takes a long time to learn – as Pericles himself noted[5] – and that this oar system eventually drove *Olympias* at very respectable speeds, albeit about three-quarters of a knot short of what had been hoped for (Morrison *et al.* 2000: 259–67). In fact, none of the difficulties came as any surprise to the coaches in charge of rowing *Olympias*, nor did the fact that they were overcome and that it became easier to achieve a good standard with each successive series of trials. On the other hand, it would still be wise for them to take another look at the epigraphic inventories, the Lenormant relief and the Zea ship-sheds which provided the parameters for the reconstruction.

The experience of the *Olympias* project, then, has been that separate disciplines do have their value in terms of maintaining depth of expertise and independent methodologies; that crossing, if not breaking down, the boundaries between disciplines requires not just a willingness to borrow and learn from another discipline, but the humility to question one's own, *on both sides*; that this dialogue and questioning needs to be sustained and never-ending; and that the humility required to do this is facilitated by the possession of some expertise in more than one discipline. It has also been the project's experience that multidisciplinarity makes it easier to persuade the non-specialist, but often impossible to convince the single-discipline expert; it also makes it much harder to explain one's work, even to a knowledgeable and favourably disposed audience.

Breaking down disciplinary boundaries, therefore, is far from straight-forward to achieve, and often leads to naive acceptance, outright hostility, or just plain incomprehension in one's audience. Is it worth it? The answer from those involved in the *Olympias* project would be very much in the affirmative. The *Newcomen Society* review, which ends by asking 'although this . . . piece of experimental work has produced a trireme, can we be sure it is *the* trireme?' (Smith 2001: 151), misses the point. Of course we cannot be sure, nor has this in fact been claimed for *Olympias*. But by working across the boundaries of many disciplines, questions have been asked and deeply ingrained assumptions challenged in ways in which they would not other-wise have been, and we are undoubtedly much closer to knowing what *the* trireme could have been, and what it could not.

Glossary of technical terms

ballast   material placed in a vessel to give it stability and enable it to float at the proper level; in the ancient Mediterranean world, large stones were commonly used for this purpose.

blade   the flattened section at the end of an oar which is placed in the water and worked against it during a stroke, forming one fulcrum of the oar (which, being a second-order lever, has two fulcra, at the thole-pin [see below] and at the blade).

canting   fixing of the rowing seats to allow the rowers to sit at an angle rather than parallel to the sides of the ship, and so face slightly outwards from the ship rather than directly towards the stern.

cross-beams   strong timbers placed at intervals across a ship from side to side to stiffen the hull.

deadeyes   two circular wooden blocks, each grooved around the circumfer-ence to allow the fixing of major ropes; these ropes can then be tightened by pulling on the end of a lanyard fixed at its other end to the centre of one of the blocks and running between them by being threaded through three holes in the centre of each block; the pull on the end of the lanyard is applied by means of a tackle (see below).

frapping   the wrapping of ropes horizontally or vertically around a wooden hull to prevent the timbers from working apart.

hogging   the tendency of a ship's hull to bend vertically, arching upwards in the middle and dropping at the bow and stern.

hogging truss   see '*hypozomata*'.

hypozomata   (Greek) ropes running inside and along the length of a hull and fixed sufficiently high at the bow and stern to counter the hogging (see above) stresses working on the hull.

keel   the timber running along the base of a ship.

knot   a speed of one nautical mile (2,025 yards = 1,852 metres) per hour.

mortise-and-tenon construction   a method of joining together planks of wood edge-to-edge by fixing small rectangular pieces of hardwood (tenons) into slots (mortises) cut within the thickness of the planks to be joined; this, the standard method of construction in the ancient Mediterranean world, allows a ship to be built shell-first (i.e. with the ribs added only after the outer shell or skin has been fixed together) and with a smooth skin (i.e. without overlapping planks). The *Olympias* reconstruction is held together by 20,000 tenons fixed into a total of 40,000 mortises.

oar-rig   the positioning, attachment and gearing of the oars in a rowing vessel.

outrigger   a frame built along either side of the hull of a trireme to support the thole-pins (see below) and oars of the topmost level of rowers.

rockered keel   a keel (see above) which is curved vertically along its length (as opposed to a straight keel, as in the *Olympias* reconstruction).

sliding-seats   seats which allow a rower to slide fore-and-aft within a rowing vessel in order to allow a longer stroke and greater use of the legs, achieved either by providing a polished or greased surface along which the rower's bottom or rowing cushion can slide, or (in modern rowing) by fixing a seat on wheels which can move along a flat surface or rails.

Spanish windlass   a device to twist and so tighten parallel ropes whose fibres have relaxed, by placing a bar between them at their mid-point and turning it.

tackle   a system of ropes and pulleys for lifting or for applying a force.

tension tourniquet   see 'Spanish windlass'.

thole-pin, thole   a wooden pin fixed to the hull of a ship and to which an oar is attached by means of a strap or loop of leather or rope; the thole-pin and oar-strap form one fulcrum of the oar (see 'blade' above).

trieres   (Greek) see 'trireme'.

trireme   the standard warship-type of the ancient Mediterranean world, powered in battle by 170 oars and designed mainly for ramming.

Notes

1   The evidence and the development of the design are discussed in detail in Morrison *et al.* (2000).

2   See Maier (1985: 32), who notes that archaeology as a discipline is especially prone to creating factoids, citing Snodgrass (1983: 142–6) on the dangers of this tendency when attempting to reconcile archaeological and literary evidence. Snodgrass rightly argues that both archaeological and historical evidence should be interpreted on their own terms, and allows that where they conflict both archaeological and historical interpretation may be at fault. It is interesting, nevertheless, that in his chosen example, of the discrepancy between Herodotus' account of the Greek settlements in Egypt (2.154; 178–9) and recent archaeological discoveries in the area, he, as an archaeologist, comes down in favour of modifying the Herodotean account in the light of the archaeology, rather than the other way around.

3 Tarn (1905). For an entertaining critique of Tarn's views, see Lehmann (1995: 160–3). Tarn's ideas had some longevity, cf. Starr (1970): 'the long-accepted view that the rowers sat in three superimposed banks is now generally rejected'; the edition of the *Oxford Classical Dictionary* in which Starr's remarks appear was superseded only in 1996.
4 Coates (1993). To the evidence for rigging oars forward of the thole-pins, which is cited by Coates, should be added (1) the position of the thole-pins shown in the oar-holes of the *Argo* on a sixth-century BC metope from the Sicyonian Treasury at Delphi (clearly visible in Basch 1987a: 240 pl. 503), (2) the evidence of wear forward of the thole-pins on oar-blocks on the upper wale in one of the Oberstimm Roman ships of the late first/early second century AD (Bockius 2002: 12, 22, 28–9, 78, figs. 9, 17, pl. 20.1–2, 21.5–6, 36.4), and (3) the rowing geometry and the positioning of the thole-pins within the oar-blocks on the upper wale of Mainz Roman Ship 1 of the late fourth century AD (Rankov forthcoming).
5 Thuc. 1.142.9: 'sea power is a matter of skill . . . and it is not possible to get practice in the odd moment when the chance occurs, but it is a full-time occupation, leaving no moment for other things'. It is irrelevant for the present argument whether the words attributed to Pericles were his own or composed by Thucydides, since the latter had himself commanded a fleet of triremes in 424 BC.

Bibliography

Basch, L. (1987a) *Le musée imaginaire de la marine antique*, Athens: The Hellenic Institute for the Preservation of Nautical Tradition.

—— (1987b) Review article on Morrison and Coates (1986), in *The Mariner's Mirror*, 73: 93–105.

Basch, L. and Frost, H. (1975) 'Another Punic wreck in Sicily: its ram', *International Journal of Nautical Archaeology*, 4.3: 201–28.

Bill, J. (1996) Review of Coles *et al.* (1993), in *International Journal of Nautical Archaeology*, 25.1: 71–2.

Blackman, D.J. (1968) 'The ship-sheds', in Morrison and Williams (1968): 181–92.

—— (ed.) (1973) *Marine Archaeology: Proceedings of the twenty-third symposium of the Colston Research Society held in the University of Bristol, April 4th to 8th, 1971* (Colston Papers, 23), London: Butterworths.

Bockius, R. 2002 *Die römerzeitlichen Schiffsfunde von Oberstimm in Bayern*, Monographien des Römisch-Germanischen Zentralmuseums Mainz, 50, Mainz: Verlag des Römisch-Germanischen Zentralmuseums.

Casson, L. (1971) *Ships and Seamanship in the Ancient World*, Princeton, N.J.: Princeton University Press.

Casson, L. and Steffy, J.R. (1991) *The Athlit Ram*, College Station, Tex.: Texas A & M University Press.

Coates, J.F. (1987) 'The strength and behaviour of tension tourniquets, or Spanish windlasses of natural fibre ropes', *International Journal of Nautical Archaeology*, 16.3: 207–11.

—— (1993) 'Should the oars be rigged aft or forward of the tholepins?', in Shaw (1993): 48–9.

Coates, J.F. and McGrail, S. (eds) (1984) *The Greek Trireme of the Fifth Century BC: Discussion of a projected reconstruction at the National Maritime Museum, Greenwich*, Greenwich: National Maritime Museum.

Coates, J.F. and Shaw, J.T. (1993) 'Speculations on fitting *hypozomata*', in Shaw (1993): 82–6.

Coles, J., Fenwick, V. and Hutchinson, G. (1993) *A Spirit of Enquiry. Essays for Ted Wright* (WARP Occasional Papers, 7), Exeter: Wetland Archaeology Research Project, Nautical Archaeology Society, National Maritime Museum.

Crawford, M.H. (ed.) (1983) *Sources for Ancient History*, Cambridge: Cambridge University Press.

Crumlin-Pedersen, O. (1993) 'Les lignes élégantes du navire de guerre de Marsala', *Les Dossiers d'Archéologie*, 183: 58–65.

—— (1995) 'Experimental archaeology and ships – bridging the arts and sciences', *International Journal of Nautical Archaeology*, 24.4: 303–6.

Dragatzes, I.C. (1886) 'Report of the excavations in Peiraeus', *Praktika of 1885*: 63–8.

Frost, H. (1972) 'The discovery of a Punic ship', *International Journal of Nautical Archaeology*, 1.2: 113–17.

—— (1973) 'First season of excavation on the Punic wreck in Sicily', *International Journal of Nautical Archaeology*, 2.1: 33–49.

—— (1974a) 'The Punic wreck in Sicily', *International Journal of Nautical Archaeology*, 3.1: 35–54.

—— (1974b) 'The third campaign of excavation on the Punic ship, Marsala, Sicily', *The Mariner's Mirror*, 60.3: 265–6.

—— (1981) *Lilybaeum. The Punic Ship: Final excavation report*, Supplement to *Notizie degli Scavi di Antichità*, 8th Ser., 30 [1976].

Hammond, N.G.L. and Scullard, H.H. (eds) (1970) *The Oxford Classical Dictionary* (2nd edn), Oxford: Oxford University Press.

Landels, J.G. (2000) *Engineering in the Ancient World* (rev. edn), London: Constable.

Lehmann, L.T. (1995) *The Polyeric Quest. Renaissance and Baroque theories about ancient men-of-war*, Amsterdam: De Gouden Real.

Linder, E. and Ramon, Y. (1981) 'A bronze ram from the sea off Athlit, Israel', *Archaeology*, 34: 62–4.

McGrail, S. (1992) 'Replicas, reconstructions and floating hypotheses', *International Journal of Nautical Archaeology*, 21.4: 353–5.

Maier, F.G. (1985) 'Factoids in ancient history: the case of fifth-century Cyprus', *Journal of Hellenic Studies*, 105: 32–9.

Morrison, J.S. (1941) 'The Greek trireme', *The Mariner's Mirror*, 27.1: 14–44.

—— (1955) 'Parmenides and Er', *Journal of Hellenic Studies*, 75: 59–68.

Morrison, J.S. and Coates, J.F. (1986) *The Athenian Trireme. The history and reconstruction of an ancient Greek warship*, Cambridge: Cambridge University Press.

Morrison, J.S. and Williams, R.T. (1968) *Greek Oared Ships 900–322 BC*, Cambridge: Cambridge University Press.

Morrison, J.S., Coates, J.F. and Rankov, N.B. (2000) *The Athenian Trireme. The history and reconstruction of an ancient Greek warship* (2nd edn), Cambridge: Cambridge University Press.

Rankov, N.B. (forthcoming) 'Ancient oar-rigs: the evidence of the Mainz Roman ships', in Tzalas (forthcoming).

Shaw, J.T. (ed.) (1993) *The Trireme Project. Operational experience 1987–90. Lessons learnt*, Oxbow Monograph 31, Oxford: Oxbow Books.

Smith, N.A.F. (2001) Review of Morrison *et al.* (2000), in *Transactions of the Newcomen Society for the Study of Engineering and Technology*, 72.1, 147–51.

Snodgrass, A.M. (1983) 'Archaeology', in Crawford (1983): 137–84.

Starr, C.G. (1970) 'Trireme', in Hammond and Scullard (1970): 1095.

Steffy, J.R. (1983) 'The Athlit ram: a preliminary investigation of its structure', *The Mariner's Mirror*, 69.3: 229–50.

—— (1985) 'The Kyrenia ship: an interim report on its hull construction', *American Journal of Archaeology*, 89.1: 75–101.

—— (1994) *Wooden Ship Building and the Interpretation of Shipwrecks*, College Station, Tex.: Texas A & M University Press.

Swiny, H.W. and Katzev, M.L. (1973) 'The Kyrenia shipwreck: a fourth-century BC Greek merchant ship', in Blackman (1973): 339–59.

Tarn, W.W. (1905) 'The Greek warship', *Journal of Hellenic Studies*, 25: 137–73, 204–24.

Tzalas, H. (ed.) (forthcoming) *Tropis VIII. 8th International Symposium on Shipbuilding in Antiquity, Hydra 2002*, Athens: The Hellenic Institute for the Preservation of the Nautical Tradition.

Ward, C. (2001) Review of Morrison *et al.* (2000), in *American Journal of Archaeology*, 105: 555–6.

Welsh, F. (1988) *Building the Trireme*, London: Constable.

Westerdahl, C. (1992) Review of Welsh (1988), in *International Journal of Nautical Archaeology*, 21.4: 84–5.

—— (1993) 'The trireme – an experimental form?', *International Journal of Nautical Archaeology*, 22.3: 205–7.

4

THE AEGEAN MELTING POT

History and archaeology for historians and prehistorians

Alkis Dialismas

Introduction[1]

This volume aims at 'breaking down the boundaries' between archaeology and ancient history; as most of the contributors work within the field of historical archaeology, defined as the 'archaeology of any period for which written record exists' (Orser 1996: 11), their shared aim is to facilitate inter-disciplinary communication in the study of the literate periods of the ancient world. While this chapter has in principle the same objective, there is a significant difference as far as the period of interest is concerned. My research focus lies within the last phases of the Late Bronze Age and the first centuries of the Early Iron Age Aegean,[2] a time that can hardly be described as 'a period for which written record exists'. Typically, we have written documents for the earlier part in the form of Linear B tablets. These, however, are mere administrative catalogues that do not provide much food for thought for historians, and they are restricted to a small number of administrative centres and palaces.[3] Homer's and Hesiod's works appear to fall outside this period, if we follow recent scholars who in the majority nowadays assign the compilation of these texts to the late eighth and early seventh centuries BC, and not to the previous centuries (Morris and Powell 1997; Bennet 1997; Mazarakis-Ainian 2000; Whitley 2002: 217–18).[4]

Therefore the task of the researchers of this period is closer to that of prehistorians than of historical archaeologists. However, I hope to show that the limited availability of literary data for this period, and their frequent ambiguity, allows two important conclusions to be reached. The first is that we should be less concerned with an integration of data at a basic level (i.e. to simply verify or falsify the information that derives from either archaeological or historical sources). Instead, we should try to integrate and combine the interpretations, explanations and reconstructions that each discipline produces, or, as Halsall (1997: 821) postulates, 'we have to eliminate the cross-disciplinary comparisons and borrowings from all but the highest and most sophisticated levels of interpretation'. Second, a reference solely to historical periods limits the scope of the dialogue between archaeology and ancient history. I would argue that it is not only archaeologists of semi-historical periods who should incorporate explanations and theories from ancient history in their discussions but that even those concerned with pre-literate cultures would benefit from this kind of rapprochement.

The interrelation between history and archaeology

The necessity of interdisciplinary dialogue has already been powerfully advocated by several contemporary scholars. They have postulated that those dealing with the historical periods should either merge the two disciplines (e.g. Morris 2000 claims that archaeology is cultural history) or be inspired by the comparison and mutual appropriation of archaeological and historical data (e.g. Hills 1997), even if very carefully applied (Halsall 1997: 821). Carver summarized his views as follows:

> We should not therefore insist on an intellectual divide between the text-user and the earth-mover. There may be a divide between the act of pattern-seeking using analysis and the act of interpretation using analogy, but it ought not to be a divide between disciplines or between theory; just two consecutive stages of the same project. So neither theory nor medium offers an obvious basis for separating the students of literate peoples into different departments.
>
> (Carver 2002: 488)

Andrén (1998: 181) went a step further and made a strong case that all archaeologists, not just those primarily concerned with literate cultures, should be interested in historical archaeology. In his view this particular branch of the discipline can act as a testing field for archaeological theory and provide models for other branches of archaeology, especially for prehistoric archaeology. Interestingly enough, this is exactly what Renfrew (1980) has advocated for one of the most studied fields of historical archaeology – that of the classical world. Hawkes (1954) was even more radical when he was constructing his often-cited 'ladder of inference'. He was quite confident that an archaeologist can investigate technology and subsistence economy while relying exclusively on material culture, but claimed that for a successful appraisal of social structure and cosmological beliefs more concrete information was necessary and that there was a need to turn, besides other disciplines and methods, to historical archaeology, which offers copious examples for analogical thinking.

There are significant advantages in using case studies from historical archaeology as analogies for other, less data-rich, periods. Indeed, the estrangement of the disciplines derives not so much from methodological differences as from 'simply poor communication and blinkered attitudes to our real context as one branch of the human sciences' (Bintliff 1991: 2). The correctness of Bintliff's first observation (i.e. 'poor communication') becomes apparent from the observation that departments of archaeology and history tend to belong to different faculties. In the few cases where they are included in the same corporate scheme (such as faculties of 'classics', 'oriental studies' or even more loose academic institutions such as 'arts' or 'humanities'), strong internal divisions tend to prevail and interdisciplinary seminars or courses are at best an occasional phenomenon. In the Faculty of Classics at Cambridge, for example, the 'official' seminars of the archaeological and historical sectors are rarely attended by practitioners of the other discipline, except for the notable exception of some graduate students. However, in 2000/01 a graduate interdisciplinary seminar was organized for the first time as an optional part of the graduate studies programme. The endeavour was successful and resulted in stimulating lectures and discussions. Unfortunately, and in spite of its success, the experiment has not been repeated so far. While there seems to be a growing desire to overcome the communication barriers, other obstacles stand in the way of 'breaking down the boundaries'.

It might be argued that these obstacles include the sheer abundance of publications produced within both disciplines during the past decades and the increased amount of responsibilities of the academic community, so that it is scarcely possible for its members to inform themselves about the intellectual developments in the other discipline, let alone to incorporate them appropriately into their work. However, this assumption is undermined by the fact that both historians and archaeologists seem capable of studying and making use of a variety of other theoretical proposals derived from disciplines as diverse as sociology, philosophy, anthropology, ethnology, linguistics, semiotics, etc. Why not then from archaeology or history respectively?

This question is better answered by Bintliff's second comment, that of 'blinkered attitudes'. The frequent polemic against, or pure indifference towards, the 'other' in the relationship of the two disciplines has its roots in the heated debates about the nature and the appropriate methodology of archaeology from the mid-1960s onwards. The general spirit can be summarized in Clarke's words:

> The danger of historical narrative as a vehicle for archaeological results is that it pleases by virtue of its smooth coverage and apparent finality, whilst the data on which it is based are never comprehensive, never capable of supporting but one interpretation and rest

upon complex probabilities. Archaeological data are not historical data and consequently archaeology is not history.

(Clarke 1968: 12)

'New archaeology',[5] in its effort to be detached from the traditions that tantalized the archaeology of the time, dismissed all methodology and explanation based on or presented as historical narrative, and consequently its proponents aborted not only all bonds with history but also those with the field of historical archaeology.

Another problem preventing effective communication is the widely held view that archaeology is a 'subservient' discipline to history; John Moreland (2001: 10–16) has recently demonstrated that this concept has even been adopted by historical archaeologists themselves. The attitude that the role of archaeology is confined to being illustrative, justificatory or 'filling in the gaps' (Halsall 1997: 819) of the literate periods has deep roots in most historians, who consequently do not bother to follow the developments in archaeological explanation. An interesting example is provided by the 'Dorian invasion'. Historical explanation, based on much later written sources, ascribed the changes that took place in the field of social practices (such as alterations of mortuary customs, use of different material culture, etc.) by the end of the Aegean Bronze Age to an invasion of a northern people, the Dorians. This theory has long ago been challenged by independent examination of the material culture (Andronikos 1954; Starr 1961; Snodgrass 1971), which showed that the chronology of these changes and the evidence for their geographical origins are incompatible with the assumption that they could have been brought about by an invasion of the Dorians; this has been confirmed by recent studies and finds (e.g. Vanschoonwinkel 1991). Notwithstanding that, this theory still dominates the papers of some historians, even if slightly altered, and despite the fact that they are aware of the archaeological finds (Thomas and Conant 1999; Pomeroy et al. 1999). Needless to say, there are some historians, such as Robin Osborne (1996), who are indeed genuinely interested in archaeological data and interpretations, even though they are mainly studying the fully literary periods.

In the field of historical archaeology there have, of course, always been scholars working with both kinds of data, but the desire to combine historical and archaeological information frequently resulted in misinterpretations. Snodgrass (1987: 36–66) has effectively shown that the effort to link archaeological data with specific historical events or information deriving from the texts has created several fallacious reconstructions of the past. Furthermore, he argues that this tendency has made 'archaeological prominence and historical importance almost interchangeable terms: in equating what is observable with what is significant' (1987: 38); such emphasis on alleged or real evidence for a few recorded historical key events disregards what is the special potential of archaeological evidence beyond illuminating texts (such as the ability to give information for everyday life, to reconstruct patterns and processes, to signify the impact of material culture, etc.).

During the past decade historical archaeology has been constantly reconsidering its scope, methodology and objectives (Moreland 2001; Carver 2002), but there has hardly been any effort, apart from a few exceptions (Knapp 1992), to create an archaeology and history that would be equally attractive to all practitioners of both subjects. Instead, efforts seem to be concentrated on demonstrating how perilous it would be to ignore either the textual sources or the material evidence. This argument cannot be challenged any more, as numerous cases have proved (for the field of Early Greek archaeology see, most recently, Morris 2000). Yet in most instances no further clarification is offered on how an effective integration of the two disciplines can be achieved. Here it is essential to bear in mind that the two disciplines have indeed different data and that these data require distinct methodologies and explanatory tools (Halsall 1997: 821), which makes integration much more difficult.

Archaeology and history as methods

It would be wrong, though, just to concentrate on differences, since both disciplines have a common goal – namely, the comprehensive study of the past. According to the generally accepted definition history studies the past through written or oral sources, whereas archaeology has exactly the same subject but relies on material remains. The problem with these widely adopted definitions is that they give the immediate impression of two separate disciplines which, by their own different means, try to understand the *totality* of past culture or, at least, make an effort to reconstruct as much of it as possible. This is an inaccurate perception, however, as a closer examination of what history and archaeology actually are concerned with might reveal.

In his groundbreaking *Study of Archaeology*, Taylor (1948) discussed the relationship of archaeology to history and anthropology. Deetz re-examined and slightly modified Taylor's conclusions in 1987 in his distinguished lecture to the Society of American Archaeology (Deetz 1988). Taylor and Deetz endeavoured to clarify the relation of archaeology, mainly with history and anthropology (including ethnology).

Ethnology, a major branch of cultural anthropology, is commonly defined as the study of culture in its living form or a 'comparative study of cultural phenomena' (Taylor 1948: 43). Deetz (1988: 17–19) summarizes the methods available to an ethnologist to study living cultures as follows: (a) to study oral and written sources, (b) to study material remains, and (c) to observe behaviour. We could define (a) as modern historiography, (b) as ethnoarchaeology and (c) as ethnography (see Figure 4.1 for a schematic

66

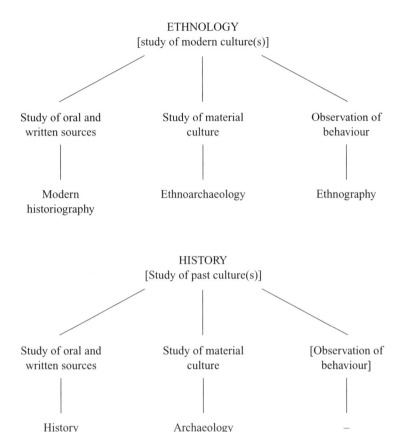

ETHNOLOGY
[study of modern culture(s)]

Study of oral and   Study of material   Observation of
written sources   culture   behaviour

Modern   Ethnoarchaeology   Ethnography
historiography

HISTORY
[Study of past culture(s)]

Study of oral and   Study of material   [Observation of
written sources   culture   behaviour]

History   Archaeology   –

Figure 4.1 Schematic representation of the relationship of history and archaeology to
the general study of past cultures

representation of the above), but we should remember that they are simply methods of collecting data of different nature and coming from different sources. Essentially the same is true for history and archaeology (Deetz 1988: 19–20). Archaeologists and historians have the same task as ethnologists or anthropologists (Deetz and Taylor used both terms), but in reference to past societies. They obtain their information (a) by studying written sources, and (b) by studying material remains; there is, of course, no opportunity for live observation of ancient behaviour. If we are to assign names to these methods, then (a) is history and (b) is archaeology (Figure 4.1). The difference between (a) and (b) lies solely in the methods used to collect different data.

It is useful to demonstrate the validity of the above schematic argument – i.e. that archaeology and history differ primarily in the methods used to approach the past – by providing a concrete example. If we investigate archaeology's contribution to the study of pottery production in the Mycenaean world, the pottery itself can tell us about quality and scale of production and distribution. Occasionally, it can also provide information about the commodities transported in specific vessels. On the other hand, the written sources of the period give us some hints about the potters and their status (Palaima 1997; Voutsa 2001), but mostly supply information about the contents of vessels, since most Linear B tablets concerned with ceramic vessels refer to them as containers of commodities (such as honey). They can occasionally even provide glimpses of details; a tablet from Knossos, for example, refers to at least 1,800 stirrup jars (Chadwick *et al.* 1986: 266),[6] thus indicating the scale of demand for these vessels. In order to reach an optimal understanding of pottery production scholars therefore need to use archaeological and historical data and methodology, and there is no need to label such synthetic researchers as either archaeologists or historians.

A suggestion for the integration of archaeological and historical data

The pottery production case illustrates why history and archaeology are essentially just different methods that are often both needed to provide a full answer to the same question. Yet, on a practical level, it is important to note that a researcher of past societies faces two significant problems. The first is that, whether we like it or not, both the archaeological and historical evidence is fragmentary and has various inherent problems. Thus different methodologies are required to generate as much information as possible, and sophisticated theoretical frameworks to interpret it. In addition, the sheer quantity of information that a scholar has to keep up with increases continuously, and new theoretical advances are being developed. Admittedly, all this cannot be effectively mastered by a single scholar – even for a single discipline, let alone for both. A second problem arises when the evidence seems to be contradictory and when there is no agreement whether the proposed interpretation of the archaeological or that of the historical sources is closer to the truth.

The dimension of these problems can be gauged on the basis of another case study from the Mycenaean period. Mycenaean archaeology still has to solve the question of whether the palace was importing and distributing bronze in its alloyed form or copper and tin separately. Bronze is an alloy of copper and tin (consisting, besides other components, of around 80 per cent copper and 10–12 per cent tin on average); tin increases the hardness of the final product. In the Late Bronze Age (and already before) all base metal objects were actually made of bronze (see Mangou and Ioannou 1997, 1998, 1999), thus the procurement of tin was as important as that of copper. The question of how the palace in Aegean communities was dealing with this is thus very interesting, since it may allow us to establish whether agents were responsible for bringing the metals to the palace and alloying them, whether the palace itself was directly involved in importing them from different sources, whether the palace played any role in the production process by alloying the metals on its premises, whether the dependent artisans who received metal allotments from the palace were allocated with bronze or copper and tin, or if they had to procure the tin by their own means, etc.

Archaeology provides the following information: the raw material was circulated in the form of ingots in the Mycenaean palatial period. The majority of these were either copper or tin ingots, bronze ingots being very rare. Luckily, two shipwrecks have been recovered whose loads comprised metal ingots of which only a tiny proportion was alloyed, the rest consisting of tin and copper (Bass 1967: 78; Pulak 1988). The majority of ingots found in mainland Greece are also unalloyed (Mangou and Ioannou 2000: 211–12, 216).

As far as the textual evidence is concerned, there are references to the term *ka-ko* and its derivatives, as well as its respective ideogram. These terms are used only as a description of the material of objects or as raw metal allocations from the palace authorities to the bronzesmiths (Smith 1992–3). The term *ka-ko* is translated with the Greek word χαλκός, which in ancient Greek (and in modern as well) is used for both bronze and copper (Gillis 1997). There is no secure reference to tin (Dialismas 2001: 125), and textual evidence provides no clues as to how the palace obtained this essential component.

At first sight the situation seems quite obscure, if not contradictory. A textual approach would lead us to doubt that *ka-ko* could refer to pure copper (de Fidio 1989: 9; Dialismas 2001: 123) because, since it is evident from the archives that the palace was highly interested in controlling the metallurgy (Killen 1987), one would have thought that in this case there should also have been a record of tin if there was any. It seems unlikely that the absence of any reference to tin is accidental, and it certainly cannot be due to limited evidence since the records that cover this specific domain are quite extensive, especially at Pylos (Smith 1992–3: 172). Thus a scholar analysing the tablets would probably conclude that the metal they refer to is bronze. However, as we have seen, archaeology suggests that the raw material arriving at the palace was unalloyed, especially in the light of the fact that we are well informed about the metal trade in the Mediterranean at the time, and since there are no tin deposits in mainland Greece which could have provided an independent supply for the palace.

In this case the combination of the data and, indeed, their interpretation, at first sight seems to lead to contradictory results, while the explanatory process in both interpretations seems appropriate and is in itself consistent. However, a clearer picture emerges if the archaeological and textual evidence are analysed separately, as suggested in the previous paragraphs, and if we only try to combine the conclusions reached independently. It is plausible to accept that the raw materials arrived separately at the palaces (the archaeo-logical proposition), that these metals (copper and tin) were alloyed in the palatial workshops, and that finally the end product (bronze) was distributed to the dependent smiths (the textual proposition). The middle part of the process (the *intra muros* alloying) does not contravene any of our evidence. Archaeologically speaking, we know that there were workshops in the palace areas (e.g. French 2002: 99), while there is no positive or negative evidence for alloying (cf. Gillis 1997: 508 who is more inclined to consider *ka-ko* to be copper). Historically speaking, the absence of any records for the import of metals is not a problem in this instance, since the archives are just concerned with distribution and collection of goods within the palace terri-tories, and we have no record of imports. Indeed, this interpretation, based on a combination of the two supposedly different sets of data, is more likely to be true than the alternatives. The option, for example, that smiths had to import their own tin (Gillis 1997: 509) can be sustained neither archaeo-logically nor historically (especially in the light of the well-known degree of control the palace exercised over metal production).

I have tried to demonstrate with this example, as well as the previous one, why, in my view, it is more fruitful to allow each method and approach (archaeological and historical) to analyse and interpret its evidence indepen-dently (as already suggested in the introduction). In this specific example a combined analysis of the data would have produced no results that histo-rians and archaeologists could have agreed on. However, if the discussion is redirected to the level of the interpretations that the Linear B specialists and the archaeologists produce, we can agree on a model, whether the explana-tion proposed here or a different one (Gillis 1997: 509).

Apart from the obvious benefit of a more persuasive interpretation, this approach also provides an answer to the problems identified at the begin-ning of this section. First, the researchers are allowed to analyse their different sets of data (historical and archaeological) separately, thus drastically reducing the amount of work for both groups. Second, the, at first sight, contradic-tory nature of the data does not prevent interpretation but raises it to a more sophisticated level.

Expanding the interpretation: prehistory and history

The question arises as to whether there is a place for a wider interdisciplin-ary dialogue for researchers of all sub-fields of human history – the second objective of the chapter. Can, for example, a scholar specializing in prehis-tory benefit from the study of historical periods and, vice versa, researchers of historical times from prehistoric archaeology?

It has indeed been suggested that historical archaeology can serve as a useful analogy or testing field for prehistoric research (Hawkes 1954; Renfrew 1980; Andrén 1998). This refers, obviously, to both the archaeology of historic periods and the textual evidence. When Homer describes the funeral of Patroclus in the *Iliad* (23.108–261), although it is extremely doubtful that every detail of the ceremony can be taken at face value and that it reflects customs of the same period, he provides nevertheless an example of how complex a cremation could be and provides one of the most revealing and vivid descriptions of such a funeral and the underlying belief system. Texts provide similar examples for several other ceremonies or practices, such as feasting. Of course, the same caution that is demanded for the ethnographic analogies (Hodder 1982) should also be applied to historical ones.

Indeed, historical parallels can provide detailed insights as to how a society was structured and on the ideologies that prevailed. These can form useful models for prehistoric times. The detailed study of Homer's epics by historians has provided a valuable picture of Homeric society from the upper levels (the kings/*basileis*, their followers/warriors and aristocrats) to the common people (slaves and a range of professions, like artisans – such as in the case of the description of Achilles' shield in the *Iliad* 18.478–609). Homer's epics also provide insights into practices that supported this structure (such as gift exchange, warfare and looting), details on the social order and appropriate social behaviour, on ideology and the impact of religion, and so on (as the analysis by Finley [1956] demonstrates). However, one problem arises; as Finley has pointed out, the Homeric society never existed in the real world. It is an amalgam of bits and pieces of real social practices of various periods and of fantastic and mythological elements, and it does not correspond to any specific archaeological period (Snodgrass 1971; Bennet 1997; Mazarakis-Ainian 2000).

However, this idealized but detailed description of an early society in the Aegean can provide useful analogies to researchers of other cultures on various aspects of real societies. There has been much debate lately on the practices of gift exchange during the period of formation of the Mycenaean society (*c.* sixteenth to fifteenth centuries BC). Voutsaki (1995a, 1995b) and Wright (1995) have suggested that gift exchange played an integral role in the rise of the Mycenaean elites and their establishment. They postulate that the ability to offer and display such gifts confirmed the status of the leader, made him part of a specific 'class', and also created the need to control resources and to obtain valuable objects, a situation reflected clearly in the shaft graves and their burial goods as evidence for the accumulated wealth. Much of this discussion derives from anthropological theory and case studies (see Thomas [1991] for a recent general account), but the Homeric society can offer even more insights: not only in the sense of enhancing the imagination of archaeologists on the exact process and conditions of the gift exchange (during warfare or official visits for example) but also in revealing crucial details. For instance, in Homeric society the whole process was accompanied by a ceremonial discussion around the valour and genealogy of the donors and recipients (see the exchange of gifts between Glaukos and Diomedes in the

Iliad 6.119–236). It was emphasized that the special items were bearing a long history of exchange (for example, the gift that Menelaus offered to Telemachus [*Odyssey* 4.612–19]) that evidently evoked memories and symbolized the great deeds and status of all previous owners. In this way the reconstruction of the Homeric society, mainly a historian's task, can be very helpful for the scholars of all societies who have reason to believe that the practice of gift exchange, or other social phenomena that appear in Homer, occurred in their period, including prehistoric ones.

I would argue that Homeric narrative is a much more interesting analogy for prehistorians (and in particular, of course, for those concerned with societies in geographical and chronological proximity to the time of Homer and his heroes), than any anthropological or ethnographical example, because it is provided by an observer much closer to the actual social context.

A final note

The case studies included here are mainly to demonstrate possible avenues of co-operation between archaeologists and historians with a research focus on the Aegean in the Late Bronze Age and Early Iron Age. Of course, there is no intention to claim that the interpretations offered here are necessarily final and correct in every detail.

What I have tried to show is that 'past actualities' (Taylor 1948: 34–5; Deetz 1988: 15) are complex phenomena and can never be even partially understood unless all the data, a wide range of analogies and the long-term processes of transformation are taken into consideration. I personally doubt that a single scholar can be in control of all the necessary specialist knowledge, methodologies and theoretical approaches in archaeology, history and their sub-disciplines. Instead, just as a competent director of an excavation does not ignore any data set and does not dispute the validity of the specialist reports when reconstructing the history of a site, the scholar aiming to reconstruct the history of a whole culture should melt all the available information together and trust the specialists who supply it.

Notes

1 I am very grateful to Professor Kourou and Professor Polychronakou-Sgouritsa, the organizers of the graduate seminar at the University of Athens, as well as to the students participating in it, for their useful comments on an earlier version of this chapter in Greek. All potential inaccuracies and errors are, of course, my own responsibility. Participation in this conference was made possible thanks to a generous grant from Jesus College, Cambridge. I am also deeply grateful to Eliana Martinis for making every possible effort to correct my English.

2 The Late Bronze Age is defined as the period from approximately the seventeenth to the eleventh centuries BC; the Early Iron Age comprises, according to common definition, the Protogeometric and Geometric periods (i.e the period from *c.* the

eleventh to the eighth centuries BC). My focus here is on the time between the thirteenth and the tenth centuries BC.

3   Linear B tablets have been found at Knossos, Pylos, Thebes and Mycenae in relatively significant quantities. The records from Tiryns, Midea, and recently Iolkos, are too few in number and too fragmentary to be relevant in our context.

4   The Linear B tablets date roughly to the period of the fourteenth and the thirteenth centuries BC. The Homeric poems were probably composed in their preserved form at the end of the eighth century and written down even later. In the same period Hesiod probably wrote his *Theogony* and the *Works and Days*. The information provided by Herodotus and Thucydides in the fifth century BC is too vague to be of any real help for the reconstruction of our period. Thus the period this chapter is concerned with is indeed at the edge of historical archaeology.

5   'New archaeology' is the name of a theoretical movement in archaeology that begun in the 1960s. It mainly opposed the traditional or normative archaeology of the time, accusing it of producing simple naive narratives. Instead it proposed a positivistic turn and suggested that the methodology of natural sciences should be applied in the archaeological interpretation as well (see Trigger 1989).

6   The tablet is KN K 700. It is broken, so it is not clear whether the record refers to an order for the production of these vases or to the number of vases stored in the palace.

Bibliography

Andrén, A. (1998) *Between Artifacts and Texts. Historical archaeology in global perspective*, New York: Plenum Press.

Andronikos, M. (1954) 'The "Dorian invasion" and the archaeological finds', *Ellinika*, 13: 221–40 (in Greek).

Bass, G.F. (1967) *Cape Gelidonya: A Bronze Age shipwreck*, Philadelphia: Transactions of the American Philosophical Society, 57.8.

Bennet, J. (1997) 'Homer and the Bronze Age', in I. Morris and B. Powell (eds) *A New Companion to Homer*, Leiden: E.J. Brill, 511–33.

Bintliff, J.L. (1991) 'The contribution of the Annaliste/structural history approach to archaeology', in J.L. Bintliff (ed.) *The Annales School and Archaeology*, Leicester: Leicester University Press, 1–33.

Carver, M. (2002) 'Marriages of true minds: archaeology with texts', in B. Cunliffe, W. Davies and C. Renfrew (eds) *Archaeology. The widening debate*, Oxford: Oxford University Press and the British Academy, 465–96.

Chadwick, J., Godart, L., Killen, J.T., Olivier, J.-P., Sacconi, A. and Sakellarakis, I.A. (1986) *Corpus of Mycenaean Inscriptions from Knossos*, Vol. 1 (1–1063), Incunabula Graeca, Vol. LXXXVIII, Cambridge: Cambridge University Press; Rome: Edizioni dell' Ateneo.

Clarke, D. (1968) *Analytical Archaeology*, London: Methuen.

—— (1973) 'Archaeology: the loss of innocence', *Antiquity*, 47: 6–18.

Deetz, J. (1988) 'History and archaeological theory: Walter Taylor revisited', *American Antiquity*, 53.1: 13–22.

Dialismas, A. (2001) 'Metal artefacts as recorded in the Linear B tablets', in Michailidou (2001): 121–43.

Fidio, P. de (1989) 'L'artigianato del bronzo nei testi micenei di Pilo', *Klio*, 71: 7–27.

Finley, M.I. (1956) *The World of Odysseus*, London: Chatto and Windus.

French, E. (2002) *Mycenae, Agamemnon's Capital. The site in its setting*, Stroud: Tempus.

Gillis, C. (1997) 'The smith in the Late Bronze Age – state employee, independent artisan, or both?', in Laffineur and Betancourt (1997): 505–13.

Halsall, G. (1997) 'Archaeology and historiography', in M. Bentley (ed.) *Companion to Historiography*, London: Routledge, 805–27.

Hawkes, C. (1954) 'Archaeological theory and method: some suggestions from the Old World', *American Anthropologist*, 56: 155–68.

Hills, C. (1997) 'History and archaeology: do words matter more than deeds?', *Cambridge Archaeological Review*, 14.1: 29–36.

Hodder, I. (1982) *The Present Past*, London: Batsford.

Killen, J.T. (1987) 'Bronzeworking at Knossos and Pylos', *Hermathena*, 143: 61–72.

Knapp, A.B. (ed.) (1992) *Archaeology, Annales and Ethnohistory*, Cambridge: Cambridge University Press.

Laffineur, R. and Betancourt, P.P. (eds) (1997) *TEXNH: Craftsmen, craftswomen and craftsmanship in the Aegean Bronze Age. Proceedings of the 6th International Aegean Conference (Philadelphia, Temple University, 18–21 April 1996), Aegaeum 16, Université de Liège, Histoire de l'art et archéologie de la Grèce antique*, Austin: University of Texas (Program in Aegean Scripts and Prehistory).

Mangou, H. and Ioannou, P.V. (1997) 'On the chemical composition of prehistoric Greek copper-based artefacts from the Aegean region', *Papers of the British School at Athens*, 92: 59–72.

—— (1998) 'On the chemical composition of prehistoric Greek copper-based artefacts from Crete', *Papers of the British School at Athens*, 93: 91–102.

—— (1999) 'On the chemical composition of prehistoric Greek copper-based artefacts from mainland Greece', *Papers of the British School at Athens*, 94: 81–100.

—— (2000) 'Studies of the Late Bronze Age copper-based ingots found in Greece', *Papers of the British School at Athens*, 95: 207–18.

Mazarakis-Ainian, A. (2000) *Omeros kai Archaiologia*, Athens: Kardamitsa.

Michailidou, A. (ed.) (2001) *Manufacture and Measurement. Counting, measuring and recording craft items in early Aegean Societies*, Meletemata, 33, Athens and Paris: NHRF Publications.

Moreland, J. (2001) *Archaeology and Text*, London: Duckworth.

Morris, I. (2000) *Archaeology as Cultural History: Words and things in Iron Age Greece*, Oxford: Blackwell.

Morris, I. and Powell, B. (eds) (1997) *A New Companion to Homer*, Leiden: E.J. Brill.

Orser, C.E. (1996) 'Introduction: images of the recent past', in C.E. Orser (ed.) *Images of the Recent Past*, London: Alta Mira, 9–13.

Osborne, R. (1996) *Greece in the Making 1200–479 BC*, London: Routledge.

Palaima, T.G. (1997) 'Potter and fuller: the royal craftsmen', in Laffineur and Betancourt (1997): 407–12.

Pomeroy, S.B., Burtein, S.M., Donlan, W. and Tolbert-Roberts, J. (1999) *Ancient Greece. A political, social, and cultural history*, Oxford: Oxford University Press.

Pulak, C. (1988) 'The Bronze Age shipwreck at Ulu Burun, Turkey: 1985 campaign', *American Journal of Archaeology*, 92: 1–38.

Renfrew, C. (1980) 'The Great Tradition versus the Great Divide', *American Journal of Archaeology*, 84: 287–98.

Smith, J.S. (1992–3) 'The Pylos Jn series', *Minos*, 27–8, 167–259.

Snodgrass, A.M. (1971) *The Dark Age of Greece*, Edinburgh: Edinburgh University Press.

—— (1987) *An Archaeology of Greece: The present state and future scope of a discipline*, Berkeley: University of California Press.

Starr, C.G. (1961) *The Origins of Greek Civilization, 1100–650 BC*, New York: Knopf.

Taylor, W.W. (1948) *A Study of Archaeology*, Menasha, Wis.: The American Anthropological Association (Memoir, 69).

Thomas, C.G. and Conant, C. (1999) *Citadel to City-state: The transformation of Greece, 1200–700 BCE*, Bloomington: Indiana University Press.

Thomas, N. (1991) *Entangled Objects: Exchange, material culture, and colonialism in the Pacific*, Cambridge, Mass.: Harvard University Press.

Trigger, B. (1989) *A History of Archaeological Thought*, Cambridge: Cambridge University Press.

Vanschoonwinkel J. (1991), *L'égée et la Méditeranée orientale à la fin du IIe millénaire, Témoignages archéologiques et sources écrites*, Louvain-la-Neuve: Archaeologia Transatlantica, 9.

Voutsa, K. (2001) 'Mycenaean craftsmen in palace archives: problems in interpretation', in Michailidou (2001): 144–65.

Voutsaki, S. (1995a) 'Value and exchange in pre-monetary societies: anthropological debates and Aegean archaeology', in C. Gillis, C. Risberg and B. Sjöberg (eds) *Trade and Production in Premonetary Greece: Aspects of trade*, Jonsered: Åström: 7–15.

—— (1995b) 'Social and political processes in the Mycenaean Argolid: the evidence from the mortuary practices', in R. Laffineur and W.-D. Niemeier (eds) *Politeia, Society and State in the Aegean Bronze Age. Proceedings of the 5th International Conference, University of Heidelberg, 10–13 April 1994*, Aegaeum, 12, Liège: Université de Liège and UT-PASP, 55–65.

Whitley, J. (2002) 'Objects with attitude: biographical facts and fallacies in the study of Late Bronze Age and Early Iron Age warrior graves', *Cambridge Archaeological Journal*, 12.2: 217–32.

Wright, J. (1995) 'From chief to king in Mycenaean society', in P. Rehak (ed.) *The Role of the Ruler in the Prehistoric Aegean. Proceedings of a panel discussion presented at the Annual Meeting of the Archaeological Institute of America, New Orleans, Louisiana, 28 December 1992*, Aegaeum, 11, Liège: Université de Liège, 63–80.

5

FIELD SPORTS

Engaging Greek archaeology and history

Lin Foxhall

Archaeology and history have long been companions in Greek studies, from the 'modern', 'scientific' beginnings of both disciplines. There is a rich range of sources for ancient Greece: written (both literary and epigraphical), iconographic and representational, and archaeological. For a very long time, for centuries even, most practitioners, whatever their intellectual or political agendas, have accepted the general principle that to understand the ancient Greek world it is necessary to somehow combine information provided by all of these different kinds of sources, even though in practice most scholars have ignored, or simply remained ignorant of, large chunks of those sub-disciplines not their own. On the whole, the close relationship between the archaeology, history and literature of the classical world remains a problematic one of squabbling siblings who, behind all the quarrels, tensions and misunderstandings, really do love each other. Why in a world of postmodern, post-processual, interdisciplinary scholarship is this relationship still so difficult? And, what is the impact of this problematic relationship on the creation of a social archaeology or a social history of the ancient Greek world?

I wonder if the fundamental aims of history and archaeology are really the same for both disciplines, as other contributors to this volume maintain? I suspect that for classical Greece the answer is 'yes', in the most general and basic sense, but 'no' in terms of the particular questions we can ask of the evidence. The result is that each discipline perceives 'the big issues' of the classical past in a different way, and may even attribute different meanings to fundamental concepts. One good example is the problem of Mediterranean 'urbanization' in the first half of the first millennium BC – the subject of a recent British Academy conference. A notion of the *polis* community appears in written sources relating to the eighth and seventh centuries BC, at least a century before there is evidence on the ground of settlements that one could legitimately call cities (Hansen 1997; Morgan and Coulton 1997). The problem here is not so much that different kinds of sources appear to give different kinds of information (though that is happening too), but a more fundamental difference in the terms of reference of both different kinds of sources and different kinds of practitioners. The question is whether the term *polis*, generally translated as 'city-state', is really a 'city' in Weberian terms, or a even a 'state' in the terms of processual (and even much post-processual) archaeological theory, at least before the middle of the sixth century BC?

I believe that, as in the example just cited, ultimately the problem becomes one of contextualization in several different senses:

One part of the problem of contextualization derives from the more recent historiography of the classical world; that is, how people within the past thousand years have studied the classical past and appropriated it as part of the foundations of their own cultures. A great many classical texts and objects have been removed from their original settings in all senses, not just in an archaeological sense. A classic archaeological example is the Greek painted pottery, especially Athenian figured vases, discovered by treasure hunters from the eighteenth century onwards in Etruscan tombs and looted from them. Thousands of these now sit unprovenanced in museums around the world, torn from both primary and secondary contexts, and no amount of empathetic scholarship can re-situate them into their 'original' contexts. How might that affect our interpretations of the scenes painted on them? To what piece or pieces of antiquity can we really securely relate these scenes and how can we appropriately contextualize them? This does not of course mean that it is useless to study them; however, it is worth thinking about the movement of ancient objects from one context to another and how that might add to or subtract from our ability to attribute meaning to them. How easy it is to forget this is well illustrated by Michael Shanks's (1999: 18) careful consideration of the issues of cultural biography and context, followed by his methodologically rather traditional interpretations of design elements in protocorinthian style, such as birds and dogs, in light of later Greek writing and thought or earlier epic verse (Shanks 1999: 95, 97). All of these literary contexts were, of course, completely divorced from archaic Corinth, and may or may not have shared thought-worlds with it.

It is less often recognized, especially by archaeologists, that analogous processes of decontextualization have also happened with texts. The prose writer Herodotus, an important source of information about how 'the Greeks' (or at least a few Greeks) viewed the cultures with which they came into contact, is frequently cited and exploited by archaeologists. We know that Herodotus came from Halikarnassos and that he lived and wrote in Athens. We do not know when he wrote; estimates vary from relatively early in the fifth century BC to the very end of the century, and are based purely on the internal evidence of the text. Even less do we really understand why he wrote his work. Though he tells us his aims in a grand way in Book 1, we cannot access his motivations from the work itself. Nor do we know how it was funded, or where, when, or in what circumstances it was disseminated, 'performed' or read. Although we know a great deal about the overall setting of the work – fifth-century Athens and its social and political organization – we actually have no idea about how Herodotus the writer can be fitted into what we know. In other words, we are lacking a huge portion of the context which we really ought to have if we are to understand properly those 'Greek' views of other societies.

These two examples both suggest the same fundamental methodological problem: who are we really 'finding' in literature, inscriptions, in art and monuments and in field archaeology? There is no reason to think it is the same people in all of these different kinds of sources, and there is good reason sometimes to suspect that it is not. The result is that it can be extremely difficult to link up the different Greeks we might be seeing in these different sources. It is useful to illustrate this first with a counter-example demonstrating how in more recent periods of historical archaeology such contextualization might be less of a problem. Matthew Johnson's (1993) study of vernacular housing focuses on how architectural forms changed and how buildings were modified between the sixteenth and seventeenth centuries AD in rural Suffolk, setting these changes into the larger picture of social, political and economic developments in England. Johnson draws upon both the archaeology of the standing buildings, and on some of the relevant documents, particularly a selection of inventories from wills of named individuals, generated as part of the probate process. In some cases specific documents are directly related to particular buildings, as when initials and dates carved onto architectural members can be linked directly to specific individuals detailed in a parish register (e.g. Johnson 1993: 149). Here, object and text can be interpreted together in relation to tangible people. In other cases it is clear that the kinds of people whose possessions, inventoried room by room in their houses, are listed in the probate inventories can be closely matched to specific architectural forms, so that it is generally clear what sorts of people lived in the houses we see. A good example is the evidence he cites for the appearance of 'double pile' houses (houses which are two rooms deep), where surviving buildings can be matched with such individuals as S. Beachcroft, clerk, who clearly lived in just such a 'double pile' house, judging from the description of his rooms and their contents in his will (Johnson 1993: 99–100). Such close connections in date and locality between texts and forms of material culture in well-documented social and administrative settings mean that we can firmly contextualize even otherwise anonymous bits of material culture in social and economic terms.

For classical Greece, this kind of exercise is not so easy. A good analogy to the counter-example just discussed which highlights the problem of differential contextualization of different kinds of source material is the problem of interpreting 'the classical (roughly the fifth to fourth centuries BC) Greek countryside'. Although there is a considerable amount of information, it does not join up like the data in the early modern example from Suffolk just cited.

The countryside often features in Greek literature. The most extensive source is the idealizing and moralizing treatise, the *Oikonomikos*, by Xenophon, a 'country gentleman' writing on estate management. However, there are many snippets in other genres, notably comic drama, where regularly local yokels in the countryside are caricatured. All of these literary sources were generated in and are relevant to Athens. (I am deliberately excluding the Boeotian Hesiod's poem *Works and Days* as too early to be relevant to the classical period, since it was probably written at the very end of the eighth century.)

Inscriptions present a different view. One group of fragmentary and severely problematic Athenian inscriptions (the so-called 'Attic Stelae', *IG* I³ 421–30), present inventories of property, including country houses and some (probably not all) of their contents, productive land, and slaves, belonging to a few very rich men. These documents were the result of a high-profile public prosecution for impiety, which was highly politicized at the time. The trial itself and the circumstances for the creation of these documents are put into context by two other Athenian literary texts (Thucydides 6.27–9 and Andokides 1). There are some inscriptions from elsewhere in Greece which provide information about the countryside, mostly leases. From Delos leases give details of the contents of farmsteads; from Amorgos and elsewhere we have details of land leased from temples or public institutions (Osborne 1988).

On the archaeological side, there are two excavated rural houses in Attica (the Dema and Vari Houses; see Jones *et al.* 1962, 1973); more recently another small rural site in the Peloponnese has been fully excavated, though the publication is not easily accessible (Blackman 1998; Pentinnen 2001). For a combination of reasons related to both the history of the discipline and the politics (with a big and small 'P') of archaeological practice in Greece, the main focus of recent archaeological work in the Greek countryside has been regional survey. There has been some archaeological survey in Attica, the territory of Athens (where the bulk of literary and epigraphic sources originate), especially in the relatively infertile ancient mining district of southern Attica (Lohmann 1992, 1993). Much more archaeological survey has been carried out, however, in other parts of mainland Greece and the islands. In most areas, with some interesting exceptions such as the Pylos region of Messenia, archaeological survey has revealed for the classical period a pattern of small, isolated rural sites often interpreted as 'farmsteads' (a term which is not safe if let out of its inverted commas).

It is therefore hardly surprising that viewpoints differ on how to join up all of these different kinds of sources: there is no easy or straightforward way to do it. Nor is there any generally accepted or very rigorous methodology, or sound theoretical framework, available. How different scholars join the various bits depends entirely on their overall (pretty intuitive) perspective of how 'classical Greece' (a problematic concept in its own right) worked.

Some American or American-based scholars, most prominently Victor Hanson (1995) and Ian Morris (1994, 2000), choose to synthesize these different types of evidence into an interpretation of an egalitarian countryside populated with 'middling' free citizen-farmers, living on their isolated plots. These interpretations draw heavily on the literary and historical context of fifth- to fourth-century Athenian democracy (probably combined with a certain amount of modern political baggage of their own). But there are many problems with such an interpretation. Even within our well-documented democratic city of Athens there was a relatively wide socio-economic spectrum, about which we have very little detailed information except to know that it existed. Moreover, these same literary and historical sources indicate that there were several different forms of government in different Greek cities. Not all of these were democratic; most, in fact, probably were not. With the exception of the Pylos region of Messenia (Alcock 2002), it would be impossible to detect from the findings of archaeological survey which regions had democratic cities and which did not. This creates a fundamental logical problem for interpretations of settlement and landholding such as those of Hanson and Morris which attempt to link archaeological phenomena directly to historically documented political configurations, and to use the resulting synthesis as an 'explanation' for constructing one particular narrative. The point is not that one or another narrative is right or wrong, but that there are many potential narratives depending on the way in which one connects different kinds of evidence.

An even bigger problem is the social archaeological issue of how to relate the sites and 'off sites' of rural occupation to people or types of person. Who lived there? Did the kinds of 'farmsteads' located by survey belong to a Xenophon-type people? Or were they inhabited by an anonymous Trygaios, a typical *agriokos*, or rustic smallholder, invented by the comic poet Aristophanes? Unlike the Suffolk example, we have no idea, and cannot link these small rural Greek sites securely to any particular socio-economic group. Hanson and Morris, like many other scholars, assume the Trygaios scenario on a very insecure basis. However, the excavated Attic country houses are quite large and well appointed. The Dema House (Figure 5.1) in particular looks like the country residence of relatively wealthy Athenians – more like the dwelling of a Xenophon than a Trygaios. Would the modest mudbrick, mud-roofed house that might have belonged to a small-scale classical farmer be archaeologically discernible? Or, as David Pettigrew (2001) suggests, are such dwellings lost in the welter of off-site scatter? Again, in all honesty, we have no idea. The point in this example is that the archaeological context of small, isolated rural sites or off-site scatters cannot be unambiguously located within the socio-economic or political frameworks represented in the literary and epigraphical evidence. Basically there is no simple way of joining up the texts and the material culture.

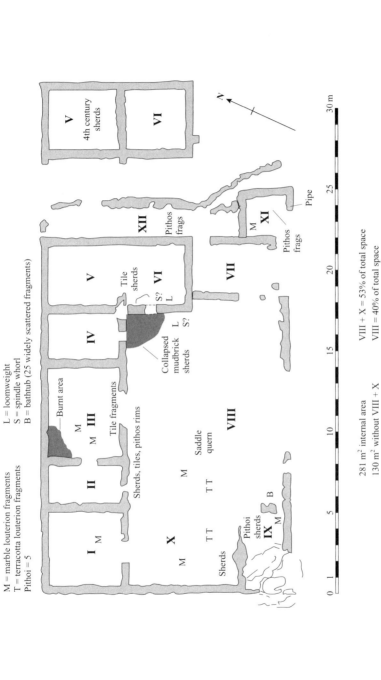

M = marble louterion fragments
T = terracotta louterion fragments
Pithoi = 5

L = loomweight
S = spindle whorl
B = bathtub (25 widely scattered fragments)

281 m² internal area
130 m² without VIII + X

VIII + X = 53% of total space
VIII = 40% of total space

Figure 5.1 The Dema House, Attica

Source: After Jones *et al.* (1962)

The core issue in this example for a social archaeology and history (that is, whom do we see in our sources?) is also related to the problem of different timescales between texts and archaeological data. An archaeological 'event' does not normally happen on the same timescale as a historical 'event'. Let me develop the above example of the Greek countryside a bit further. Although archaeological survey, our main source of information about the Greek countryside, provides invaluable long-term perspectives, for any one period – say, the classical period (roughly the fifth to fourth centuries BC) – the view presented in most survey publications is a static and synchronic one. Sites are assumed to be contemporary and all sites belonging to a 'period' of 100–200 years in length are presented as simultaneously occupied. Sometimes, as in the case of the southern Argolid survey, isolated rural sites are reconstructed as if they were central nodal points for working 'farmsteads' (Figure 5.2), each at the centre of its own consolidated plot of land (hence the Hanson/Morris reconstruction of the 'homesteading' farmer). In contrast, the textual and historical contexts of land tenure and inheritance present a landscape divided into many small plots, generally transmitted via partible inheritance, where land, houses and agricultural resources were divided into equal portions and shared among sons, with dowries provided for daughters. These historical contexts, as portrayed in the documents of Athens, Gortyn and elsewhere, directly contradict static reconstructions of the southern Argolid kind, and suggest instead a dynamic, continually shifting patchwork of landholdings. The scale of 'events' discernible in the archaeological record lacks the fine-tuning accessible in the texts. So, for example, changes from seasonal to permanent occupation, short phases of occupation and abandonment, extending or dividing a house, transfer of land to the next generation are not visible in survey data. In this case documents can lead us as archaeologists to redefine the terms of our questions about the function and meaning of small isolated rural sites, even if we cannot link the archaeological and historical evidence directly in a valid way. If we accept the kaleidoscopic countryside of the texts, how many of these sites were really occupied simultaneously, how many more might there have been, how do they fit into the overall complex of settlement hierarchies and temporal patterns, and how were they used by the people who built them to gain access to wide areas of countryside?

Conclusion

Despite their fraternal affinity, the history and archaeology of the classical world will continue to have a troubled relationship as long as each discipline forgets that the contexts of the other are different and not always straightforwardly complementary. Though we usually remember the limits of contexts in our own sub-discipline it is easy to forget them when dealing with another we know less well. Because of the history and politics of the

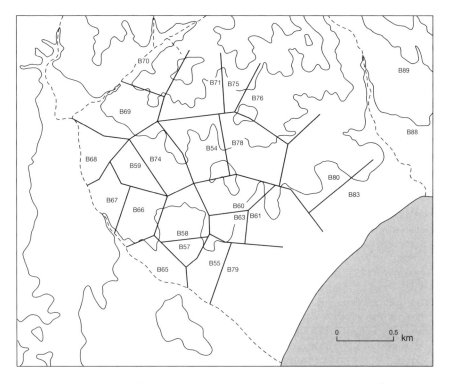

Figure 5.2 Late classical 'farmsteads' and proposed landholdings in the Flamboura area, southern Argolid

Source: Jameson *et al.* (1994: 388)

study of ancient Greece, many of our sources have been torn from their contexts, and it is easy to forget that we cannot replace them in their settings as if this had not happened. Even when dealing with modern archaeological data, these different kinds of contexts cannot be combined to produce a narrative for the classical world in the same ways as is possible for later historical periods. In the Suffolk example I cited, the scale of events and the access to individuals and contexts via texts and archaeological data converged reasonably harmoniously, with a focus on the house. For the Greek countryside the long-distance perspective of regional survey cannot pick up the kaleidoscopic detail represented in the texts, and at present there is no easy way to resolve these two viewpoints into a comfortable narrative. Perhaps this is why, at the moment, the questions asked in archaeology and history are somewhat different even if the overarching aims are the same. If we uncritically ask the same questions of different kinds of evidence we will get silly answers. However, we can, as practitioners with converging aims, try to direct our questions and investigations with an awareness of those of other sub-disciplines, to meet where we can, to recognize where we cannot, and to respect and develop our awareness of the full range of evidence for the Greek past.

Bibliography

Alcock, S.E. (2002) 'A simple case of exploitation? The helots of Messenia', in P. Cartledge, E.E. Cohen and L. Foxhall (eds) *Money, Labour and Land: Approaches to the economies of ancient Greece*, London: Routledge, 185–99.

Blackman, D.J. (1998) *Archaeology in Greece 1997–98*, Archaeological Reports, 44: 1–128.

Hansen, M.H. (1997) 'The polis as an urban centre. The literary and epigraphical evidence', in M.H. Hansen (ed.) *The Polis as an Urban Centre and as a Political Community*, Copenhagen: Munksgaard, 9–86.

Hanson, V.D. (1995) *The Other Greeks*, New York: The Free Press.

Jameson, M.H., Runnels, C.N. and Van Andel, T.H. (1994) *A Greek Countryside: The southern Argolid from prehistory to the present day*, Stanford, Calif.: Stanford University Press.

Johnson, M. (1993) *Housing Culture: Traditional architecture in an English landscape*, London: UCL Press.

Jones, J.E., Graham, A.J. and Sackett, L.H. (1973) 'An Attic country house below the Cave of Pan at Vari', *Annual of the British School at Athens*, 68: 355–452.

Jones, J.E., Sackett, L.H. and Graham, A.J. (1962) 'The Dema House in Attica', *Annual of the British School at Athens*, 57: 75–114.

Lohmann, H. (1992) 'Agriculture and country life in classical Attica', in B. Wells (ed.) *Agriculture in Ancient Greece*, Stockholm: Swedish Institute at Athens, 29–57.

—— (1993) *Atene: Forschungen zu Siedlungs- und Wirtschaftsstruktur des klassischen Attika*, Köln: Böhlau.

Morgan, C. and Coulton, J.J. (1997) 'The *polis* as a physical entity', in M.H. Hansen (ed.) *The Polis as an Urban Centre and as a Political Community*, Copenhagen: Munksgaard, 87–129.

Morris, I. (1994) 'The Athenian economy twenty years after the *Ancient Economy*', *Classical Philology*, 89: 351–66.

—— (2000) *Archaeology as Cultural History: Words and things in Iron Age Greece*, Oxford: Blackwell.

Osborne, R. (1988) 'Social and economic implications of the leasing of land and property in classical and hellenistic Greece', *Chiron*, 18: 279–323.

Pentinnen, A. (2001) *Berbati between Argos and Corinth: The excavations at Pyrgouthi in 1995 and 1997 from the Early Iron Age to the Early Roman period*, Stockholm: Swedish Institute at Athens.

Pettigrew, D. (2001) 'Chasing the classical farmstead: assessing the formation and signature of rural settlement in Greek landscape archaeology', *Journal of Mediterranean Archaeology*, 14.2: 189–209.

Shanks, M. (1999) *Art and the Early Greek State*, Cambridge: Cambridge University Press.

6

MYTH, EXPECTATIONS AND THE DIVIDE BETWEEN DISCIPLINES IN THE STUDY OF CLASSICAL GREECE

Janett Morgan

For the Greeks of the classical period a myth was a traditional story, set in the distant past, which focused on the exploits of supernatural beings such as heroes or deities. There was, however, an element of doubt as to the veracity of such tales. Their essential components, the characters and events, could not be conclusively proved as a consequence of the antiquity of their setting. As a result, any story based on a traditional narrative (*mythos*) was considered by certain writers of the classical period, such as Thucydides, to be less reliable than narratives based on investigative research (*historia*). Although both myths and histories described the past they came to be seen as opposites: the fictitious past stood in opposition to the facts of the historical past. Yet myths were much more than simple stories. They played a vital role in allowing Greeks of the classical period to form perceptions about their own past and in enabling them to explain the construction of their society and culture in the present. Myths gave expression to certain beliefs about the past. They offered a lens through which the relationship between past and present was explored and rationalized. The power of myth as a means to explain the past or justify the present made it difficult to avoid in historical narratives. Despite his misgivings about the value of traditional stories, Thucydides, in the *History of the Peloponnesian War*, attributed the development of the first navy to the legendary King Minos (1.20) and believed absolutely in the historicity of King Agamemnon and the Trojan War (1.9–12). In this chapter I wish to explore the role that stories about the past play in the construction of past and present histories. Myths, in the guise of beliefs about the past, have justified and continue to add authority to political, social and religious discourses. These, in turn, have created and maintained divisions in our approaches to the classical past, preventing the development of unified narratives or holistic studies.

One of the primary functions of ancient myth was to explain present phenomena as a consequence of past events or behaviour. Of fundamental importance to any community were notions of their origins, their genesis as a race. These origins were found by reference to the distant past and to the historical or mythical point at which the group could be clearly identified. In the ancient world, stories of the development of social and racial groups were essentially mythical. The purpose of these myths was to justify the rights of the political and social community. The Athenians explained their origins through myths about early kings such as Kekrops, who was half-man and half-snake (Euripides, *Ion* 8–27), and Ericthonius, born when Athene threw to the ground a piece of wool stained with the semen of Hephaestus (Euripides, *Ion* 265–74). These stories reinforced the Athenian belief in their antiquity as a people. They enhanced the Athenians' perception of themselves as a unique social group by providing common ancestors that were linked to the sacred pantheon and they gave authority to Athenian claims of autochthony, justifying their possession of the land of Athens. Myths of origin allowed the members of a race, or social group, to construct an identity for themselves based on perceived common origins and geographical location.

As a consequence of the opportunity that myths offered to explain, they were also a powerful and persuasive method of justification. Ancient myth could be interwoven with events in the more recent past giving legitimacy to political systems, political acts and claims of political hegemony. We see such uses most clearly in ancient tales concerning the establishment of colonial cities. Herodotus, in his *Histories* (4.150–9), writes about the origins and foundation of the city of Cyrene. He offers two distinct myths: one told by the inhabitants of the mother-city, Thera; another by the descendants of the original colonists. In the Cyrenian version, the foundation was a consequence of the expulsion of the founder Battos and his followers from Thera, following advice from the Delphic oracle. By contrast, the Theran version records a community undertaking with full Theran support. These myths reflect the differing needs of the two communities, each with an interest in the settlement. Since its establishment, Cyrene had become wealthy, whereas Thera's fortunes were dwindling. Thus, whilst the Cyrenian myth reflected their desire for independence, the Theran version showed their desire to maintain an influence and benefit from 'their' colony (Osborne 1996: 12). Myths about the past were here adapted and manipulated for present purposes. Indeed, the Therans were even able to produce a copy of the inscribed text of a seventh century BC agreement directly linking the two cities and describing the terms on which the colony was to be set up (Fornara 1983: no. 18). The cloudy nature of the distant past and of myths of origin offered the opportunity to rewrite the past to suit present needs.

Throughout European history myths have played a major role in perceptions of the past and constructions of national identities. Tales such as the

Mabinogion, a collection of medieval Welsh myths and folk tales written down in the nineteenth century, help to define cultural groups of the distant past. They can also assist in the construction of social groups in the present by creating an awareness of shared cultural links that contributes to the definition of a national identity. From the time of the Reformation in Europe, an ability to trace national origins to the past of classical Greece became highly desirable. This was largely a consequence of the need amongst the emerging Protestant nations to create a new tale of national origins that was distinctly separate from the Latin histories of Catholic countries. A separation of historical peoples, as well as religious dogma, was required. Individuals sought to read the gospels in their original language, ancient Greek, and offered new, alternative interpretations of passages in the New Testament. Knowledge of the Greek New Testament provided the theoretical basis of Martin Luther's dispute with Rome (Bernal 1987: 193). The pasts of Greece and Rome came to be placed in opposition to each other and viewed as Greek purity versus Latin corruption. Northern, Protestant countries, especially Germany, now began to identify their pasts with the mythical ideals of purity, democracy and freedom on which they had constructed the past of classical Greece. Political similarities between the federal structure of Germany and the *polis* structure of ancient Greece were emphasized in order to stake a claim to being the heirs of the classical Greeks (Bernal 1987: 213). Over succeeding centuries the religious and political interpretation of the ancient Greek past was carried through into academic spheres. Yet the past with which the German scholars identified was itself a mirage. It was as much a myth as the dazzling white statues that were created by paint erosion rather than notions of aesthetic purity. The manipulation of the past and the need to create a new myth of origins had led to a situation where the past of classical Greece had itself become a myth. It was a past constructed through the lens of political and religious discourses that served the needs of the present (Shanks 1996: 58). The ability of states to show a continuity and linear progression from this mythologized past was used as a means to legitimize claims of racial superiority and to justify political autonomy and territorial gains (Jones 2000: 445). For the countries of north-west Europe, a connection to the 'superior' culture of the classical Greeks offered confirmation of their right to political supremacy. It was used to justify imperialist aggression by both France and Britain against the Ottoman Empire (Morris 1994: 11). The potent intertwining of past with present needs saw the creation of a historical myth for political and religious purposes.

The ability to look at the political use of past mythology with the benefit of hindsight does not make our present any the less immune to creating its own myths. Morris has argued that with the removal of the social circumstances that validated Hellenism, classics as a discipline lost its validity (1994: 9). But new political and social needs continue to shape the interpretation of the past. National identities are not conclusively fixed but require redefinition as political alliances and circumstances change (Jones 2000: 448). Nowhere is this more apparent than in the evolution of the European Community. Begun primarily as a trade organization this bureaucratic monolith has metamorphosed into a geo-political entity with a drive towards political harmonization and integration. The concept of a European identity requires its own mythology, and it is here, again, that appeals to the historical past have begun to serve political ends and education has become the tool through which such myths are disseminated. The educational initiative for the study of history, CLIOH (appropriately named after the ancient Greek muse of history!), was established with the intention to find new objectives and standards for learning by looking beyond current academic structures and research traditions (François and Isaacs 2001: VII). This aim is to be achieved through the comparison of national historiographies and intensive programmes of research in thematic areas. Although the project acknowledges the diversity of European histories, the fact that the acronym CLIOH stands for 'Refounding Europe: Creating Links, Insights and Overviews for a new History agenda' suggests an awareness of the past as a political tool for the present. CLIOH's first publication, *The Sea in European History* (François and Isaacs 2001), is a study of the influence of the sea on the development of various European nations past and present. Its general, thematic approach is based on comparisons of historical traditions with a view to making connections (François and Isaacs 2001: VIII). It comes as no surprise to find that the CLIOH project is funded by the European Commission. Its aims of comparing approaches and emphasizing common elements in European history match the political agenda of the European Community. It is a form of myth-making, which implies that by focusing on common themes in the historical development of European countries we can develop a unified approach. This may, in turn, help to define the new political community. History will always be a political tool as a consequence of its value in creating political and social identities. The needs of the political present will continue to exert an influence on academic discourses and foster the development of certain beliefs about the past. This extra-disciplinary influence encourages academic separation since great and general narratives that give primacy to certain types or parts of evidence above others are easier to manipulate into an academic discourse that can be used to support political ideologies.

The close relationship between political and social discourses and education systems had a significant impact on the development of academic structures for the study of the classical past and was primarily responsible for causing divisions between the component parts of the discipline. For those who subscribed to the myth of classical Greek superiority, access to its past was considered to be through original Greek texts and access to these was controlled by academic systems (Shanks 1996: 68). The study of texts was given primacy above other sources for investigating the classical past. Texts therefore became separated, idealized and idolized by a false mythology of politically and socially influenced academic discourse. Further separation was caused by the elevated status ascribed to the material products of classical culture. This resulted in the artefacts of classical Greece being divorced from their contexts and idealized as art. The ascription of value, attribution and the evaluation of artefacts according to their place in a sequence of stylistic development became more important than the role of these artefacts in historical narratives. Art was seen as the key to understanding a culture (Shanks 1996: 56). The iconographic study of the past was absorbed into art history.

For archaeology, the advent of the scientific revolution of the nineteenth century saw profound changes in the perception of the material past and in the discipline's view of itself. Archaeology was seen as having a significant role to play in histories concerned with the scientific evolution of man and the science of man's origins. The material past of man was conceived of as a science of nature, its research methodology in opposition to art and the aesthetic humanities (Shanks 1996: 95). Archaeological writing became concerned with typology and analysis; it became scientific in its aims and literature. Classical archaeology, which had been an integral though inferior part of classical studies, began to adopt the approaches of the new prehistoric archaeology where material evidence alone was used to develop narratives about the past. The primacy of texts in interpreting the past came under question as the elite social status of the authors was deemed to make them unrepresentative of a social reality. A myth developed that archaeology as science was fact and stood in opposition to textual evidence, which was literature and therefore fiction. This myth runs deep. Even scholars who take a more holistic approach to ancient evidence, such as James Whitley, cannot resist the comparison of literary 'ideals' with archaeological 'realities' (Whitley 2001: 322). The development of different academic approaches, initiated by the influence of social and political discourses, resulted in the creation of deep schisms between those who studied archaeology, texts and artefacts.

A divide, once created, is difficult to breach. The emerging fragmentation within studies of the classical past rapidly accelerated as the different disciplines began to develop different agendas. Each component part emphasized the primacy of its form of evidence and the validity of the view of the past that it could offer. Yet the belief in primacy was itself a myth, utilized to justify the continued separation. It ignores the fundamental issue that all of our sources for the study of the past of classical Greece are equally subjective. They all require interpretation; there is no single truth. The subjective nature of each type of evidence can be illustrated in the approaches taken to investigate the notion of female seclusion in the classical Greek house. This search was instigated by the presence of the word *gunaikon* (female space) in classical texts and a belief that this referred to an architectural space.

Iconographic evidence from pottery showed images of women alone in areas that appeared to be domestic. However, it is difficult to say with any degree of certainty whether a 'real' situation is being presented or what messages we are intended to read from the images (Llewellyn-Jones 2002: 171). The archaeological search to find areas of female seclusion found no clearly identifiable or separated areas that could be strongly associated with the women of the house. In order to shed light on possible practices of female separation, material evidence was combined with modern ethnographic analogies (Nevett 1994, 1995). Through the lens of anthropology, the spatial remains of houses were interpreted to offer potential evidence to support the hypothesis that women were secluded. This interpretation was subjective, the choice of analogy being influenced by personal beliefs about the past (Hodder 1982: 19). Yet the expectations on which the initial search was based were unrealistic. They were a myth derived from the social ideology that a place should be found for women in past histories and were based on a literal reading of the word *gunaikon* in texts. *Gunaikon* certainly implies female space, but it is a rare word whose appearance in texts tells us more about social ideals than architectural realities. It illustrates the problems in extracting a single word from a text and placing a literal interpretation on it. In using texts we are looking not simply at the ideals of a culture expressed in written form and passed down through time but at a culture that has come to us through a multitude of filters. The majority of surviving texts are copies, often made long after the original text was written. Repeated copying of texts leads to a range of differences between the available copies and to a corruption of the original message (Dymond 1974: 111). It is not always possible to understand the 'true' meaning of an individual word. Translation also involves the ascription of meaning, and the meanings that we give words are subject to influences from modern ideologies and views. With regard to technical words, such as the names of domestic spaces, the desire to give a definitive translation obscures the potential range of meanings that the word might convey and limits our understanding of it (Kurtz and Boardman 1985). The myths of primacy and incompatibility began as a result of external influences derived from contemporary social and political needs. These beliefs led to divisions between the component parts in the academic study of the classical past and continue to justify separate agendas in the present.

As well as playing a vital role in grand political discourses, mythology can also be used to confer legitimacy on the ambitions of individuals. As such, myth is a powerful tool in the hands of those who would shape the past to present their own, individual agenda. The mythologizing or use of the idealized past by strong political leaders was a feature of ancient politics. This usage could take a direct form, such as the appearance of the tyrant Pisistratus at the side of the 'goddess' Athene when entering Athens to retake power (Herodotus, *Histories* 1.60). It could also involve the creation of myths based around the individual, such as Alexander's divine descent from the god Zeus

(Arrian, *Campaigns of Alexander* 7.30), or the later use of Alexander's throne and regalia by his generals Perdiccas and Eumenes to justify their hold on power after his death (Green 1990: 19). The use of myth to justify the political actions of individuals is as much a feature of modern as ancient history. Napoleon Bonaparte used symbols and political ideas from the ancient pasts of Rome and Greece to both reinforce and justify his self-conferred status as Emperor. He made a direct visual link between his assumption of power and the rule of strong ancient leaders such as Alexander and Caesar through the erection of public statues. His use of all forms of propaganda, whether written or visual, enhanced and manipulated his own image and allowed him to create a legend around his person (Grabsky 1993: 120). In a similar manner, Adolf Hitler also appealed to the myth of a divinely inspired leader to create a legend for himself by publishing the tale of his quasi-religious vision at Pasewalk. Here he claimed to have realized that his role should be to liberate the German people and restore them to greatness (Kershaw 1998: 103). Such tales create an aura around an individual. They set him apart from other men, indicating a superiority that can be used to justify his particular vision of the present. In the hands of powerful individuals, history and myth can be used to manipulate public opinion and justify individual political agendas.

A divided discipline is more vulnerable to the academic agendas of individuals with strong beliefs about the past. Within the field of classical archaeology myths have been used to catch the public eye, or to justify a particular interpretation of the past. For Schliemann, the tales of the mythical past told in the *Iliad* offered a potential means to locate material remains. His insistence on treating the *Iliad* and the *Odyssey* as historical documents caused an outcry amongst academic scholars for whom they were no more than stories (Finley 1974: 6–7). Schliemann's methodology and research were constantly questioned and frequently derided by scholars. However, unpopular as his work was with academic scholars, it was well received by the general public (MacGillivray 2001: 70–1). The Trojan War had been brought to life and the romance of Schliemann's discovery, allied with the romance of his own story, amateur versus academic establishment, touched a chord in the public consciousness (Herrmann 1981: 128). The myth of the man and the excavation was as potent as the myth of Troy. Mythology also played a major role in the excavations of Sir Arthur Evans. In naming his discovered people the Minoans, he tapped into the legend of King Minos. He gave his excavations a dimension that non-academics could relate to. In much the same way as Schliemann, Evans's use of the Minotaur myth appealed to the public's love of stories. His vision of the peaceful Minoans captured public imagination at a time of political instability and world war. It was a utopia that offered hope for the future as well as illustrating the concerns of the present. The construction of the Minoans reflected the beliefs of Evans himself who proceeded to interpret the site and its chronology according to his personal views. He attempted to suppress evidence that did not fit into his preordained pattern (MacGillivray 2001: 284–6). The strength of Evans's opinions led to an extremely persuasive interpretation of the past that still holds sway today, despite material evidence that appears to refute many of his assertions. The histories of the discovery and excavation of both Troy and Knossos have themselves become myths.

Both grand and individual mythological discourses are largely reliant on the same key factor in achieving their full potential – that of public opinion. To become successful and remain relevant, a myth must reflect its time, or have a particular relevance to the people of that time. The previous examples of successful manipulations of myth by politicians and academics all share a common feature in that they were influenced by the social circumstances of their time, as much as they were the product of individual agendas. These were myths that were accessed or created as a response to prevailing social ideologies. Whilst I am wholly in agreement with Hodder (1986: 180) that the contemporary social basis of our reconstructions of the past does not invalidate those reconstructions, the influence of modern social and political ideologies on academic discourses has enhanced separation in the study of classical Greece. The interests of the contemporary generation will always be reflected in their approaches to the past. It is possible to see in the studies of academics of the nineteenth and early twentieth centuries a focus on male public life that mirrors the interests and predominant social group of that era. The emphasis on political and religious life was enhanced by the nature of ancient texts remaining to us, which were predominantly written by a male, citizen elite. By contrast, the emergence of New Archaeology, with its emphasis on the systemic structure of society, might be seen as a reflection on the questioning of the political establishment and traditional values of contemporary society in the 1960s. The genesis of politicized approaches to the past based on modern theories such as Marxism and feminism are simply examples of the many lenses through which the past can be accessed. They are methodological narratives that enable the construction of a dialogue between past histories and contemporary beliefs. As a result of the multiplicity of approaches employed by those who research the classical past not only is the discipline structurally divided but even within the component parts there is no consensus or common dogma. The past remains open to interpretation and individual myth-making.

Myths are not only influenced by social discourses, they also have the power to shape and create public beliefs about the past. This is achieved through their role as entertainment. In the ancient world myths were told through the medium of poetry, plays at festival competitions and banquets. Within the modern world myths about the past can be disseminated through the medium of television. The current proliferation of history and archaeology programmes in television schedules shows that the past is an area of great interest to the viewing public. The ability of the past to capture public attention and appeal to public imagination, as witnessed in the stories of

Schliemann and Evans, continues today in the role of history as entertainment. Television programmes focus on the romantic stories of the past – the travels of Alexander the Great, the demise of the Minoan civilization, Atlantis and missing treasures. These are the stories that sell television programmes. This is the past that the public wishes to see. Although there can be benefits to the popularization of the past – such as the rumoured increase in applications for Roman history courses following the film *Gladiator* – there can also be a significant divergence between the interpretations of the past presented on television and those offered by academics. Balanced arguments are not as intriguing as a more entrenched position. In the recent programme *The Search for Troy* (*Lost Worlds*, Channel Four, 11 November 2002), despite constant assertions that the evidence did not support a firm identification of the site with ancient Troy, the purpose of the programme appeared to be to drive the viewer towards that very conclusion. Arguments to the contrary were presented as academic gripes whilst the views of the excavator, Professor Manfred Korfmann, were romanticized in much the same way as the views of Schliemann: one man versus academic establishment. The end result was a skewed programme. Similarly, in the programme *Ancient Greece and Rome* (*Sex BC*, Channel Four, 12 August 2002) the editorial narrative that ran through the programme contained a number of fundamental errors. Although the past cannot always be seen clearly without interpretation, there are some events that have been described in a straightforward manner and on which we can rely. Harmodius and Aristogeiton, the Tyrannicides, killed a son of the tyrant Pisistratus whose family had been ruling in Athens for the previous forty years. They did not kill the leaders of a rebellion, as the above programme suggested. Those who study the ancient past are more aware of the danger of taking sources literally, a danger that television programmes are quite happy to ignore. In the introduction to the series *The Spartans* (Channel Four, 17 November 2002), myths of Spartan rulers, such as Menelaus and Helen, were presented as historical fact. Where inaccuracy becomes excused for narrative then the past that is put on general release is a myth, a fantasy that appeals to a public starved of stories. This creates a divide between the histories of academics and history according to public perception that further fragments the image and study of the classical past.

As a consequence of its historical role in social and political discourses, the division of the classical disciplines has become enshrined in academic organization. A brief study of history and archaeology departments in British universities reveals this to be the case. As a result of the separation, the classical past continues to be prey to wider social and political discourses. The circle is completed, the division perpetuates itself. This situation appears to cry out for integrated approaches and for boundaries to be overcome. To a certain extent this has taken place. Fortunately, adherence to administrative divisions has never been an essential component of academic research. The emergence of more thematic approaches to the study of the past has led to the development of research centres, allowing academics of many disciplines to meet on neutral ground, to combine their different strengths and provide new insights into the ancient past. The principle of interdisciplinary co-operation is frequently a stated objective, as can be seen in the literature describing the aims of such centres – for example, on the web pages of the Exeter Centre for Hellenistic and Greco-Roman Culture (http://www.ex.ac. uk/classics/research/hell2.htm). The inclusive nature of thematic research allows a checked and balanced picture of the classical past to emerge. The validity and desirability of such approaches is beyond doubt. And yet I feel I must strike a cautionary note. Interdisciplinary approaches offer further insights into the ancient past, but the study of the past remains and will always be a subjective discipline. Interdisciplinary research offers another history that stands alongside those created by earlier and contemporary needs. The result is a plethora of different attitudes, approaches and beliefs about the classical past that can often contradict each other. However, in encompassing as wide a range of agendas as possible, academic discourse can be kept interesting as well as elucidative. History shows that the past will always be subject to the needs of the present. As long as we acknowledge the essential role of interpretation in studies of the past then we cannot complain about the wide range of pasts that exist. The past is a myth waiting to be told and, in stating our beliefs, we learn not only about the past but also about our present. The abundance of different beliefs about the past certainly fuels and maintains the academic divide in the study of classical Greece, but it also acts as a check. The existence of many views prevents the dominance of any single dogma. It allows the individual to make of the past what he or she wants and, as a result, keeps the study of classical Greece relevant.

Note

This article was written during my Doctoral Award from the Arts and Humanities Research Board, to whom I offer grateful thanks.

Bibliography

Bernal, M. (1987) *Black Athena. The Afroasiatic roots of classical civilisation. Volume 1: The Fabrication of Ancient Greece 1785–1985*, London: Free Association Books.

Dymond, D.P. (1974) *Archaeology and History. A plea for reconciliation*, London: Thames and Hudson.

Finley, M.I. (1974) *Schliemann's Troy – One Hundred Years After*, London: British Academy.

Fornara, C.W. (1983) *Archaic Times to the End of the Peloponnesian War*. Translated Documents of Greece and Rome, 1, Cambridge: Cambridge University Press.

François, L. and Isaacs, A.K. (2001) *The Sea in European History*, Pisa: Edizioni Plus.

Grabsky, P. (1993) *The Great Commanders*, London: BCA.

Green, P. (1990) *Alexander to Actium. The historical evolution of the Hellenistic age*, Berkeley: University of California Press.

Herrmann, J. (1981) 'Heinrich Schliemann and Rudolph Virchow: their contributions towards developing historical archaeology', in G. Daniel (ed.) *Towards a History of Archaeology*, London: Thames and Hudson, 127–32.

Hodder, I. (1982) *The Present Past*, London: Batsford.

—— (1986) *Reading the Past*, Cambridge: Cambridge University Press.

Johnson, M. (1999) *Archaeological Theory. An introduction*, Oxford: Blackwell.

Jones, S. (2000) 'Discourses of identity in the interpretation of the past', in J. Thomas (ed.) *Interpretive Archaeology. A reader*, London: Leicester University Press, 445–57.

Kershaw, I. (1998) *Hitler 1889–1936: Hubris*, London: Penguin Books.

Kurtz, D.C. and Boardman, J. (1985) 'Booners', in *Greek Vases in the J. Paul Getty Museum*, Malibu: Occasional Papers on Antiquities, 2: 35–70.

Llewellyn-Jones, L.J. (2002) 'A woman's view? Dress, eroticism and the ideal female body in Athenian art', in L.J. Llewellyn-Jones (ed.) *Women's Dress in the Ancient Greek World*, London and Swansea: Duckworth Classical Press of Wales, 171–202.

MacGillivray, J.A. (2001) *Minotaur. Sir Arthur Evans and the archaeology of the Minoan myth*, London: Pimlico.

Morris, I. (1994) 'Archaeologies of Greece', in I. Morris (ed.) *Classical Greece: Ancient histories and modern archaeologies*, Cambridge: Cambridge University Press, 8–47.

Nevett, L.C. (1994) 'Separation or seclusion? Towards an archaeological approach to investigating women in the Greek household in the third to fifth centuries BC', in M. Parker-Pearson and C. Richards (eds) *Architecture and Order: Approaches to social space*, London: Routledge, 98–112.

—— (1995) 'Gender relations in the classical Greek household', *Annual of the British School at Athens*, 90: 363–81.

—— (1999) *House and Society in the Ancient Greek World*, Cambridge: Cambridge University Press.

Osborne, R. (1996) *Greece in the Making 1200–479 BC*, London: Routledge.

Shanks, M. (1996) *Classical Archaeology of Greece. Experiences of the discipline*, London: Routledge.

Snodgrass, A. (1980) *Archaic Greece. The age of experiment*, London: J.M. Dent & Sons.

Whitley, J. (2001) *The Archaeology of Ancient Greece*, Cambridge: Cambridge University Press.

Part III

ROME

7

THE UNEASY
DIALOGUE BETWEEN
ANCIENT HISTORY AND
ARCHAEOLOGY

Ray Laurence

Archaeologists do not discover the past but take shattered remains
and make something of them. This is what makes archaeology so
fascinating.

Michael Shanks (1996: 4)

There is an urgent need to improve communication across geographical, chronological and not least professional and disciplinary
boundaries.

Simon James and Martin Millett (2001: 2)

The public and the academic

Major changes have taken place in the interaction of the disciplines that
study the human past. The numbers applying in Britain to study for a joint
honours degree in ancient history and archaeology continue to rise and are
at present on the verge of outnumbering applicants for single honours degrees
in either ancient history or archaeology. The reason for this is that the
prospective student has grown up in a world that does not differentiate
between archaeology and history. There is a demand amongst the student
body for a joint approach, and universities have responded with imaginative
course structures. However, the way in which these degrees are taught across
the UK is far from integrated. As a discipline, archaeology is firmly rooted
in the human and physical sciences; in contrast, ancient history is located
within the humanities usually within a classics department – a home that
places a particular emphasis on the reading of texts. The degree structure is
derived from single honours degrees in archaeology and ancient history with
a reduction of each element to cause it to be manageable in three years and
of a comparable number of credits as the single honours degrees. Efforts have

been made towards equality of learning for students taking joint degrees, but the delivery is in two parts by two departments, even via two faculties as an increasing number of archaeology departments realize the advantages of science-based funding. The aims of the degrees are set out in two separate benchmarking documents produced by practitioners within the two academic disciplines and published as gospel via the Quality Assurance Agency, subsequently being combined to produce the learning outcomes of the joint degree in ancient history and archaeology. Students taking the degree report back that they develop a certain academic schizophrenia when writing coursework for each department. However, on graduation, these students may be the ones who will be able to combine the two disciplinary approaches more effectively than their single honours counterparts who have a narrower vision of their subject. This is particularly true of those who are studying Roman archaeology. What prevents a full integration in postgraduate study is an unwillingness of institutions to value the interdisciplinary premise under which MA and doctoral activities need to take place, and most students are forced into one or other academic department with a toehold in the other. Often, the forcing of individuals into one or other department is arbitrary and follows an instinctive competitiveness of departments for resources, whether financial or ones of prestige.

The public perception of the study of the past does not recognize these academic divisions created within university power structures. This fact is recognized by a leading academic tour provider, Andante Travels, in their brochure to highlight the differences between their guide lecturers drawn from a variety of disciplines; it is worth quoting in full:

- Archaeology is the study of humankind through their remains.
- Classical Archaeology concentrates on the archaeology of Greece and Rome.
- Ancient History studies humankind's past through ancient texts.

It is important that these distinctions are borne in mind because your guide lecturer's learning and approach will depend on their discipline. An archaeologist is more likely to explain practical considerations such as water supplies, building techniques and how people lived, whilst an ancient historian will be at home translating epigraphs and using textual evidence.

The need for explanation by a company run by former archaeologists reveals the misconception amongst the public that the study of the past is in some way uniform. It also identifies a failure of academia to fulfil the expectations of the public and instead a tendency to be directed by the politics of disciplinary separation, self-justification and the creation of an academic identity through difference.

Into the academy

Going to university in the mid-1980s I was presented with the option of switching to a new single honours degree course in ancient history and archaeology with the additional bribe of a field course in Pompeii. All seemed ideal, with integrated units taught across the two departments, but the teaching, marking and reading lists revealed and highlighted the existing academic divisions with the challenge to create some form of unity. The ideology of separation and the definition of the relatively new discipline of archaeology that had emerged from its origins in classics or history departments were paramount at the time. Archaeology as a discipline required archaeological answers that were based on material culture. This factor, and the discipline as a whole, was often open to ridicule by historians and classicists finding their answers in texts and viewing the results of archaeology as unsurprising. Nearly twenty years on from my entry into university as a student, the rivalry seems to have changed. Archaeology is well established as a discipline and those from its former homes in history and classics view the increasing interest in this 'new' discipline as disturbing and often through the traditional academic lens of jealousy at the success of others. Many of those in post today did not experience the moment at which archaeology left classics or history as a prodigal son. However, the ideological opposition seems to still exist to the detriment of the study of the past.

Looking back over my own work in its published formats, from my current position in a classics department, I see in it the attempt to combine textual and material evidence – whether in the study of Pompeii (Laurence 1994), land transportation (Laurence 1999), geography (Adams and Laurence 2001) or less so in human ageing (Harlow and Laurence 2002). The latter may have been a final attempt to be a historian, but it was thwarted by an invitation to publish on this subject in *World Archaeology* (Laurence 2000), thus revealing the futility of resisting the interdisciplinary approach to the past. It is this final anecdotal personal experience that the reader needs to bear in mind when reading what follows: the observations made are subjective and relevant to my own academic identity that continues to emerge and, at present, seems to be going full circle in a swing towards archaeology.

Viewing the dialogue

There are those disciplinary fundamentalists who seriously believe that either archaeology or the study of texts is a waste of time. The expression is usually found in statements to the effect that archaeology does not answer my historical questions or that the texts do not aid me with the explanation of my material evidence. These statements made by academics, often in conversation, are from positions of ignorance: they simply cannot understand the nature of the discipline or the evidence in front of them, and hence cannot rethink their questions into a format by which they might be answered. Such colleagues should not be forgotten when we attempt to explain why ancient history and archaeology have failed to integrate. These practitioners of their individual disciplines wish to dismiss what they cannot understand – it may not be their fault, they simply were not exposed to the strategies for interpretation that have developed separately in the two academic disciplines.

I find that one of the more dangerous aspects of the intersection of archaeology and history is the reduction of the complexity of the past or the possibility of more interesting questions about the past in favour of chronological outlines made available from dated evidence. To give a semi-fictional example: a site has been located from its standing remains, a geophysical survey has been conducted with great success in the location of a villa and an amphitheatre on the site, and excavations follow to date the structures and to create sequences. The textual evidence is sought out to identify further information. The town was designated as such in the Augustan lists of places found in Pliny's *Natural History* 3; olive production is mentioned in Strabo's *Geography*; Livy mentions the action of conquest; the *agrimensores* record the format of centuriation for which there is no archaeological evidence; and finally the place is recorded as a market and religious centre in relation to the martyrdom of a saint. These snippets are supplemented by epigraphy, notably an inscription recording the building of baths, water supply, and, unusually, a *campus* (whatever that might refer to) for the *municipium*, alongside a number of funerary inscriptions, some freedmen, etc. The problem then is what to do with the information. Often a narrative of conquest–colonization–town building–municipalization–survival into Late Antiquity is then produced. Luckily, this approach is being superseded by an emphasis on why this place is recorded in this way – a strategy that is not incompatible with the emphasis within archaeology on the phenomenology of places in the landscape. The end result is a mutation of the traditional narrative of both disciplines towards an understanding of the phenomenology of landscape in texts and how the materiality of place was represented.

If we take the relationship in the other direction – the ancient historian using archaeology – can we identify similar pitfalls? There might be an expectation of the textually minded to be able to see on the ground the material manifestation of what they have read about – for example, drinking practices in bars or inns (*thermopolia, popinae, cauponae, tabernae*) in say Pompeii or Ostia (Hermansen 1982; Defelice 2001). This practice is beset with perils, not least in our example where different terms are used for a similar material object. We need simply to remember that in our own language there is a multiplicity of words for similar establishments: bar, pub, hotel, inn, lounge; or for restaurants: hostaria, ristorante, gastro-pub, taverna, etc. One of the greatest limits to our understanding of the material evidence is our uncertainty of how it was categorized linguistically. What was the relationship in antiquity between material culture and texts? Little work has been done to date on this subject, but it is worth noting Riggsby's (1997) study of the *cubiculum*, and Leach's (1997) study of the *vestibulum*. However, these have not led to a theory of representation of the material world in language. This would seem to be absent. There is a tendency among those who risk the perils of working in two disciplines to combine the two types of evidence within an apparatus of juncture that is seldom made explicit.

The greatest point of departure of the two disciplines is over the details of how each uses its evidence to form interpretative strategies. There is an expectation in some quarters (Allison 2001) that it should be possible to let the evidence speak for itself and to let the two disciplines form hypotheses that could be tested against each other (compare Shanks 1996 on this). Key cases are whether texts represent material reality accurately. The answer is inevitably no, since texts and material culture form two different modes of representation. Both are capable of obscuring the actuality of human action (Moore 1986) and marginalizeing, for example, a presence of children or adult women or the old. There is an unsaid complexity to our fragmentary archaeo-historical record of antiquity that we struggle to understand.

Cultural factors: modernity

The relationship between ancient history and archaeology has not existed in isolation from other cultural trends of the twentieth century. In many ways, reading the debate over the resurgence of classical architecture in the 1980s, with Prince Charles involved in a public slanging match with the architectural establishment (Jencks 1988a), I was reminded of the minor debate or squabble of ancient historians and archaeologists over the correct use of evidence. The nineteenth century – and to a greater extent the twentieth – rejected classical architecture on the very grounds that had defined its nature – a textual statement by Aulus Gellius (19.8.15). He categorizes two types of writing: one of a high standard referred to as a classic and one that was of a poor standard identified as proletarian. The former had justified the use of the classical style in the construction of the British Museum or other Regency buildings in London and, at the same time, was to become the architecture of government in Washington, D.C. – the newfound capital of ex-colonialism (see Broadbent 1991). In the twentieth century, the statement of Aulus Gellius was turned on its head to reject such architecture as elitist in favour of a new architecture for a new age of the masses – a modern style derived by Le Corbusier from the Parthenon in Athens and then transformed via a technology of reinforced concrete to produce, on a good day, modern classics (Goalen 1995; Greenhalgh 1990; Jencks 1991). Unfortunately, the architecture of modernism was reduced to the cheap, mass-produced, low-cost elements that from the 1970s onwards are being torn down by the very local authorities that created them.

The debate over architecture was never polite: modernists were labelled as Stalinists, classicists as Nazis (Curl 1992: 169–70). The aspiration of modernism to create architecture for the masses is one that is concurrent with the ideal that archaeology can rediscover the lives of the everyday as a counter to the textual remnants left by the elite that so transfix ancient historians.

The oppositional nature of the debate between modernism and classicism ran out of steam in the 1990s with the appearance of the freestyle of postmodernism. Classicists waved banners of victory over a corpse of failure within modernism to create a new society and celebrated the survival of classicism (Aslet 1988; compare Jencks 1988b). For others, there was a realization that architecture did not create a new spirit of the age, let alone new behaviours (Watkin 1977). Equally, there is little 'natural' in classicism, as anyone who has visited the bars of Richmond Riverside realizes (compare the reality with the architectural photos on completion [Terry 1988]). More interestingly, for the disciplines that study antiquity, architecture created some new hybrids that looked for meaning in the urban landscape alongside a hermeneutic interpretation of home and a sense of place (Jencks 1987: 43). The rules of modernism and classicism were distorted, as opposed to disregarded, in favour of creativity based on parody, nostalgia, pastiche and inter-textuality (Jencks 1987: 330–50). At the same time, within the disciplines of history and archaeology there was a fundamental questioning of the rules of evidence, interpretation and the aspiration of recovering lives actually lived in the past. John Barrett (1997a, 1997b) led the way in questioning whether it would ever be possible to recover the lives of those 'without history' or simply absent from the textual remains. Similarly, a greater awareness of the role of material culture as a language of representation was advocated. In this case, it was realized that the people without history from the past were probably also making a limited appearance in the material record. Simply put, the power relations of antiquity marginalized traces of women, children and the old whether in texts or material culture. Like modern architecture's death, modern archaeology's aspiration to define a people without history in direct opposition to the textual evidence also saw its demise before the turn of the twenty-first century.

The return to disciplinary praxis

In 2001, the *American Journal of Archaeology* published an article entitled 'Using the Material and Written Sources: Turn of the Millennium Approaches to Roman Domestic Space' by Penelope Allison. The text of the twenty-eight pages reads as a manifesto as to why ancient historians and archaeologists should study their separate but entwined disciplines without reference to each other's evidence or interpretations. On completion of such study, the results should be in some way tested against each other. The article reveals one archaeologist's view of the interaction of the disciplines and reveals an overall ignorance of the current practice of ancient history. The message of the article is that anybody attempting to utilize both sets of evidence is in the wrong and has transgressed the established boundaries. She opens with the familiar comment made by a Roman historian revealing ignorance of the subject of archaeology, but then suggests that Roman history is the study of personalities such as Julius Caesar or interpersonal relations in the past. In the discussion of the data, or more correctly the texts, Allison misconstrues the recent interpretations of texts; for example, in the discussion of Vitruvius she suggests that ancient historians view his work as a 'description' of domestic space (compare actual usage in articles in Laurence and Wallace-Hadrill 1997). However, it is clear from the text of Vitruvius that the work is creating a contrast between Italian and Greek architectural practices. Few ancient historians view such works as descriptions of what happened in the past; texts are always representations of practice. Few would say that the domestic spaces of Pompeii and Herculaneum only illuminate the text of Vitruvius today (Allison 2001: 188). What it can do, though, is to create an understanding of the relationship between what he wrote and a lived experience. This is to draw on the philosophical work of Henri Lefebvre, in which he observes and formulates a relation between lived experience and its representation (Laurence 1997). For Allison, such an action is found to be unsettling: 'I am perplexed that a Roman historian would use a philosopher's perceptions of the nature of space in the Roman world to set the framework for an investigation of that space' (Allison 2001: 199). It is extraordinary to read this; archaeology has always drawn on the work of others whether philosophers, sociologists or anthropologists in the formulation of theoretical positions (Shanks 1996, for example). The rejection of the use of one of the most influential thinkers for the study of space within the geographical sciences (Shields 1999: 141–85; Soja 1996) leads to the depressing conclusion that archaeology wishes to set itself in isolation, not just from Roman history but from all disciplines with the exception of anthropology. In effect, what Allison argues for is the academic isolation of archaeology from ancient history and other humanities subjects, including philosophy, and the hope that in no way would a Roman historian studying Pompeii influence the discipline of archaeology (Allison 2001: 199). We should also note here that Allison should not be seen as representative of her discipline (see comments on use of theory: Allison 2001: 200), even though the paper was published in a major international journal for the discipline of archaeology.

If a dialogue is to be achieved between ancient history and archaeology, how can it include both historians who see no value in the study of archaeology and archaeologists, such as Allison, who cannot tolerate interests of ancient historians in her subject area of archaeology? The latter has produced a reaction and that at least means there is communication. The greatest problem at the heart of the squabble is the relative weighting of evidence.

Should archaeological sites be seen in the chronological context of their time? For example, most sites in Britain from the Roman period tend to be seen within the context of the Claudian campaigns of AD 43 and the subsequent conquest, and a model of acculturation that might see the inhabitants of those places as adapting to Romanness or resisting it (see Laurence 2001 for discussion). This is to relate the material culture to the political superstructure of history in a very specific, if somewhat haphazard manner. The advent of Roman social history, with its focus on demography, the family, gender, children and ageing, over the last twenty-plus years presents new challenges and new opportunities for the relationship between the disciplines.

A different dialogue

A key problem for the relationship of ancient history and archaeology is a sense of underdevelopment of these two disciplines in their dialogue with each other. The key problem for all practitioners is how to utilize the other discipline in the interests of their own. Evidence or interpretations are plucked from one and applied in another. For example, Martin Millett broke new ground in the relationship between the disciplines in his book *The Romanization of Britain* (1990) by placing his interpretation of the process of acculturation within a context of a Roman Empire drawing on the work of ancient historians. The emphasis of the work on socio-economic institutions was in keeping with the key questions under debate within ancient history on taxation, trade and economic theory. Here, we find the historical texts creating the big picture or wider context, with archaeological evidence at the heart of the endeavour. The effect of this work on a decade of scholarship or a generation of scholars can be found in the Proceedings of the Theoretical Roman Archaeology Conference (Barrett 1997b). The movement from this work, written within the Department of Archaeology at Durham, via fieldwork in Spain and then Italy to the Faculty of Classics in Cambridge, shows the possibility of crossing the disciplinary boundary or simply of making one's work of relevance to both classicists and archaeologists.

It is a case of formulating the questions so that both disciplines may contribute to their solution. The hurdle that needs to be overcome is that those within the disciplines train students in techniques of their own discipline and to have a pride in the uniqueness or contribution of their discipline to the study of the past. Hence, what students need not understand is a sense of how another discipline may contribute to the solution of a question of one's own (see Allison 2001 for an example of such thinking). This is true of both single honours and joint honours students. There is a sense within course units of the contribution of other disciplines, but often a lack of understanding of the nature of evidence or basis of interpretation. However, fundamental to the development of a dialogue is the creation of new questions that might bring the subject areas together; or create, for the first time, a unified approach to the human past that is expected by the public, and presented to them via the powerful mediums of television and film.

Towards intersection and the mutation of disciplinary endeavour

At this stage, I wish to offer a case study of the possibility of redefining our questions and approaches to a single subject: that of dwelling. It draws on and follows from work by the sociologist John Urry (2000), who suggests a totally redefined approach for the discipline of sociology that in many ways posits an intersection of the language of society with the materiality of living. It is Urry's summation of dwelling, based on the original analysis of Heidegger, that I wish to focus on to illustrate how archaeology and ancient history may make a significant contribution together, as opposed to apart. The first step towards co-operation here is to look beyond the two disciplines for new ideas or reworkings of traditional concepts – in this case, cities, houses and landscapes. Urry sees dwelling as a state of being or staying with things. It is also based on a sense of community in terms of topographical location, a localized social system and its associated social interaction, but he adds much more: a materiality of place, a role for objects in the creation of imagined communities, and a role for objects in the creation of notions of home and belonging, alongside a community of metaphors that mask inequality in both texts and material objects. It is with this view of the community dwelling in a place that I wish to show how, in contradistinction to Allison (2001), archaeologists and ancient historians have made, or may in the future make, a unified contribution to our understanding of Pompeii in AD 79. It will be noted that much of this we already do, but in isolation or without the unifying concepts. The suggestion made here is aspirational and experimental, hence is intended as a focus of thought rather than a research design.

At the heart of a sense of community is that of history or a memory or temporality of place. Here, we can envisage the study of literary texts to understand the meta-narrative of history that could include or exclude colonization as a fundamental event horizon. This would exist alongside a memory of the construction of public monuments and private dwellings, including their destruction via seismic activity, and reconstruction for a future place of dwelling for descendants. Alternative narratives of individual lives and those of ancestors would need to be considered, based on textual analogies (see Flower 1996) alongside the study of excavated remains that provide evidence of diachronic change (e.g. Fulford and Wallace-Hadrill 1999). The utilization of the concept of the life cycle of things and people would be applied: to evaluate subjective temporal thought and the temporal survival of objects through time, and their disposal and incorporation into the archaeological record. The intersection or separation of the life cycle of people and things would contribute to an understanding of temporal senses of home and belonging. The role of monuments and monumental writing, alongside statuary, in the creation of an imagined identification with emperors past and present would be a focus for archaeologists, architects, and epigraphers. The role of writing in the creation of the imagined presence of the emperor, or in some cases their absence, would be evaluated as an identifier of community or maybe multiple identities of citizenship – the mention of Roman tribal identities in funerary epigraphy would provide a parallel study of imagined community beyond that of the locality.

The landscape of dwelling is one that is felt by the senses, yet to date little work on this has been conducted (see Hopkins 1999: 7–45 for an attempt to recreate the senses of Pompeii). We have yet to see arising from the study of architectural space or wall frescoes a model or theory of visual perception. This sense, alongside those of smell and touch, remains underdeveloped in both disciplines. It should be noted that colour and its use, and hence perception, is something we have a vast amount of data for in Pompeii. The seating in theatres and amphitheatres provides an area for the study of visual and aural perceptions, alongside the limits to the human voice. Parallel studies of the very largest structures would provide a maximum limit on the distance a voice or human action can carry across space (I would like to thank Peter Rose for these observations; see Rose 2001). Equally, domestic dwellings provide a mass of information on the use of perspective, vanishing point and the positioning of objects for visual display. Although these subjects have been studied, their interaction has not been reformulated into a theory of perception. Moreover, such analysis may allow us to understand the representation of perception in textual sources.

Maybe the greatest contribution to our understanding of the sense of dwelling has been made by Jashemski's work on plants and gardens within the Vesuvian sites. The position and layout of gardens and plots is now well known. When we think of domestic space, we should also consider the garden as part of that space and part of the conception of home or dwelling. There is a role for the natural environment in the creation of the material culture of home; these constitute part of a landscape that is both in the mind and on the ground. It can be found through extension in fresco decoration and in the representations of houses and villas in literary texts. What Jashemski (1979, 1993, Jashemski and Meyer 2002) has shown both archaeologists and ancient historians is the relevance of the intersection of material culture and text, whilst utilizing the full extent of scientific techniques. The results of her study and publication of the data allow for the consideration of the temporality of planting trees and the creation of garden aspects through time. It may be possible to calibrate the use of space and design through an analysis of the age of trees within gardens and courtyards. Further, we may consider the creation of light and shade across the dwellings and interpret its value.(I owe these observations to Diana Rowell.)

The built environment itself can become the object of study in terms of its setting as a place of consumption. Here, I am thinking not so much of the daily life of the economy, but rather of the establishment of a network of connections beyond the city. The best-known forms of such analysis are those of pottery; we can find amphorae from right across the Mediterranean and beyond. There are other materials for analysis, notably building materials and specialized use of stone. Marble is a frequently studied item, but there are others such as basalts, bricks, travertines and limestones. The advances in geo-archaeology permit identification of the geological sources of these (see, for example, Peacock 1989 on millstones). Similarly, the movement of local materials further afield provides the possibility of viewing the network of relationships beyond the locality of the city itself. This raises the question of the meaning of such networks; do they for example represent a pattern of landownership across space with an individual supplying a city with materials from an estate? How are alien materials, such as marble, incorporated into a concept of home and dwelling that can utilize the exotic to create a notion of superiority over other inhabitants?

In approaching objects that are part of dwelling, I feel there is a need to begin again. Many objects are labelled with reference to texts (Allison 2001), and hence are categorized together. The problem for us is to break away from such categories and to examine their role in the creation of dwelling and their relationship to furniture and space. The representation of such objects in texts can be approached in a similar manner to ask: why were they written about? What was their purpose in the etymological and antiquarian literature of Varro and Festus? The latter may reveal not so much what they were for, but an understanding of the role of material objects in texts – a subject to date uninvestigated.

Above, I have suggested possibilities of a dialogue to understand a sense of place or dwelling at a single site destroyed at a specific moment. The emphasis is not on how people lived but on what the conception of dwelling meant – whether represented in texts or material culture. The possibility of interaction lies in the alteration of what we wish to know. It is not a dialogue to recreate the lives of the past or the inhabitants' everyday life, and we need to recognize that such an ambition is beyond the capability of either discipline. By refiguring the question and the possibility or attainment of an answer, which is obtainable, it is possible to open a dialogue. In other words, the two disciplines need to rethink their priorities away from specifics of the past towards a historical sociology of habitation and of what constitutes a community or home in the material and written record. Unless we reformulate the questions, we will be unable to progress in an engagement across the disciplinary divide.

A future before us

Generally, there is recognition within academia that both disciplines have much to offer each other. The boundary between the two subject areas is in many ways artificial, but part of the architecture or organization of universities. It is worth noting here that in the UK the AHRB (Arts and Humanities Research Board) and the LTSN (Learning and Teaching Support Network) group archaeology, classics and history together, yet few universities place these disciplines together in a single school or mega-department. Within archaeology, ancient historians have a marginal position to the discipline maybe similar to that of zooarchaeologists (see Dobney 2001). The central area of the discipline's focus continues to be on settlements and material culture, with a willingness but inability to incorporate all the available evidence into this package to include the human endeavour of representation and the results of archaeological science into such matters as food consumption and horticulture. Texts are simply another form of evidence available to archaeology; unfortunately, few archaeology degrees incorporate an understanding of the written evidence into their curriculum.

The posing of new questions would seem to be a way forward towards interaction as opposed to mutual separation. There has been a tendency for many in the two disciplines to ask quite different questions of the past to begin with, and then upon making a conclusion from their respective evidence to ask the same question of the other discipline's evidence. The result is an inevitable disjuncture confirming the extant academic division. The problem for us, if we want to interact, is to define topics of analysis that can be addressed via all the evidence available (as I have attempted to suggest above for Pompeii). The level of interaction need not be that of primary research – for example fieldwork or textual analysis – but rather one of synthesis and narrative. The way we present material in narrative form is essential for the development of the subject (the study of the past). By altering the traditional subject – historical narrative or descriptions of settlement or artefactual records – we can begin to consider formats that are open to universal contribution from across the two disciplines. Hill (2001) suggests the following areas for the study of identity: the body, foodways, settlement space and consumption. (I would add some others; see Laurence 2001.)

The question arises, inevitably, as to how we might achieve such bold aims to bring the two disciplines together. There is an untapped resource: those who have graduated in both subjects. They have been trained in both subjects, have abilities in both disciplines (contrary to the view put forward by Allison 2001), and have an understanding of how the academic structure of the two disciplines creates separation in the study of antiquity. It is a question of reorganization to provide a structure for these graduates within directed masters and doctoral programmes that can produce the synthesis that is desired and needed (Hill 2001: 15), rather than the current emphasis of students following the politics of division created by the universities across (and beyond) the UK. These students on entry into university saw ancient history and archaeology as a unity with different evidence deployed, but discovered during their degree there had developed contrasting academic cultures in their respective departments. In some ways, there is already a movement towards such an outcome. Those of the TRAC generation (on which see Allison 2001: 200; Hill 2001: 12 for very different views) have taken the first steps towards such a juncture with frequent reference to the literary and archaeological sources and experimental uses of theory, with a move away from, but a lingering obsession with, Romanization and ethnic or cultural identity. If we are going to encourage our students to study across the united discipline, a shift in the attitude has to occur within academia to permit it. All subscribe to interdisciplinary studies in principle, but in practice many will find that there will be a reason for confining a person to a discipline or a department. The Research Assessment Exercise encourages universities to categorize an academic singularly as an ancient historian or an archaeologist. Being half of each does not work; hence there is a choice to be made – colleagues who had been appointed to be in two departments end up retreating to the most secure, with their two heads of department fighting to secure them into their own political world. This process begins at the level of postgraduate students and a squabble for the diminishing human resource – those prepared or able to endure the debts associated with full-time study in Britain's universities.

However, we should recognize that there has been a change generally from the dialogue that focuses on whose evidence might be best and the assumption by some of the superiority of written evidence (see Reece 1988 for a view from our past). There is a difference in the disciplines from the positions of the 1980s: the outlook has become more European and more confident about the importance of material culture's contribution to human society. The question of whether you are or are not an ancient historian or archaeologist ceases to have meaning today (apart from the moments of entrenchment, such as academic appointments and interviews – i.e. in the context of the architecture of or expressions of power in universities). The discipline of Roman archaeology seems to have become more comfortable with itself, and also with ancient historians striving to develop answers to different, but relevant questions. The reason for these changes may lie in the recognition within postmodernist cultures that there is no right way to approach the past and an emphasis on the celebration of the pluralism that may be carried over into the academic study of the past. Where the relationship between the two disciplines goes from here is up to us – and that means you.

Bibliography

Adams, C. and Laurence, R. (2001) *Travel and Geography in the Roman Empire*, London: Routledge.

Allison, P.M. (2001) 'Using the material and written sources: turn of the millennium approaches to Roman domestic space', *American Journal of Archaeology*, 105: 181–208.

Aslet, C. (1988) 'Classicism for the year 2000', *Architectural Design Profile*, 71: 5–9.

Barrett, J.C. (1997a) 'Romanization: a critical comment', in D. Mattingly (ed.) *Dialogues in Roman Imperialism*, Portsmouth, R.I.: Journal of Roman Archaeology Suppl., 23: 51–66.

—— (1997b) 'Theorising Roman archaeology', in K. Meadows, C. Lemke and J. Heron (eds) *TRAC 96. Proceedings of the Sixth Annual Theoretical Roman Archaeology Conference, Sheffield, 1996*, Oxford: Oxbow Books, 1–7.

Broadbent, G. (1991) 'Neo-classicism', *Architectural Design Profile*, Special issue, 23.

Curl, S. (1992) *Classical Architecture*, London: Batsford.

Defelice, J. (2001) *Roman Hospitality: The professional women of Pompeii*, Warren Center, Pa.: Shangri-La Publications.

Dobney, K. (2001) 'A place at the table: the role of vertebrate zooarchaeology within a Roman research agenda for Britain', in S. James and M. Millett (eds) *Britons and Romans: Advancing an archaeological agenda*, York: CBA Research Report 125, 36–45.

Flower, H.I. (1996) *Ancestor Masks and Aristocratic Power in Roman Culture*, Oxford: Clarendon Press.

Fulford, M. and Wallace-Hadrill, A. (1999) 'Towards a history of pre-Roman Pompeii: excavations beneath the House of Amarantus (I.9.11–12), 1995–8', *Papers of the British School at Rome*, 67: 37–144.

Goalen, M. (1995) 'The idea of the city and the excavations at Pompeii', in T. Cornell and K. Lomas (eds) *Urban Society in Roman Italy*, London: UCL Press, 181–202.

Greenhalgh, M. (1990) *What is Classicism?*, London.

Harlow, M. and Laurence, R. (2002) *Growing Up and Growing Old in Ancient Rome*, London: Routledge.

Hermansen, G. (1982) *Ostia: Aspects of city life*, Alberta: University of Alberta Press.

Hill, J.D. (2001) 'Romanisation, gender and class: recent approaches to identity in Britain and their possible consequences', in S. James and M. Millett (eds) *Britons and Romans: Advancing an archaeological agenda*, York: CBA Research Report 125, 12–18.

Hopkins, K. (1999) *A World Full of Gods*, London: Weidenfeld and Nicolson.

James, S. and Millett, M. (2001) 'Introduction', in S. James and M. Millett (eds) *Britons and Romans: Advancing an archaeological agenda*, York: CBA Research Report 125, 1–3.

Jashemski, W.F. (1979) *The Gardens of Pompeii*, Vol. 1, New York: Caratzas Brothers.

—— (1993) *The Gardens of Pompeii*, Vol. 2, New York: Caratzas Brothers.

—— and Meyer, F.G. (eds) (2002) *The Natural History of Pompeii*, Cambridge, Cambridge University Press.

Jencks, C. (1987) *Post-modernism. The new classicism in art and architecture*, London: Academy Editions.

—— (1988a) *The Prince, the Architects and New Wave Monarchy*, London: Academy.

—— (1988b) 'The new classicism and its emergent rules', *Architectural Design Profile*, 71: 23–31.

—— (1991) 'Post-modern triumphs in London', *Architectural Design Profile*, 91: 8–13.

Laurence, R. (1994) *Roman Pompeii: Space and society*, London: Routledge.

—— (1997) 'Space and text', in Laurence and Wallace-Hadrill (1997): 7–14.

—— (1999) *The Roads of Roman Italy: Mobility and cultural change*, London: Routledge

—— (2000) 'Metaphors, monuments and texts: the life course in Roman culture', *World Archaeology*, 31: 442–55.

—— (2001) 'Roman narratives: the writing of archaeological discourse – a view from Britain', *Archaeological Dialogues*, 8: 90–123.

Laurence, R. and Wallace-Hadrill, A. (eds) (1997) *Domestic Space in the Roman World: Pompeii and beyond*, Portsmouth, R.I.: Journal of Roman Archaeology Suppl., 22.

Leach, E.W. (1997) 'Oecus on Ibycus: investigating the vocabulary of the Roman house', in S.E. Bon and R. Jones (eds) *Sequence and Space in Pompeii*, Oxford: Oxbow Monograph, 77: 50–72.

Millett, M. (1981) 'Whose crisis? The archaeology of the third century: a warning', in A. King and M. Henig (eds) *The Roman West in the Third Century*, Oxford: BAR Int. Ser., 109: 525–30.

—— (1990) *The Romanization of Britain*, Cambridge: Cambridge University Press.

Moore, H.L. (1986) *Space, Text and Gender. An anthropological study of the Marakwet of Kenya*, New York and London: Guildford Press.

Peacock, D.P.S. (1989) 'The mills of Pompeii', *Antiquity*, 63: 205–14.

Reece, R. (1988) *My Roman Britain*, Cotswold Studies 3, Cirencester: Cotswold Studies and Oxbow.

Riggsby, A.M. (1997) '"Public" and "private" in Roman culture: the case of the *cubiculum*', *Journal of Roman Archaeology*, 10: 36–56.

Rose, P. (2001) 'Spectators and Spectator Comfort in Roman Entertainment Buildings', unpublished MA dissertation, University of Reading.

Shanks, M. (1996) *Classical Archaeology of Greece: Experiences of the discipline*, London: Routledge.

Shields, R. (1999) *Lefebvre, Love and Struggle*, London: Routledge.

Soja, E.W. (1996) *Thirdspace: Journeys to Los Angeles and other real-and-imagined places*, Oxford: Blackwell.

Terry, Q. (1988) 'Richmond Riverside', *Architectural Design Profile*, 75: 32–7.

Urry, J. (2000) *Sociology Beyond Societies: Mobilities for the twenty-first century*, London: Routledge.

Wallace-Hadrill, A. (1997) 'Rethinking the Roman atrium house', in Laurence and Wallace-Hadrill (1997): 219–40.

Watkin, D. (1977) *Morality and Architecture*, Oxford: Clarendon Press.

8

A MATTER OF PERSONAL PREFERENCE?

The relevance of different territories and types of evidence for Roman history

Eberhard W. Sauer[1]

One to four per cent of territory: more than enough to understand an Empire?

No other state has ever controlled all of the Mediterranean for a single day; the Roman Empire did so for almost 400 years, from the first to the early fifth century AD. Yet, while many classical scholars and university departments define their study area as the Mediterranean, or parts thereof, the Roman Empire stretched far beyond areas of Mediterranean climate and vegetation; namely, to the Iberian and Gallic Atlantic coast, to Britain, to the Rhine and Danube (and for about two centuries substantially beyond these rivers), to eastern Anatolia, the Syrian desert and southern Egypt and there and elsewhere in Africa into the Sahara.[2] During the early and high Empire members of the senatorial class (and often also those of equestrian rank) who pursued a career appropriate to their status normally held a range of offices, often in several different frontier and core provinces far apart from each other. They experienced personally the vastness of the Empire and its astonishing cultural diversity. They owned houses decorated with fashionable interior design, including wall paintings and mosaic floors, they were familiar with some classical authors, but they frequently also spent years of their lives in military bases at the very margins of Empire and saw with their own eyes rural dwellings of indigenous type in the frontier zone.

Yet the cosmopolitan nature of the Empire and the similarly cosmopolitan perspective of the key figures in running the Empire are in sharp contrast to the narrow geographic and thematic scope of a high proportion of those who study it. A whole range of specialist disciplines is devoted to its investigation: ancient history, with Late Antiquity sometimes being separated from Republican and high imperial history, classical archaeology (sometimes confined to art history in selected Mediterranean centres), the archaeology of the Roman Empire, sometimes also called provincial Roman archaeology (with less attention to art and, depending on the university, often with particular attention to Roman archaeology within the confines of the modern state the institution happens to be part of), Christian archaeology, Latin and Greek philology, sub-sections of theology, Egyptology and oriental studies, not to mention the often semi-independent subjects of epigraphy, numismatics, papyrology, etc. and further institutional specialization within different departments. This diversity of specialisms would in principle, of course, be an advantage, especially since it would be beyond human capability for an individual to master all the languages and methodologies of the sub-disciplines in all their intricacies; the danger lies not in some degree of specialization but in studying different types of evidence or geographic areas to the near total exclusion of others (i.e. without trying to place the subject of one's study, where possible, into an Empire-wide context or without taking all sources of evidence into account).

This chapter does not propose a utopian and unworkable ideal that all scholars with an interest in Roman studies should spread their interests equally across the whole of the Empire; instead it argues against mental iron curtains (such as the Alps for many scholars with interests in the Mediterranean) beyond which we do not look for the wider context or parallels because what is on the other side (even though we may scarcely know it or even want to know it) is thought to be so different from what we are doing that we can tacitly ignore it. It also advocates that university curricula should be designed in such a way that all students specializing in this period have to study different parts of the Empire and not just focus on one segment (no matter whether this happens to be Asia Minor or the north-western provinces), and that adopting a more narrow focus later should only be permissible once they are aware of the wider context.

Indeed, one wonders whether Rome's elite would have understood how modern scholars could develop an interest in wall paintings and sculpture or poetry but none whatsoever in military matters and economics, or vice versa – or how they could devote their entire professional lives to studying either Roman Britain or central Italy or another similarly small fraction of the Empire without showing much interest in the remaining 96 to 99 per cent of its land mass (or even just conceive the idea that 1–4 per cent can be understood in isolation from the rest). Even if the average peasant living in a round house in Cornwall or in a mud-brick building in an Egyptian village would not have been likely to have travelled anywhere near as far as a high proportion of members of the Roman elite, even he or she would have been confronted with Empire-wide institutions and networks of long-distance exchange of material goods.

Only a small proportion of the phenomena which still matter to us today, and are thus vital in persuading the public that the study of 'dead' cultures is a worthwhile investment, can be understood within the framework of any single discipline with a narrow geographic or methodological scope. This is particularly true for those which go beyond the legitimate aims of satisfying the curiosity of a greater or smaller number of people about the past or giving them a sense of local identity; and these phenomena can be subdivided into two groups: (1) developments that have shaped history to the present and whose origins go back to the Roman period, and (2) successes and failures in dealing with situations and problems similar to those we are facing today. Examples of the former include the rise and victory of Christianity, the emergence of a codified legal system, or the establishment of a road network which is partially still in use today. The most obvious examples of the latter are the Empire's overexploitation (though with considerable regional variations) of its natural resources, such as wild animals and forests (e.g. Kuhnen 1992: 36–9, 71–81); but also its success in farming arid regions, a model for sustainable agriculture on nowadays abandoned land (Barker 1996); parallels between the cosmopolitan nature of the Roman Empire and the current phenomena of globalization and European integration, as opposed to the much smaller political units in the European Middle Ages. One of these parallels is the religious diversity in pagan Rome, similar to the emerging multiplicity of religious and secular world-views in the west today and quite separate from the enforced dominance of a single religious doctrine in the intervening period (notwithstanding the schisms and infighting in medieval and post-medieval Christianity).

Equally, it is only an awareness of the history of the Empire as a whole, I would argue, that makes us recognize and appreciate what is special about the Roman state and helps us to explain why for a period of no less than some 800 years, from the second century BC to the seventh century AD, it was the most dominant military and economic power in Europe, the Mediterranean and the Near East – longer than any Empire before or after it. Nothing could be further from the truth (or indeed explain this superlative, no matter whether we consider it to be a positive or negative superlative from a moral perspective) than to assume that it is easy to draw parallels between the Roman Empire and post-medieval colonial empires, and that they were essentially similar. This is where scholars with anthropological training, and often specializing in a limited geographic area, frequently produce highly questionable theories; they are often inspired by the assumption that otherwise unproven resistance which, in their view, one ought to expect continually in any empire, must have left its mark in the material record and thus is there to be revealed to the discerning archaeologist. Peter Wells (1999: 170, 196–8), for example, interprets the 'reproduction of traditional houses, pottery, fibulae, burial practices, and ritual behaviors' in Roman Germany as 'cultural resistance' of the 'colonized' against the 'colonizers', seen as a foreign authority as late as the second half of the second century AD. Also worth noting in this context is Jane Webster's research on presumed resistance as, according to her hypothesis, expressed through the Roman interpretation of native deities attested by inscriptions, literature and art; her research is novel and stimulating, yet some of her conclusions about alleged deliberate and malicious interference and resistance are debatable and have, in my view, already been powerfully rejected by Wolfgang Spickermann (1997: 151–2; cf. 147–8). There is no space here to discuss her extensive research in any detail. It is, nevertheless, interesting to note that in one of Webster's publications on the subject (1997), while warning us of the difficulties in making comparisons between the Catholic Church 'committed to the eradication of indigenous beliefs' (indeed!) in Spanish Latin America and Roman paganism (1997: 179), she still claims that 'syncretism in colonial contexts is rarely benign' (e.g. 1997: 172) and that this equally applies to pagan religion in the Roman north-west. She also refers in passing to open rebellion and nationalism in Peru and Mexico (1997: 175, 179), while acknowledging the scarcity of rebellions in the west of the Empire (1997: 169–70).

The central question here, as in case of Wells's research, has to be, if there was indeed such widespread covert resistance in the Roman as well as modern colonial empires, why was the threshold to open rebellion crossed so much more frequently in the case of the latter and why did none of them maintain their extensive colonial dominions for the same length of time? The very fact that the Batavian uprising of AD 69 was the last revolt in Europe which one could term 'politically separatist' and that outside Europe there were no separatist rebellions either, except for the special case of the Jewish Wars, the last of which was crushed in AD 135 – though the Empire continued to exist for centuries – should sound a note of caution against assumptions that the population in the provinces continued to strive for independence generations after their ancestors had been brought under Roman control. Given the vast territorial extent of the Empire and its long duration it is indeed remarkable that there are virtually no later separatist rebellions, if we exclude internal struggles for imperial power which were not separatist in nature, but occasionally resulted in a temporary power stalemate (such as between the Gallic, Palmyrene and central empires in the early 270s). John Drinkwater (1992, esp. 208; cf. Urban 1999: 94–6, 114–16, 121–2) has argued that the later uprisings of the Bagaudae in Gaul and on the Iberian peninsula were caused by a 'disintegration of local systems of order' rather than being peasant revolutions; but even if the latter should be true, there is no evidence to suggest they were seen as freedom fights against 'foreign' occupiers. That there appears to have been a higher level of discontent in the later Roman period in comparison with the second and early third century was probably the result of a number of factors, such as temporary breakdowns of security as a result of civil wars and invasions, the economic downturn, the replacement of the comparatively fair taxation system of the early Empire with an increasingly uneven spread of the burden (Neesen

1980), not to mention later religious suppression. Banditry, while being widespread (Grünewald 1999; MacMullen 1966: 190–248, 255–68), virtually never escalated into serious armed rebellion or led to the total loss of control over territories. Apart from that only the revolt of the Isaurians in the south of Asia Minor, which developed into a long war, springs to mind (Hellenkemper 1986; Hild and Hellenkemper 1990: 34–42), and it may conceivably have been separatist in nature. David Mattingly (1997b: 20) rightly describes the idea of 'unremitting nationalistic and armed resistance' as 'a false vision'.

Such a scarcity of separatist rebellions in the high Empire cannot be a result of incomplete coverage by written sources, since these pay particular attention to military conflicts throughout Roman history; in my view, it suggests that Rome used the 'carrot and stick approach' much more successfully than most other empires. The Roman state was at least as brutal as the dominant colonial empires of post-medieval times (and arguably much more than some of them) in the methods used to establish control over peoples who were unwilling to become subjects voluntarily. It did not shrink from indiscriminate mass killings if this seemed the only way to gain or maintain control over a territory (e.g. Caes., *B. Gall.* 6.34, 43; Joseph, *BJ* 5.446–51, 7.414–34); unlike the darkest episodes of the twentieth century, however, this did not happen for irrational (e.g. racist) reasons, but simply in the ruthless pursuit of power. Those who submitted without offering armed resistance (however unreasonable it may have been to expect them to do so) could, irrespective of their ethnicity, count on being spared excessive violence (notwithstanding a few cases of corrupt or insensitive magistrates).

However, the same pragmatism also led to an exceptionally successful integration of conquered populations. It entrusted co-operative members of the native elite with key positions in provincial society and allowed them to maintain or enlarge their personal wealth. The opportunity to gain citizenship, however, was not confined to the elite but also open to others (for example, to those choosing a military career), and the social system gave people a realistic hope of improving their financial situation and social status and of gradually working their way up in local society if they were free, hardworking and successful. The majority at the bottom of society were linked with the elite through sophisticated networks of mutual dependence (Alföldy 1985: 150–6, 162–85). In terms of religion Rome pursued a *laissez-faire* policy, allowing the continuation of virtually all cults with the exception only of a minute fraction of religious movements and phenomena (Bendlin 1997; Sauer 2003a: 45–52). Because of such successful integration, rather than military pressure, separatist rebellions normally ceased within a few generations of Rome having established control, notwithstanding the fact that military garrisons in almost all but the frontier provinces were reduced to a token presence as early as the first century AD. Italy lost its military and economic dominance in the same century, and by the early third century all free citizens gained citizenship while the emperors themselves from then onwards were mostly descended from provincial and not Italian families; Rome even lost its role as the imperial capital in the late Roman period.

All of this is in striking contrast to developments in recent colonial empires (though there are, of course, major differences between them as well). Any approach presuming that there is a permanent dichotomy between occupiers and those subdued by these 'foreigners', that this subdued population of the provinces or of the colonies of empires is always suppressed by the centre and consequently always and perpetually strives towards independence, and that one needs to find proof of this in the archaeological record, constitutes a misguided research strategy and results from an ahistorical approach and an often too narrow geographical focus. The anti-colonialist mission of some modern authors may well have influenced their belief that genuinely ambiguous material culture is the sole evidence for otherwise unrecorded widespread resistance against, and dissatisfaction with, imperial rule during the high Empire. Yet there is no argument here that Roman rule was more benign in intention than that of modern colonial empires, only that it was more effective in practice. Those who maintain that there were such high levels of resistance really ought to provide an explanation for the Empire's exceptional longevity. It is certainly safer to interpret native elements in material culture as signs of traditionalism than of political resistance similar to the cultural diversity of the early immigrant population of the United States (Sauer 2001: 128). I would thus argue that the essence of what is special about the Roman Empire is its cosmopolitan nature, and that if one is specializing too narrowly and excludes large parts of its territories (even if impressively wide-ranging 'parallels' from other periods and areas are used) one might be at risk of not seeing the wood for the trees.

Narrowness of specialization or width of coverage can, of course, be defined by chronological, geographical and methodological parameters. Chronological specialization tends to be wider amongst scholars of the ancient world than is the case amongst modern historians, because there is often insufficient or insufficiently closely dated evidence to study phenomena within a short period (a single century for example) in isolation. In comparing the approaches adopted by archaeologists based in different states it is important to avoid clichés, yet few would dispute that is hard to find examples of scholars from universities in Mediterranean countries who conduct fieldwork at Roman sites in north-west Europe, while examples for the opposite phenomenon abound. Northern European and North American scholars cover on average probably the widest terrain. This, however, is no more than a tendency; there are also many who confine their interests to a small part of the ancient world (Italy or parts thereof, for example), often studied in complete isolation from the rest of the Empire and frequently even without any acknowledgement that the work of those who study frontier provinces has anything whatever to do with their research. This seems curious since it ought to be obvious that the impact of Rome on the history and culture of the world would have been infinitesimal had its dominion remained confined to the Italian peninsula, let alone central Italy. Archaeology in Germany, France and, to a lesser extent, Britain tends to have a strong regional focus as well. This regional focus partially has organizational reasons and is partially the result of the explosion of information resulting from decades of rescue archaeology and centuries of research.

It would undoubtedly take years to read all the recent books and research papers on the archaeology of Roman Britain alone (and several lives to work one's way through the existing archives). Yet the population of Roman Britain constituted, at a very rough estimate, perhaps just one-twentieth of that of the Empire.[3] Like all other parts of this vast political entity, Britain shared so many elements of its material culture and its political and administrative organization with other provinces of the Empire that it is impossible to comprehend Romano-British developments in a vacuum (cf. Sauer 2002). (This is, of course, not to say that indigenous roots of cultural phenomena and developments are not equally important for our understanding of Roman Britain or, indeed, any other part of the Roman world.) Notwithstanding the fact that those parts of Britain under Roman rule had never before or since, until the creation of the British Empire, been part of such a vast political unity, a not insignificant proportion of recent studies on Roman Britain suffer from a tendency to covert isolationism. In a recent volume of the *Proceedings of the Theoretical Roman Archaeology Conference* (Davies *et al.* 2001), for example, no less than four papers (amongst thirteen) are included which omit any reference to Britain in the title or even any hint of this geographical focus, thus implying an Empire-wide, if not universal scope, while they deal in fact exclusively or almost exclusively with Roman Britain. It may also be of interest that none of the reasonably extensive bibliographies of these four papers lists a single title in a language other than English. And yet Britain has only been chosen as a case study here. Indeed, regional specialization is even more pronounced in other countries, while there are probably more monographs of a synthetic nature available dealing with Britain as a whole than is the case for any other modern country or ancient geographic unit within the former Roman Empire.

How do we square the seemingly irreconcilable observations that there is more material and information available on Roman Britain – or, indeed, on Roman Gaul, Germany or Italy – than any individual can study and synthesize and that these are, nevertheless, geographical areas too small and too interconnected with neighbouring territories to be studied in isolation? I would argue that we need to restructure the way archaeology and history are approached and taught. At a time when publication of academic texts increases in volume year by year, while the time available to each scholar remains a constant (or is even reduced as a result of a burgeoning bureaucracy), we thus need to get away from the expectation that there is an ever-growing canon of general books and articles which each and every scholar working in the field *must* have read (let alone the illusory aim to be comprehensive in anything other than a narrowly defined topic). This expectation reduces the time available to venture into new territories or, indeed, to re-examine the primary evidence upon which unproven assumptions frequently repeated in textbooks are based. I am by no means advocating that we go from one extreme to another and ignore groundbreaking new research and theory, but a balance needs to be struck between being up to date and being able to cover a wide field. Areas of specialization must not increasingly shrink as the amount of published information explodes. We must accept that we cannot know everything, but should be able to contextualize, or, at least, be able to find further information on virtually everything related to the culture or the phenomena we study. At university level there has to be more emphasis on guiding students to find their own way through the 'jungle' of publications in as wide an area as possible (and not necessarily within the confines of Roman studies), rather than to follow the lecturer blindly and getting to know merely 'isolated trees in the jungle'. The student specializing in Roman Britain, Roman Italy or any other area of similar size for a dissertation or other major piece of work, still ought to be able to find on his or her own relevant information on any other part of the Empire (e.g. Roman Syria) by being introduced to relevant recent works of reference and leading journals. The effective use of encyclopaedias, historical atlases, general bibliographies on a wide range of subjects and prosopographical literature should be a key learning objective for all students in Roman studies. Most importantly, curiosity to venture into different geographical territories, periods or methodologies should be encouraged rather than curtailed. Such an approach will require unlimited curiosity on the part of university teachers, combined with the humility of admitting they are not omniscient.

Disciplinary separatists, supremacists and unifiers

This applies equally to breaking down geographic barriers and barriers between material culture and text. It is well known that, at least in the northern provinces of the Empire, the Roman period is a phase of hitherto unparalleled numerical scale in the production of artefacts and construction of buildings of permanent materials. It is, however, also a time when significant textual evidence is available for much of those territories. While classical sources already shed significant light on societies of the Late Pre-Roman Iron Age (whose study cannot and should not strictly be separated from post-conquest history), the amount of written information, especially that with a precise geographical focus, tends to increase markedly in Roman times. Furthermore, the interpretation of many objects and installations requires background knowledge of textual evidence (e.g. a statue of a deity known from classical mythology, literature and inscriptions to name just one example). The density of written coverage of some aspects of Roman culture (with or without regional focus) contrasts sharply with the virtual absence of any information on others. It is a period in which both textual and material evidence are of crucial significance, and we obtain an unbalanced view and a picture full of gaps if we prioritize one over the other.

Of interest in this context are the very different ways in which Fergus Millar, one of the most distinguished, productive and wide-ranging ancient historians of our times, and Warwick Ball, an archaeologist by training whose research interests stretch from the Mediterranean coast to India, have approached the study of the Roman Near East. It ought to be stressed that the subject areas of the works produced by Millar (1993) and Ball (2000) differ in some respects. Millar's work impresses by his mastery of the relevant non-European languages, in addition to Greek and Latin, and his conse-quential ability to cover a remarkable and unequalled range of the textual evidence. Ball's study has a wider chronological and geographical scope (including also the late Roman period, contacts with India, etc.). Ball is more concerned to present evidence for the east influencing the west rather than vice versa (e.g. Ball 2000: 303) and to stress the achievements of eastern cultures within and outside the Empire. Indeed, while Millar is accused of being partisan for the west (Ball 2000: 2–3, 317), Ball undoubtedly shows the opposite bias – for example, by overplaying Persian and underplaying Roman military successes in the third century (Ball 2000: 22–3) and without acknowledging that the Persians not only failed to take over any note-worthy stretch of Rome's territories in this century permanently (let alone realize their stated aim of reconquering the vast areas in the Levant that had been under Persian control centuries earlier) but even had to cede some land on the upper Tigris to the Romans in *c*. AD 298. Regardless of such details, Ball's work is on the whole admirably accurate, wide-ranging and informative.

From our point of view both books are of interest insofar as they focus on essentially the same subject, notwithstanding these differences – namely, the general history of the Roman Near East – though they are written from very different perspectives. Ball has produced a much more comprehensive history because he has dared to cross the subject boundary and devoted considerable attention to the textual in addition to the archaeological evidence. There can indeed be little doubt, in my view, that Ball, who discusses the political and military history of the region as well as religion in its multifarious mani-festations, the development and character of towns and the countryside, the complex interplay of a plethora of different artistic, architectural and other cultural influences, etc., presents the fuller picture since he bases his study in equal measure on the written, visual and other material evidence. Millar, by contrast includes only the occasional reference to archaeological remains and very much presents a history as told by the surviving texts, thus excluding virtually all subjects which they do not cover. Millar (1993:

xiii–xiv), it ought to be stressed, does not claim comprehensive coverage of the physical evidence and, indeed, has succeeded more than anybody before him in his stated aims of producing a history of political structures and language in the Roman Near East; yet he has equally demonstrated the incapacity of the written record available for the subject to illuminate more than certain aspects of its history (and the same, of course, would be true for material evidence taken on its own).

Breaking down the boundaries between archaeology and ancient history in the Roman period requires more than the mere inclusion of some evidence from the 'other' side of the divide where it is useful to illustrate phenomena and does not contravene the theories based on the interpretation of the 'own' discipline's evidence (as Ball, notwithstanding some debatable details, has done in an exemplary manner). The way it should not be done has been aptly characterized by Graeme Barker (1985: 121), referring specifically to studies of the agricultural economy in the Mediterranean: 'At worst, historians have regarded archaeology as a source of useful secondary information if it fitted in with existing historical models, and as a collection of misleading or irrelevant pots and pans if it did not.' It is essential that an effort is made to be open-minded towards unfamiliar methodology, especially in areas where the conclusions differ. Instead, representatives of both disciplines frequently excel themselves to propagate their credo that the evidence the 'other' discipline uses (while of interest) is of much more limited potential than the representatives of the discipline themselves mistakenly think it is.

A concrete example of such an attitude is provided by the recent discussion on the discoveries from Kalkriese in northern Germany. It is well known that the most devastating defeat the Roman army suffered against an external enemy under the reign of Augustus took place somewhere in the forests of northern Germany in AD 9, when no less than three legions with supporting auxiliary troops under the command of Publius Quinctilius Varus were annihilated in the *Teutoburgiensis saltus* (not identical with the modern Teutoburg Forest) by a force of native Germans led by Arminius. Arguably this battle prevented much of Germany from becoming a part of the Empire, and much effort has been invested by academics, as well as by amateur researchers, in trying to find the locality of this momentous Roman defeat. Rudolf Pörtner (1959: 23), in his popular introduction to Roman Germany, counted no less than some thirty candidates for the battlefield, 'each one of them', as he remarked ironically, 'superbly investigated and proven'. It can come as no great surprise, in the light of this multitude of places with a claim to be the site of a single event, that the news in the early 1990s that it now had indeed been located at Kalkriese has been greeted with caution by parts of the scholarly community.

Whether this was caution or over-caution can only be decided from the evidence. This consists of a considerable number of finds typical for the Augustan period, notably coins and pieces of military equipment (Schlüter

1993, 1999a, 1999b). The *c.* 620 copper alloy coins (as far as they are datable) and all countermarks on them, pre-date AD 9. Amongst the almost 600 precious metal coins (partially deposited in hoards and partially as site finds), only one from an area some 5.5 km across is later than AD 9 (Berger 1996, 1999, 2000a, 2000b); this dates to AD 69 and is thus certain to have been deposited on a different occasion (Berger 1996: 158–60). The wide distribution of the finds would correspond to the historical record that the army perished while being attacked on the march. The natural terrain, forested hills at the edge of an extensive bog, would equally fit perfectly with the textual evidence (Cass. Dio 56.19–22; Tac., *Ann.* 1.60–1, 1.65; Flor. 2.30.34–9; Vell. Pat. 2.119), though this observation on its own would, of course, by no means limit the circle of potential sites to this one locality.

The wide scattering of military equipment nowhere near an army base (as far as we know) is best explained by combat in the area; but is the discovery necessarily to be explained by the events of AD 9? Not if we follow the ancient historian Peter Kehne. Kehne (2000; cf. Wolters 2000; Berger 2000b) believes that it might just as well be associated with minor combat between Germans and fleeing troops in AD 9 away from the main battle, or, more probably, with later campaigns – notably those of Germanicus in AD 15 or 16 in northern Germany. His main arguments are as follows:

1 The finds (over 4,000) are far fewer than one would expect at such a major battle site.
2 The coins only prove that the event is later than AD 6/7, but not how much later. The absence of coins minted after AD 9 does not prove anything.
3 The mutilation of some coins is best explained by the troop revolts following the death of Augustus in AD 14, probably allowing us to exclude that it was the site of the Varus battle (Kehne 2000: 70; cf. 59–60).

He concludes (Kehne 2000: 74 in translation): 'The possibility of dating an archaeological assemblage precisely on the basis of finds of Roman coins is being vastly overestimated, as this colloquium has decisively shown.'

Kehne certainly cannot be accused of having failed to take material evidence into consideration; quite the reverse. Yet he concludes that representatives of the 'other' discipline(s) vastly overestimate the potential of their material. It is legitimate to raise such a question, but it is equally permissible to ask whether Kehne has been able to show that he is in full control of the methodologies (i.e. mainly statistical analysis and interpretation of archaeological and numismatic data) whose validity he has questioned.

The first argument relies on the following calculations: each soldier would have carried, on Kehne's (2000: 73–4) estimate, around 1,000 metal parts which roughly equals 18,000,000 for the whole army as an absolute minimum. Even if just 1 per cent had been found, we should still expect to find 180,000. There is no need here to point out the difficulties in reaching a high recovery rate when exploring a vast area. It is more important to stress that the bulk of Kehne's estimated 1,000 metal parts per soldier would have formed part of the body armour or other large items which were easy to spot and could be collected in one piece. Metal was valuable, and if the remains at Kalkriese are those of the famous Varus battle of AD 9, the Germans had years to rob the corpses of their body armour and all metal items lying next to them. The fact alone that, to my knowledge (cf. Coulston 2001: 25–31), not a single battlefield in the whole of the Roman Empire has been identified (other than those associated with a siege) which has yielded more finds than Kalkriese demonstrates just how efficient the victors tended to be in robbing and reusing most metal items (cf. Cass. Dio 56.21–2; Tac., *Ann.* 1.68; Agathias 2.10). If Kehne's argument is accepted that over 4,000 items are too few for a major battle, he would not only have disproved that Kalkriese was the site of the Varus battle but also that there were ever any major battles in antiquity at all (despite the wealth of literary evidence to the contrary).

There is insufficient space here to scrutinize Kehne's second argument, which has been discussed in detail elsewhere (Sauer 2003b). Suffice it to say that coin composition changed rapidly at military sites at the time, as has been pointed out most powerfully by David Wigg (1997). Kehne (2000: 53) holds on to the old idea that coins reached military sites via slow 'coin drift' which, according to him, makes it impossible to read much into the absence of coin types post-dating AD 9 and by no means excludes the possibility that the Kalkriese assemblage dates to AD 15 or 16 (as he believes it could). He does not appear to be aware of the mounting evidence presented by Wigg and others that copper alloy coins were largely minted for, and directly distributed to, the army in the Julio-Claudian period and that it thus makes little sense to assume that it took years for the army to receive new coin types minted in significant numbers. Nor does he take statistics into account; namely, that it has been shown by Wigg and others that the composition of coin series at military sites changed rapidly, with similar tendencies over wide territories within a few years as a result of this direct supply of fresh coinage.

The third argument, that stab marks on coins were probably inflicted in AD 14, is particularly astonishing as coins with similar forms of mutilation also occur at Lahnau-Waldgirmes (Kehne 2000: 59), an urban settlement east of the Rhine which not even Kehne claims to have been reoccupied in or after AD 14.

One cannot help getting the impression that this is a case not of breaking down the boundaries but simply of transgressing them in order to postulate that the 'other' disciplines cannot contribute as much as one's own (without the willingness or sufficient attempts at getting familiar with their methodologies beforehand).

As early as 1885 Theodor Mommsen (1885) had postulated that the site of the Varus battle had been in the area of Kalkriese on the basis of the concentration of coins, even though far fewer were known then. Mommsen, the only Roman historian (or, indeed, archaeologist) ever to have been awarded the Nobel Prize (Schlange-Schöningen 2002), proved to be far ahead of his time. In our context it is important that it was by no means just a lucky guess which enabled him to identify the correct site at such an early date. Mommsen's research interests spanned a far wider range of fields, chronologically, geographically and methodologically, than those of most Romanists before or after him. Not only did he write on all periods of Roman history and all parts of the Empire, as well as on Roman law and numerous other aspects of ancient history, but he also played a key role in the systematic compilation of Latin inscriptions and early medieval sources. The former were compiled Empire-wide into the *Corpus Inscriptionum Latinarum* which took full account of what was known about their findspots. He was even the driving force behind the creation of a large archaeological research project to investigate the forts along the German frontier (Hartmann 1908; Braun 1992). In addition, he not only ventured into the wide field of numismatics but was able to put coins into context by taking into account, like a good modern archaeologist would do, date, location, number and patina (even if this was based on the numismatist Julius Menadier's report rather than on autopsy), and distribution over the landscape (e.g. Mommsen 1885: 53). It was Mommsen's open-mindedness and his willingness and capacity to master diverse sources of evidence and methodologies which allowed him to come to a correct interpretation where so many others before and after him failed.

Cases of scholars who declare evidence from other disciplines inadmissible when it is incompatible with hypotheses formed on the basis of sources from their own subject (even where scanty) abound. This is striking, for example, in the question as to how much or how little direct violent Christian intervention against pagan cult objects was involved in transforming the ancient world from a pagan into a Christian society. Some text-centred academics who believe in an early decline of paganism as a whole and of Mithraism in particular find it acceptable to discount the abundant evidence for late fourth-century coin offerings in numerous temples of Mithras as rubbish deposition. Some classical scholars equally make little mention of, let alone discuss, the numerous instances of image-destruction reported in post-classical biographies of Christian saints, in this case being hampered by a chronological rather than a methodological boundary (Sauer 1996, 2003a, 2003c with references).

Centrifugal and centripetal forces at present and the silent majority

It would be unfair, however, to conclude that classical scholars are generally unaware of the dangers of scientific separatism. There are many notable examples of scholars whose competence reaches across the disciplinary divide, such as Greg Woolf, or who have ranged geographically very widely, like the late Barri Jones. Whether, however, the majority sees the subdivision of classical scholarship by disciplinary or geographic boundaries as a major issue seems much more doubtful, as is most powerfully demonstrated by their silence on this subject. Most historical archaeologists and ancient historians would tacitly or openly (e.g. Cornell 1995: 28–30) acknowledge that, to a greater or lesser extent, they need 'each other's' evidence, yet they would not normally go as far as to argue for the dissolution of the boundaries, sometimes not even for a shift of emphasis. Some classical scholars consider material evidence scarcely worth mentioning or its omission worth explaining. Peter Wiseman's (2002b: xiii; cf. xv–xvi) definition of classics is symptomatic: it is the 'study of Greco-Roman civilisation itself, one and a half millennia of literature, politics, philosophy, law, religion and art'. One could thus paraphrase Wiseman's definition of the subject area of classics as follows: it comprises Graeco-Roman civilization and all evidence to illuminate it except for those categories of the material evidence which do not please the aesthete or any aspect of history for which they form the main source of information. Amongst the seventeen essays in Wiseman's (2002a) collection, *Classics in Progress*, literature features most prominently and wider historical themes strongly, while the relationship between visual history and ancient history is afforded one contribution and other archaeological subjects appear in none of the titles at all, notwithstanding Wiseman's (2002b: xiii) claim that the selection places 'a deliberately eclectic emphasis on its [i.e. classics'] range of subject matter', the idea being 'to offer examples of the interest and variety of the subject'. While he also stresses that the survey is not meant to be exhaustive, the emphasis on literary and, to a far lesser degree, art-historical evidence in the titles of the selection is so pronounced that it can be scarcely accidental. Even though one has to agree with Wiseman (2002b: xiii–xiv) that there are examples for chronologically more narrow and purely philological approaches in the past (Platnauer 1954), one would have wished to see the logic behind focusing on literature, including art, but excluding the rest of archaeology made explicit. Not all classicists would agree with such an exclusive literature-centred approach. Indeed, most encouragingly, Averil Cameron (2002: 185) and Alan Bowman (2002: 219–20), in their contributions to the same volume, stress the inseparability of literary and archaeological evidence. There is thus no consensus amongst classicists as to how relevant or irrelevant material evidence is; the impression remains, nevertheless, that a high proportion of them are so convinced that a sophisticated understanding of Graeco-Roman culture can be achieved without taking into account archaeological evidence (except, occasionally, works of art) that they do not even consider it necessary to acknowledge this omission, let alone to provide any justification.

Interesting in this context is also a recent provocative work by Jerry Toner (2002) which seeks answers for the declining interest in classics over the past century (notwithstanding a minor resurgence of interest in ancient history in recent years). In sharp contrast to Wiseman (2002b), he laments the focus the subject places on selected works of literature whose relevance is difficult to convey to a wide audience:

> Let's face it, how many people want to read Homer in the original these days? What students want nowadays is to be able to study topics like the growth of early Christianity, the start of empire, or the role of women.
>
> (Toner 2002: 12)

Two of the main goals according to Toner ought to be:

- to offer a broader range of subjects so as to attract as wide an intake as possible.
- to place more emphasis on cultural knowledge rather than technical knowledge such as Latin or Greek. That kind of technical skill can come later to those who have a particular propensity and interest in it.

> (Toner 2002: 132)

Yet, strangely, despite Toner's emphasis on the need to widen the subject to make it relevant to wider circles of the population, history is still very much presented as self-sufficient and archaeology makes only the odd random appearance (e.g. Toner 2002: 55–6, 71–2). One would have thought that the next logical step from Toner's claim that the field should be widened would be to offer a holistic approach to the ancient world which no longer presents the literary wisdom – no matter how progressive the approaches applied to contextualize it – largely in isolation from all other sources of evidence (or vice versa). In their attitude to disciplinary identities one does not sense much difference on average between traditionalists and 'modernizers' or 'revolutionaries'.

The situation could hardly be described more aptly than by Martin Carver (2002: 467): 'The problem for some Atlantic countries is that due to incidents of temporary power in university administrations, those that study the same past of the same people do not necessarily work together.' Yet, sadly, the problem is by no means confined to countries bordering the Atlantic Ocean (and certainly not to those bordering its core belt); it is a problem of global dimensions even if there is no space here to discuss the structure of universities in all countries where Roman studies are taught. One more example may, however, be useful. Tonio Hölscher, writing from a continental European perspective, reaches very similar conclusions:

What danger there was in this [i.e. specialization] is apparent from the development, particularly since the early twentieth century when the histories of ancient art, ancient literature or political institutions were treated so categorically as autonomous phenomena that they largely lost connection to ancient society and its complex culture. Later, the internal divisions within archaeology have frequently led to research, into architecture, coins or Roman Germany, for example, being conducted like an independent game, played according to self-defined rules and the connection with the culture of antiquity as a whole was more or less lost.

(Hölscher 2002: 12, in translation)

However, Hölscher (2002: 16) not only considers scientific separatism to be a past error but sees the acute risk that the situation will deteriorate still further: 'On the whole more and more specialist subjects strive towards academic autonomy. If we are concerned about understanding the whole culture and not just about achieving perfect working techniques, we vehemently have to oppose such a fragmentation.' These statements form part of the first chapter of an introduction to classical archaeology which still places the main emphasis on art, architecture, towns and major monuments in selected parts of the Greek and Roman Mediterranean. This (i.e. the concentration on a limited field of research within Greek and Roman studies) is justified with the abundance of data and scientific literature – too much, in his opinion, for an individual to master without becoming an amateur. However, encouragingly, Hölscher (2002: 12–13) believes that boundaries between specialist disciplines have to be flexible. He laments that the specialist disciplines have been defined primarily according to method and material (e.g. philology for linguistic sources, archaeology for visual and material evidence, and, similarly, history, history of architecture, epigraphy, numismatics and papyrology): 'One very much hopes that in future these mechanical and unproductive material-disciplines are supplemented or replaced by thematically defined subjects.'

One would like to see Hölscher's wishes come true, yet it is to be feared that his concerns about further fragmentation in future are at least as likely to be proved correct.

Notes

1 I would like to thank Dr Peter Haarer and Dr Martin Henig for reading this chapter, and for their most valuable linguistic improvements and comments on various aspects of the subject.
2 Even by the Hellenistic period it makes no sense to confine the classical world to the Mediterranean, even if we maintained the traditional Greek and Rome-centred world-views, as the territory of states with Greek governments (not to mention their cultural influences) comprised temporarily even parts of the Indian subcontinent.

3   For the size of the population of the Empire, see Frier (2000: 811–16), though note that he adopts from McEvedy and Jones (1978) what are probably underestimates at least for the population of the post-AD 14 annexations in the west (cf. Millett 1990: 181–6 on Britain alone) and east. Needless to say, estimates vary substantially and give us no more than an approximate idea of population size. Even for Egypt, the best-recorded part of the Roman world in terms of demography, estimates vary considerably and range from the 4.5–5 million adopted by Frier (cf. Bagnall and Frier 1994: 53–4, Beloch 1886: 254–9; Rathbone 1990) to Josephus' figure of 7.5 million inhabitants (*BJ* 2.385, powerfully supported by Lo Cascio 1999; cf. Bowman 1986: 17–18) (not counting an additional 500,000 for Alexandria), or somewhere in between (Scheidel 2001: 246–8 with references). It is in any case certain, in parallel with the much-better-documented demography of the late Middle Ages and early post-medieval period in Europe, that there must have been substantial fluctuations in the population size of the provinces of the Empire over time.

Bibliography

Alföldy, G. (1985) *The Social History of Rome*, London and Sydney: Croom Helm.

Bagnall, R. and Frier, B.W. (1994) *The Demography of Roman Egypt*, Cambridge: Cambridge University Press.

Ball, W. (2000) *Rome in the East. The transformation of an empire*, London and New York: Routledge.

Barker, G. (1985) 'Agricultural organisation in classical Cyrenaica: the potential of subsistence and survey data', in G. Barker, J. Lloyd and J. Reynolds (eds) *Cyrenaica in Antiquity*, Oxford: BAR Int. Ser., 236, 121–34.

Barker, G., with contr. by Gilbertson, D.D. (1996) 'Farming the desert: retrospective and prospect', in G. Barker (ed.) *Farming the Desert. The UNESCO Libyan Valleys Archaeological Survey, 1: Synthesis*, Tripoli and London: UNESCO, Department of Antiquities and Society for Libyan Studies, 343–63.

Beloch, J. (1886) *Die Bevölkerung der griechisch-römischen Welt*, Leipzig: Duncker & Humblot.

Bendlin, A. (1997) 'Peripheral centres – central peripheries: religious communication in the Roman Empire', in Cancik and Rüpke (1997): 35–68.

Berger, F. (1996) *Kalkriese 1. Die römischen Fundmünzen*, Mainz: Philipp von Zabern.

—— (1999) 'Kalkriese: Die römischen Fundmünzen', in Schlüter and Wiegels (1999): 271–7.

—— (2000a), 'Die Münzfunde von Kalkriese. Neufunde und Ausblick', in Wiegels (2000): 11–45.

—— (2000b) 'Replik zu den Beiträgen von Peter Kehne und Reinhard Wolters', in Wiegels (2000): 253–8.

Bowman, A.K. (1986) *Egypt After the Pharaohs: 332 BC–AD 642: from Alexander to the Arab conquest*, London: British Museum Publications.

—— (2002) 'Recolonising Egypt', in Wiseman (2002a): 193–223.

Braun, R. (1992) 'Die Geschichte der Reichs-Limeskommission und ihre Forschungen', in *Der römische Limes in Deutschland*, Archäologie in Deutschland Sonderheft 1992, Stuttgart: Theiss, 9–32.

Cameron, A. (2002) 'The "long" late antiquity: a late twentieth-century model', in Wiseman (2002a): 165–91.

Cancik, H. and Rüpke J. (eds) (1997) *Römische Reichsreligion und Provinzialreligion*, Tübingen: Mohr Siebeck.

Carver, M. (2002) 'Marriages of true minds: archaeology with texts', in B. Cunliffe, W. Davies and C. Renfrew (eds) *Archaeology. The widening debate*, Oxford: Oxford University Press and the British Academy, 465–96.

Cornell, T.J. (1995) *The Beginnings of Rome: Italy and Rome from the Bronze Age to the Punic Wars (c. 1000–264 BC)*, London and New York: Routledge.

Coulston, J. (2001) 'The archaeology of Roman conflict', in P.W.M. Freeman and A. Pollard (eds) *Fields of Conflict: Progress and prospect in battlefield archaeology. Proceedings of a conference held in the Department of Archaeology University of Glasgow, April 2000*, Oxford: BAR Int. Ser., 958, 23–49.

Davies, G., Gardner, A. and Lockyear, K. (eds) (2001) *TRAC 2000, Proceedings of the Tenth Annual Theoretical Archaeology Conference*, London: Oxbow Books.

Drinkwater, J. (1992) 'The Bacaudae of fifth-century Gaul', in J. Drinkwater and H. Elton (eds) *Fifth-century Gaul: A crisis of identity*, Cambridge: Cambridge University Press, 208–17.

Frier, B.W. (2000) 'Demography', in A.K. Bowman, P. Garnsey and D. Rathbone (eds) *The Cambridge Ancient History, XI: The High Empire* (2nd edn), Cambridge: Cambridge University Press, 787–816.

Grünewald, T. (1999) *Räuber, Rebellen, Rivalen, Rächer. Studien zu latrones im Römischen Reich*, Stuttgart: Steiner.

Hartmann, L.M. (1908) *Theodor Mommsen. Eine biographische Skizze*, Gotha: Friedrich Andreas Perthes.

Hellenkemper, H. (1986) 'Legionen im Bandenkrieg – Isaurien im 4. Jahrhundert', in *Studien zu den Militärgrenzen Roms, III, 13. Internationaler Limeskongreß, Aalen 1983*, Stuttgart: Theiss, 625–34.

Hild, F. and Hellenkemper, H. (1990) *Tabula Imperii Byzantini, 5.1, Kilikien und Isaurien*, Vienna: Verlag der Österreichischen Akademie der Wissenschaften.

Hölscher, T. (2002) *Klassische Archäologie, Grundwissen*, Darmstadt: Wissenschaftliche Buchgesellschaft.

Kehne, P. (2000) 'Zur Datierung von Fundmünzen aus Kalkriese und zur Verlegung des Enddatums des Halterner Hauptlagers in die Zeit der Germanienkriege unter Tiberius und Germanicus (10–16 n.Chr.)', in Wiegels (2000): 47–79.

Kuhnen, H.-P. (ed.) 1992 *Gestürmt, geräumt, vergessen? Der Limesfall und das Ende der Römerherrschaft in Südwestdeutschland*, Stuttgart: Württembergisches Landesmuseum.

Lo Cascio, E. (1999) 'La populazione dell'Egitto romano', in M. Bellancourt-Valdher and J.-N. Corvisier (eds) *La démographie historique antique*, Cahiers Scientifiques de l'Université d'Artois, 11/1999, Arras: Artois Presses Université, 153–69.

McEvedy, C. and Jones, R. (1978) *Atlas of World Population History*, Harmondsworth: Penguin Books.

MacMullen, R. (1966) *Enemies of Roman Order. Treason, unrest and alienation in the Empire*, Cambridge, Mass. and London: Harvard University Press.

Mattingly, D. (ed.) (1997a) *Dialogues in Roman Imperialism. Power, discourse, and discrepant experience in the Roman Empire*, Portsmouth, R.I.: Journal of Roman Archaeology Suppl., 23.

—— (1997b) 'Introduction. Dialogues of power and experience in the Roman Empire', in Mattingly (1997a): 7–24.

Millar, F. (1993) *The Roman Near East, 31 BC–AD 337*, Cambridge, Mass. and London: Harvard University Press.

Millett, M. (1990) *The Romanization of Britain. An essay in archaeological interpretation*, Cambridge: Cambridge University Press.

131

Mommsen, T. (1885) *Die Örtlichkeit der Varusschlacht*, Berlin: Weidmannsche Buchhandlung.

Neesen, L. (1980) *Untersuchungen zu den direkten Staatsabgaben der römischen Kaiserzeit (27 v. Chr.–284 n. Chr.)*, Antiquitas, 1.32, Bonn: Habelt.

Platnauer, M. (ed.) (1954) *Fifty Years of Classical Scholarship*, Oxford: Blackwell.

Pörtner, R. (1959) *Mit dem Fahrstuhl in die Römerzeit*, Düsseldorf (Munich and Zürich [reprinted 1979]: Droemer/ Knaur).

Rathbone, D.W. (1990) 'Villages, land and population in Graeco-Roman Egypt', *Proceedings of the Cambridge Philological Society*, 216 (New Ser., 36): 103–42.

Sauer, E. (1996) *The End of Paganism in the North-Western Provinces of the Roman Empire. The example of the Mithras cult*, Oxford: BAR Int. Ser., 634.

—— (2001) 'Going native, review of Wells 1999', *Classical Review*, 51.1: 127–8.

—— (2002) 'The Roman invasion of Britain (AD 43) in imperial perspective: a response to Frere and Fulford', *Oxford Journal of Archaeology*, 21.4: 333–63.

—— (2003a) *The Archaeology of Religious Hatred in the Roman and Early Medieval World*, Stroud: Tempus.

—— (forthcoming 2003b) *Coins, Cult and Cultural Identity: Augustan coins, hot springs and the early Roman baths at Bourbonne-les-Bains*, Leicester: Leicester Archaeology Monographs, 10.

—— (forthcoming 2003c) 'Not just small change – coins in Mithraea', in M. Martens and G. De Boe (eds) *Proceeding of the International Conference on Roman Mithraism: The evidence of the small finds, 7–8 November 2001, Tienen, Belgium*.

Scheidel, W. (2001) *Death on the Nile: Disease and the demography of Roman Egypt*, Mnemosyne, 228, Leiden, Boston and Cologne: Brill.

Schlange-Schöningen, H. (2002) 'Theodor Mommsen (1817–1903)', *Antike Welt*, 33.6: 698–703.

Schlüter, W. (ed.) (1993) *Kalkriese – Römer im Osnabrücker Land. Archäologische Forschungen zur Varusschlacht*, Bramsche: Rasch.

—— (1999a) 'The Battle of the Teutoburg Forest: archaeological research at Kalkriese near Osnabrück', in J.D. Creighton and R.J.A. Wilson (eds) *Roman Germany: Studies in cultural interaction*, Portsmouth, R.I.: Journal of Roman Archaeology Suppl., 32: 125–59.

—— (1999b) 'Zum Stand der archäologischen Erforschung der Kalkrieser-Niewedder Senke', in Schlüter and Wiegels (1999): 13–60.

Schlüter, W. and Wiegels, R. (eds) (1999) *Rom, Germanien und Kalkriese*, Osnabrück: Osnabrücker Forschungen zu Altertum und Antike-Rezeption, 1.

Spickermann, W. (1997) 'Aspekte einer "neuen" regionalen Religion und der Prozeß der "interpretatio" im römischen Germanien, Rätien und Noricum', in Cancik and Rüpke (1997): 145–67.

Toner, J. (2002) *Rethinking Roman History*, Cambridge: Oleander Press.

Urban, R. (1999) *Gallia rebellis. Erhebungen in Gallien im Spiegel antiker Zeugnisse*, Historia Einzelschriften, 129, Stuttgart: Steiner.

Webster, J. (1997) 'A negotiated syncretism: readings on the development of Romano-Celtic religion', in Mattingly (1997a): 165–84.

Wells, P.S. (1999) *The Barbarians Speak. How the conquered peoples shaped Roman Europe*, Princeton: Princeton University Press.

Wiegels, R. (ed.) (2000) *Die Fundmünzen von Kalkriese und die frühkaiserzeitliche Münzprägung*, Möhnesee: Osnabrücker Forschungen zu Altertum und Antike-Rezeption, 3.

Wigg, D.G. (1997) 'Coin supply and the Roman army', in W. Groenman-van Waater-inge, B.L. van Beek, W.J.H. Willems and S.L. Wynia (eds) *Roman Frontier Studies 1995. Proceedings of the XVIth International Congress of Roman Frontier Studies*, Oxford: Oxbow Monograph, 91, 281–8.

Wiseman, T.P. (ed.) (2002a) *Classics in Progress. Essays on ancient Greece and Rome*, Oxford: Oxford University Press and the British Academy.

—— (2002b) 'Preface', in Wiseman (2002a): xiii–xvi.

Wolters, R. (2000) 'Anmerkungen zur Münzdatierung spätaugusteischer Fundplätze', in Wiegels (2000): 81–117.

9

A HOUSE DIVIDED

The study of Roman art and the art of Roman Britain

Martin Henig

This case study is based on the personal experiences of the writer, who has worked in Oxford for over thirty years, and because of his interests often found himself in a liminal position between 'classical' and 'European' archaeology. One part of his academic life has been concerned with teaching mainstream Roman art for the classics faculty, and researching Greek and Roman gemstones; the other with various aspects of the art of Roman Britain. In his own eyes these are simply two aspects of a seamless tapestry embracing the entire Roman Empire, and if other scholars saw things in the same way there would be little need for this volume and none at all for the present contribution. In fact it was clear to me from the start that my work was regarded differently by two quite discrete groups of colleagues. On the one hand the majority of members of the classics faculty apparently assess and value my work largely in its relationship to Mediterranean culture. Thus, for them, I have been from first to last an authority on intaglios and cameos, and no encouragement has ever been given to me to teach any course centred on Roman Britain or north-west Europe. For the other constituency, which comprises archaeologists in the University School of Archaeology as well as local excavators, museum curators and the like, it is precisely the British, insular aspect of my work that is of importance and the gems and sculpture I study are *only* of interest when they are local finds; there is almost never any interest in iconography here for its own sake, nor is the relationship of (for example) British gem finds, or for that matter bronzes, sculptures or mosaics to works of art found in other lands part of the mental landscape of most of these people. For them the primary interest of a site appears to lie in occupation patterns, economy and pottery. Any artwork is regarded as, at best, an exotic diversion from the main area of interest and is the subject of an appendix where I am called in as an 'expert'. Of course the analysis presented here is personal and circumstantial, but to a large degree it can be presented as something tangible, with a long historical ancestry which needs to be explored before remedies can be suggested.

Classical archaeology and British antiquity

The division between the archaeology of Greece and Rome and the archaeology of northern and western Europe is a very old one which, even in England, goes back to the sixteenth and seventeenth centuries. Rich aristocrats or their benefactors travelled to Italy (and occasionally beyond) as tourists and collectors, bringing back with them Greek and Roman gems, coins and sculptures as well as more modern pictures, manuscripts and books; these they kept in galleries and libraries in town and country houses whose architecture increasingly came to resemble the sumptuous splendours of antiquity. Further, the collections came to be published in sumptuous catalogues, especially in the eighteenth century (see Haskell and Penny 1981). The long list of virtuosi or dilettanti would include Thomas Howard, Earl of Arundel and Charles Townley. Lesser men with an interest in the past, doctors and parsons, gardeners and academics had to be content with the world immediately around them – with 'British antiquity' in fact. Representatives of these local scholars include William Camden and John Cotton, William Stukeley and Thomas Hearne (Piggott 1985, 1989; Wright 1997; on Roman antiquities see Munby 1977). Although they were concerned with the same culture and might also collect coins and books, they did not have the resources to gather collections of gems and statues, and lacked the space for the latter. Their interests inevitably turned to topography, identifying Roman roads and camps in the English, Welsh and Scottish countryside. Apart from coin collecting, opportunities to indulge in the world of classical archaeology were relatively few and far between. Rather poignantly, Stukeley attempted to describe the classical statuary at Wilton, but this was not his world. He did, however, produce a treatise on a silver lanx from Risley Park in Derbyshire and a volume on the coinage of the British 'usurper' Carausius. The latter volume, *The Medallic History of Carausius*, published 1757–9, has often been criticized for the idiosyncrasies of some of the author's ideas, but the drawings and descriptions are objective. Hearne was an even finer numismatist, possessing a good collection himself and capable of describing issues with all the classical learning of an Oxford scholar. He is perhaps better known for his part in the description and debate centring on the mosaic found at Stonesfield in Oxfordshire in 1712 (see Freshwater *et al.* 2000). His ability as an observer was perhaps sharper than that of his opponents such as the Merton don, John Pointer, but lack of contact with comparanda led him to misidentify the mosaic as depicting Apollo rather than Bacchus. It is of some interest that the Stonesfield mosaic, albeit in a rather poor engraving, achieved sufficient celebrity to be included in the leading European classical encyclopaedia of its day, that of Montfaucon (published in 1719). For the most part, however, the world of the local antiquary was very different from that of those better-favoured scholars who could travel, observe and collect in Europe. Only briefly during the Napoleonic Wars when travel to the Continent was disrupted were de-luxe volumes of antiquities produced by Samuel Lysons (1797, 1813–17), no doubt mainly for country house libraries. Here sculpture from the temple of Bath and mosaics from great villas like Bignor, Frampton and Woodchester were displayed in a style normally reserved for prize antiquities from the Mediterranean (see Henig 1995: 178–81).

That moment was never to recur. The growth of British power and the increasing availability of travel for the well-to-do meant that Greece, the Near East and India were added to Italy and southern Gaul. The occasional excavation report, such as that on the Bartlow Barrows by John Gage, and the altogether exceptional acuteness of the writings of the London antiquary and collector Charles Roach Smith stand out for their European awareness. For the most part, as the Victorian age progressed the study of Romano-British archaeology had different aims. These hardly changed for more than a hundred years. Primacy was given to military antiquities which seemed to show how the Romans had managed a rather similar empire. Towns and villas were of interest as revealing how Romans, or natives who had been Romanized in the manner Tacitus described in *Agricola* 21, lived their lives. Art only had a passing interest for Francis Haverfield (1915) who saw it as being largely mechanical and uninspired save for folk crafts; for Collingwood (Collingwood and Myres 1937: 247–50) Roman art itself was seen as being totalitarian, and Romano-British art even more vulgar and inept than that produced abroad. The present writer took classical civilization A-level in 1960 with the Roman Britain option. Topics were almost entirely concerned with the army and towns. Any question on art would have expected a disparaging answer. Certainly no careful analysis of a British sculpture or mosaic against a prototype from the Mediterranean area would have been expected or required. It should be added that my initial training was as a modern historian who had chosen to take a course in ancient history with the special paper in Roman Britain under my own volition; none of the classicists in the school took this option, which I sensed was despised by them.

Jocelyn Toynbee and the two archaeologies

We did not know it at the time, but 1960 was almost the last year when the art of Roman Britain could be ignored, for in 1962 an exhibition was held in the Goldsmiths' Hall, London backed by a superb catalogue by the Lawrence Professor of Classical Archaeology at Cambridge, Jocelyn Toynbee. This was later expanded into a massive book, *Art in Britain under the Romans* (1964). The writer had lectured and produced very distinguished work on classical archaeology, such as *The Hadrianic School* (1934). The essence of her achievement was that she was the first Mediterranean archaeologist to take the objects displayed in local museums in Britain seriously. To her colleagues she must have seemed a bit eccentric, but professors of her eminence are allowed to have hobbies: hers happened to be 'Roman Britain' rather than stamp-collecting! For the present writer, who knew her only comparatively late in her life, she still stands as one of the very few scholars with feet in what had become two quite distinct worlds. The opportunity to lay on a weekend conference in Oxford to mark her eightieth birthday was too good an opportunity to be missed. Julian Munby and I (Munby and Henig 1977) decided to concentrate on her special Romano-British achievement, but not exclusively. Jocelyn was not in the plot and, against all convention, she was herself asked to contribute and produced a splendid study of mythology on medallions. The *Festschrift* also included papers on amber carvings from Aquileia and on bone pins depicting hands holding fruit or eggs. An especially charming tribute came from Professor Martin Robertson (1977), a Hellenist who at least appreciated Jocelyn's work. Most of the Roman Britain papers (including seminal studies of mosaics) had ramifications outside the province. Nevertheless one reviewer (Ling 1979) at least was rather disparaging because we had picked up only on one of the honorand's achievements and (maybe by implication) the least important of them.

A trail had been blazed and the ramifications were many, but thirty or forty years is not long enough to remove all distinctions. Moving away from the strictly historical, the rest of this chapter will deal with how I have perceived the study of culture in Roman Britain through my own career. First, why did I and contemporaries at the Institute of Archaeology at London all choose to work on Britain and the north-west provinces? There was not really much choice. Apart from a post or two at the British Museum and perhaps at the British School in Rome, opportunities to work abroad were almost non-existent. And if one had wanted to research material in a foreign country there was the additional problem of funding. My contemporaries at the Institute of Archaeology took up posts or subsequently worked in Lincolnshire, Derbyshire, Leicester, Surrey, Wiltshire and London. The tradition into which we all fitted was the topographical one started by Camden. Art only came in incidentally and was almost invariably regarded as a matter which Jocelyn Toynbee alone could pronounce upon. Before her, of course, it would for the most part have been dismissed with little more than a shrug of the shoulder.

But if the prospect of working in the Mediterranean remained distant, the acute student of Roman archaeology was about to sample a measure of it in Britain. A young field archaeologist, Barry Cunliffe, trained in the same way as his predecessors such as Richmond and Frere on British antiquity, found himself in 1961 excavating a Campanian-type villa (or even the palace of a client king) at Fishbourne in Sussex. Subsequently he was to sort out and publish the important temple and bath complex at Bath, Somerset, though

Figure 9.1 First-century mosaic at Fishbourne Roman palace, Sussex
(photo Grahame Soffe)

here he was building on the work of predecessors back to the eighteenth century, as well as on that of Toynbee and Richmond more recently. This demanded that he turn himself for the purpose into a full-blooded classical archaeologist, where necessary calling in expertise from scholars who normally worked only in Italy and the Mediterranean. Finds from such sites as Bath and Fishbourne of course included some material that might as well have been found in Italy (Figure 9.1), but this had always been true of other much less glamorous sites as well. Thus when the writer of this chapter decided to study the engraved gemstones found in Britain, he was mainly making comparisons with gems from outside Britain and, with regard to iconography, working solely with classical archaeologists.

Engraved gems had, indeed, been one of the earliest fields of classical archaeological research in England, with the advent in the reign of James I of royal and ducal collecting by Prince Henry and the Earl of Arundel, who were only following in the wake of the princely collecting in continental courts during the previous century and more. In part this was because gems were regarded as both valuable and collectable. Normally findspots were not recorded as they were acquired on the market and provenance meant: 'what earlier collection did these come from?' While there is a certain historical interest in knowing that a gem was in the former Arundel collection and had passed to that of the Dukes of Marlborough, for a student trained in the traditions of the archaeology of context the study left a great deal to be desired. Attitudes to my dissertation epitomized the two approaches. Thus for John Boardman, always an enthusiastic supporter but trained (as a Greek archaeologist) through the British School in Athens, my work essentially brought together a large number of gems which would otherwise lie in complete obscurity in provincial British museums. For Romano-British colleagues, such as my supervisor Professor Sheppard Frere, the study threw a little light on 'Romanization' and my training rendered me a useful 'specialist' who would write up objects that the excavator did not understand or, in truth (alas), care very much about.

A curious reversal

To judge by the reception of the volume (Henig 1974) which eventually appeared, its impact in Britain was entirely confined to the classical archaeologists and collectors, although it was interesting to see that about the same time, and later, studies of gems as site finds were published in Germany and France. In other words, awareness of the 'classical archaeological' element in the finds from the northern provinces was firmly established, if only as a minority taste. The interest of classical archaeologists might seem to contradict the premise of the two cultures within archaeology which underlies this chapter, but it is explicable. Intaglios and cameos were probably engraved throughout the Empire, but on the whole they were standardized and for the most part show little sign of local style. What I had done was to collect together intaglios and cameos from many local museums (into which it may be fancied most classical archaeologists would not think it very worth while to set foot) and make them available to 'refined' scholarship. Thus the interest of glyptic specialists in, say, a Hellenistic gem depicting Ptolemy XII was for them intrinsic (Plantzos 1999: 46 no. 19); it did not lie in its being found in Wroxeter, although to me part of its fascination lay in the way in which it epitomizes the complex temporal and spatial links between cities in the ancient world (Figure 9.2a). Similarly a unique Italic (Roman Republican) gem from Verulamium showing Diomedes stealing the Palladium (Figure 9.2b) was of far greater importance to the classical gem specialists for its iconography (Moret 1997: 90 no. 130) than it was to the excavator, for whom it was simply an exotic find; but again the perceptive cultural historian could use such a find to illustrate one way in which knowledge of Graeco-Roman myth entered Roman Britain. Thirty more years of fighting the prejudices of the two sides have not very materially changed a curious situation wherein Romano-British glyptics remains an outstation of classical archaeology.

A more normal position is that posed by scholarship dealing with the other arts which have a provincial flavour and have achieved fairly widespread acceptance by mainline Romano-British (and north-west European) archaeologists,

Figure 9.2a
Hellenistic intaglio cut upon a sardonyx
depicting Ptolemy XII, from Wroxeter,
Shropshire (scale 5.6:1)

Figure 9.2b
Italic (Roman Republican) intaglio
of sard showing Diomedes stealing
the Palladium, from Verulamium,
Hertfordshire (scale 4:1)

but at the same time have been dismissed by classical archaeologists as
barbarous because they appear to lack the quality of Mediterranean finds.
Again this writer and others have had to contend with prejudice – but here
from the contrary direction.

The Cinderella of Roman art studies

Another project which had its genesis in the 1960s, but only started to appear
ten years later, was the British section of the international *Corpus Signorum
Imperii Romani* (CSIR). This was to be issued under the auspices of the British
Academy and was thus rather better funded. Clearly the thought behind the
publication of all the sculptures of the Roman world was ambitious and there
was co-operation by other countries including Germany and Austria.
Nevertheless, this essentially north European project, with its array of fasci-
cules on Germany and Austria as well as Britain, was not followed by scholars
working in Mediterranean lands, although a link of a sort with the classical,
Mediterranean archaeology was established by separate publications: as part
of the British CSIR of some of the Roman sculpture in the British Museum

and (by the Archaeological Institute of the University of Cologne) of Roman sculpture in English private collections. The fact that the latter project had to be undertaken by a German university is a reflection of the paucity in numbers of classical archaeologists in Great Britain.

For the most part classical archaeologists are only concerned with marbles (very occasionally limestones) from the Mediterranean region. In some instances they are dealing with the sculptural embellishment of famous buildings (such as the *Ara Pacis*), but generally they deal with works from a geographical area, like Campania or a single city, such as Aphrodisias. It is hard to see that the *historical* importance of such assemblages is, objectively, any greater than that of the limestone sculptures from studios at Cirencester (chief city of the Dobunni and eventually a provincial capital) and Bath, or the sandstone reliefs from the legionary fortress of Chester. Working on the sculpture from the Cotswold region, the writer (Henig 1993) has again and again been struck by the stylistic interest and iconographic variety of the better work, which includes the remarkably inventive pediment of the Temple of Sulis Minerva at Bath with its political message (Henig 1999; Figure 9.3) and a capital inhabited by Bacchus and his entourage which surmounted a Jupiter column in Cirencester, which both deserve illustration

Figure 9.3 Pediment of the Temple of Sulis Minerva, Bath, Somerset
(photo Nick Pollard and Robert Wilkins)

141

in any book on Roman art. Dealing with Chester (Henig forthcoming), there were fewer works of top quality; but there was compensation in being able to read associated inscriptions and thus to link carvings on altars and tomb-stones with named members of the Imperial army and what appears to have been, in the middle Empire, a flourishing civilian settlement. Questions about style and patronage were very much to the fore and it was by no means apparent that in art-historical terms my work was any less worthy, any less intellectually respectable, than if I had been studying sculpture in Rome or Athens.

Amongst the sculptures from Roman Britain published in various fasci-cules of the Corpus there is a great deal of work of real quality which shows how local artists in Britain combined 'classicism' with a distinctive feeling for texture and pattern – qualities that students of the medieval sculpture of north-west Europe seem to appreciate and value, though it would seem that the only standard which classical archaeologists appreciate is fairly slavish copying of metropolitan work. Notions that many of the sculptures and bronzes from Roman Britain are freer and in a sense better than their prototypes as works of art would be anathema to them.

It is difficult to account rationally for the profound lack of curiosity over more than one decade from classical archaeologists working less than a hundred yards from my office in such work. This can be contrasted with the cosmopolitan attitude of epigraphers, presumably because they have long realized that a name or a phrase from an inscription in one province can have resonance elsewhere.

Wall-painting and mosaics

The quantity of Roman wall-painting from Campania and Rome gives it a commanding position, but a considerable quantity of schemes of decoration can be examined in Britain, where the late Joan Liversidge (e.g. 1969, 1984) and Professor Roger Ling (Davey and Ling 1981) have produced important work. The latter is interesting in the context of this chapter as a rare example of a scholar who does bridge the divide between disciplines; this catholicity gives his work on the British material considerable breadth, especially in drawing on comparanda, though I sense that he would regard himself first and foremost as a classical archaeologist (after all that is the area he is paid to teach in Manchester University) and (like Jocelyn Toynbee) his British studies can be seen as an agreeable pastime, interesting but (of course) infe-rior to the serious business of classical archaeology.

A corpus of mosaics from Britain is in progress, edited and largely illus-trated by David Neal and Stephen Cosh (2002–). Although ASPROM and the Society of Antiquaries of London, the sponsors of the publication, have links with wider European scholarship, this is basically a work in the tradi-tion of Samuel Lysons (1797, 1813–17), and the old British topographical tradition has played a large part in the work. The interest of those mainly concerned with Mediterranean mosaics remains to be seen; the impression one gets from both Katherine Dunbabin's (1999) and Roger Ling's (1998) recent books on mosaics is that what is found in Britain is held to be distinctly odd and parochial. David Neal, who comes directly from the local (English Heritage) tradition, is a very talented, professional draughtsman, and the beauty of the production will undoubtedly bring it to the attention of some scholars who hitherto have avoided Romano-British studies. Taking what are the most attractive artworks from Britain, and doing them full justice, Neal and his colleagues have set up the most powerful challenge to the classical archaeology tradition in modern times. Nevertheless, it will be very interesting to see whether this Corpus will be ultimately marginalized by the classical archaeologists, like the British volumes of CSIR or most of the rest of the evidence for vibrant artistic activity in Roman Britain and elsewhere in the north-west provinces.

Reassessing Romano-British art

Looking at the arts, category by category, has its uses but it is also useful to look at the field as a whole, bringing in from the cold other categories such as the multifarious achievements of the bronzesmith. While most continental countries have issued corpora, there has been little in the way of sustained work in Britain – although my own studies of individual works from Britain, ranging from tiny figurines and votive masks to the great head of Hadrian from the Thames at London, are summarized in my *The Art of Roman Britain* (Henig 1995). The better works are of the highest distinction and interest. The same feeling that the classical archaeologists are missing something can be seen with regard to jewellery, likewise discussed in my book and more fully by Dr Catherine Johns in *The Jewellery of Roman Britain* (1996). Who could consider the Thetford and Hoxne treasures without being deeply moved by the quality and the strangeness of some individual pieces? It is not even necessary for the classical archaeologist in London to read these books, only to visit the Weston Gallery of Roman Britain in the British Museum where glittering gold and silver, fine bronzes, mosaics, wall-paintings, sculpture and gems provide an intellectual and aesthetic treat for the visitor.

The disdain of the classical archaeologists suggests that such books are not read and that galleries like that in the British Museum are not much visited by them. Presumably, this is the result of ignorance and prejudice: for a classical archaeologist, the art produced in a 'provincial' centre in north-west Europe must appear by its very nature inferior to art produced in the centre. Even Jocelyn Toynbee was not immune from establishing a hierarchy of excellence, with imports from Italy at the top, Gaulish works second and last of all Romano-British. Even though writers on Romano-British mosaics, wall-painting, sculpture and gems had bucked the trend, on the whole the Toynbee distinction has been allowed to remain. In Oxford University, for example, there has been no enthusiasm amongst the powers in classical archaeology to establish courses to include such 'degenerate' material! If 'the proper study of Mankind is Man' (Alexander Pope, *An Essay on Man*, Epistle 2, line 2) it is hard to privilege one part of the ancient world as opposed to another, even if the productions of one area please an average viewer more than those of another. An 'art historian' is, after all, a historian and not an aesthete.

But we cannot let those responsible for European archaeology off the hook. For them excavation and settlement archaeology are primary and such Roman art which impinges is highly marginal. In over ten years of archaeology and anthropology at Oxford, the writer has not once been asked to make a real contribution to the course by lecturing on his specialities – notably the art and culture of the province in which Oxford lies! Apart from the waste of resources, the result has been to deny to students the possibility of widening their horizons and of healing the centuries-old divide.

Divided we fall!

Recently I have attempted to address the whole question of Roman culture in Britain in *The Heirs of King Verica* (Henig 2002). The book is aimed at a readership beyond students of the north-west provinces and the early medieval historian, for it asks us about the nature of classical culture as a whole, a culture in which to a degree the educated classes of Roman Britain and those of our own day share (I make no apology at all for being elitist!), with some suggestions of how the classical inheritance was passed on through the first millennium AD. Unfortunately, if there is anything that so many classical archaeologists seem to find more distasteful than the subject of Roman Britain it is the culture of the Middle Ages, where it is so often the north that plays a premier role. Perhaps this is best epitomized by an experience last year when a classical archaeologist to whom I was talking expressed blank amazement that I should be deeply concerned with the British Archaeological Association (BAA), which although interested in Roman culture from the time of its founders Charles Roach Smith and Thomas Wright in the mid-nineteenth century, has its major concerns in the millennium which follows the Roman period. A moment's reflection should show how these are not really widely separated cultures but linked phases of the same civilization.

For their own purposes many medieval archaeologists and historians prefer a *tabula rasa* and disregard what went before. Alongside telling the classicists what they are missing, the writer, as honorary editor of the BAA, has to remind his friends in the organization that Roman art, especially Roman provincial art, has a key part to play in their own study, for history is a seamless web, both temporal and spatial. Indeed, readers from China (let alone from space) would be justified in asking what all the fuss is about as 'classical', 'north-west European' and 'medieval' archaeology are all only related aspects of culture in a very small part of the earth's surface. Here, a very old friend, Professor John Onians, who is both a classical archaeologist and a student of Renaissance architecture, has introduced the writer (and his students) to the liberating concept of World Art. At a personal, ideological level there is no problem, and we can move on, but of course such enlargement of perspectives does not solve anything when confronted by vested interests. The one area where the north-west Europeans, the classical archaeologists and (it is to be feared) the medievalists are united is in distrust of the polymath or the person interested in everything. One is tempted to write that Pliny the Elder would have had a hard time today, but Pliny was immensely rich so he could have financed himself as an eccentric 'amateur'.

Can anything be done to heal divisions born of ancient suspicions and snobberies? It is undoubtedly easier to travel today than it was a few decades ago, and there are very many more opportunities for students to work abroad, even to dig in places like Rome, Pompeii and a myriad other ancient sites from Turkey to Spain, opportunities that simply did not exist for earlier generations. EEC membership has helped to a degree by making it possible to work abroad, if the lack of language skills in Britain (not just in the ancient languages) causes problems still. But it is disturbing that people go to dig and study the antiquities of Italy without at the same time, or earlier, becoming *au fait* (as did an earlier generation) with sites at home and the collections of local museums. It is alarming that to a large degree the study of the art of Roman Britain is in the hands of people at or near retirement age without many obvious successors in the wings. Archaeological units perform a highly professional job but entirely lack specialists in art, and the number of amateurs with all-round interests seems fewer as there are other calls on leisure.

The old snobbery was essentially one of wealth, coupled with a classical education (in Greek and Latin); the new snobbery would, no doubt, reverse these desiderata. But it is still alive. There is no reason why classical archaeologists should not practise their skills with the Roman period art of the north-west. One small sign of hope is that the new *Lexicon Iconographicum Mythologiae Classicae* (1981–99) has attempted to bring together representations of classical myth from throughout the Roman Empire, and thus quite a number of works of art from what was once *terra incognita* are displayed to classical archaeologists wherever they work, many more than in the days of Montfaucon. It is harder, however, to persuade them that everything should not be judged by the procrustean canons of Graeco-Roman taste.

Even if an individual finds it hard not to privilege his subject, one route out of an extremely narrowly centred world-view was brilliantly pioneered by the leading Hellenic archaeologist during my time in Oxford, Professor John Boardman, in his important study *The Diffusion of Classical Art in*

Antiquity (1994), even though in regard to the north-west it has limitations. People throughout Eurasia took up many aspects of classical art and ornament; the process was not just confined to northern Europe. If one looks at what one knows about, takes it beyond its current limits and can get it into a teaching syllabus this would of itself break down barriers. I am not sure that Boardman quite arrives at the point where the part-Hellenized art of a region is itself a legitimate centre for study, but logically it must do so. After all, what would Greek art have been without foreign, 'barbarous', largely oriental influences? Whether of course a faculty – a group of people in what is admittedly now not likely to be a male-dominated, smoke-filled room, though ideologically still highly resistant to change – will be prepared to use imagination in making appointments and constructing syllabuses is another matter.

What of the archaeologists of the local Roman scene? Few, if any, oppose the study of the heartlands of the Roman Empire, but the interests of the dominant figures among them (such as Professor Martin Millett and Professor Barry Cunliffe) lie in field survey and excavation rather than in art history; in contrast to the succeeding so-called 'Dark Ages' no institution (other than the British Museum) has ever bothered to create posts in the arts of provincial Rome, and the effect has often been to leave scholars who dare to work in this area unemployed, partially employed or on the edge of academic discourse with the effect that, for economic reasons, the Mediterranean remains to a degree outside the experience of the few committed art historians who do try to build bridges between the north-west and the classical world, save as a holiday destination. The main enemy here for the art historian leaving our shores is what it has always been: largely a matter of money. Unless the scholar has contacts and funding it is hard to operate abroad. And the interested amateur is inevitably going to work from home. When addressing a local society even a mile or two from a university which is one of the centres of classical archaeology in Britain, the writer of this chapter feels himself to be in a different intellectual world because, to those often-derided amateurs, Rome self-evidently means both the Arch of Titus (seen on a summer holiday) and the local villa. A metaphor of what should be the seamless fabric of Roman archaeology is displayed in the Oxfordshire Museum at Woodstock. Here the whole process of study, acquisition, display and publication of an early eighteenth-century embroidery showing the Stonesfield mosaic (a mosaic which actually 'made it' to the European consciousness soon after it was discovered) is a poignant reminder of what our subject should be about. Essentially this was a wonderful meeting point for all interested in Roman art to come together, but in practice the resonance of the find was largely with local students of Roman Oxfordshire rather than with international scholars working on the cult of Bacchus and its art throughout the ancient world. What did we expect?

On the whole the Roman interests of readers of the journal *Britannia*, purchasers of the many books on Roman Britain published by Tempus, and members of the Association for Roman Archaeology remain obstinately local, with art accorded a very humble place. Education would help, but this needs to start in the schools; and in an artistically deprived society, where even western art history forms no part of the syllabus, how can one expect widespread understanding of Greek and Roman art? Surely the visual arts, together with literature, should be an integral and compulsory part of the National Curriculum, with Greek and Roman art and culture forming a good part of this. Maybe nascent classical archaeologists could be introduced early on to the realization that art did not end with the Pantheon, and they might appreciate not only western art in general but the local areas of Roman art from which western art sprang.

A very small sign of hope, at least increasing the number of people 'on the margins' who are just not satisfied with the *status quo*, is the invention of the subject of World Art, outlined above. It is now, at least, a vital undergraduate subject at the University of East Anglia. At its centre is the idea that we have to be anthropologists of art, looking at the productions of diverse places and simply be prepared to enjoy the differences caused by different climates, resources and natural histories. In miniature the culture of Italy or Britain or Germany in the Roman period will have had similarities and differences produced by manifold factors. A few scholars, notably John Onians (1999) at the University of East Anglia and Jaś Elsner (1995, 1998) at Oxford, are attempting in their own ways to break the mould and no longer privilege one period over another. It is a logical step from their work, even if they have not done it themselves, to focus on a particular artefact – let us say the Bath gorgon or the Thetford treasure – and ask why these works are different from other objects made in Italy, and not dismiss them, as I fear John Boardman (1994: 308–9) appeared to do in the former case, with a shrug: 'it might have meant something to a Briton'. Yes, indeed, but what did it mean to the Briton? The Thetford and Hoxne treasures, in the opinion of this writer, contain the most visually exciting examples of Roman jewellery in existence; there is nothing like them in Italy because they were produced by a different, a provincial, culture, but they deserve a positive response from classical archaeologists, not just from specialists in Roman Britain, both for their aesthetic content and for what they tell us of a Roman Empire at the cusp of its transformation. The former treasure was dedicated to Faunus, a god familiar to readers of Virgil, Ovid and Horace, urging us in our studies to bring the south into the north, take the north into the south and when we have absorbed the implications to rise above the mentality of Plato's proverbial frogs around a pond and seize on all our imaginative instincts. And the Orpheus mosaics invented in Cirencester early in the fourth century, of which the finest example was that laid in the palatial villa at Woodchester (Figure 9.4), display local themes, for Orpheus is

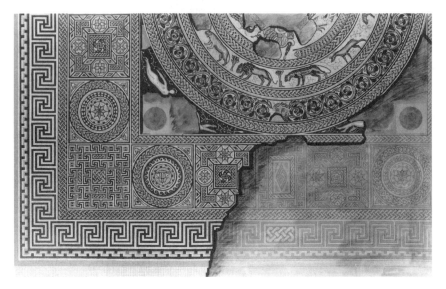

Figure 9.4 Orpheus mosaic from the villa at Woodchester, Gloucestershire
Source: After Lysons (1797)

conflated with the regional hunter god and imbued with the neo-Platonism of the age, as shown by placing the divine hero at the centre of a turning world, in the midst of three concentric circles of birds, mammals and foliage. What such works of art tell us is of abiding importance. Alas I fear, after a lifetime of effort and observation of the self-interested way in which establishments work, that institutional narrowness will triumph. As in the past, gains in understanding will be the work of individuals battling against prejudice and the odds against a powerful mediocrity.

Bibliography

Boardman, J. (1994) *The Diffusion of Classical Art in Antiquity*, London and New York: Thames and Hudson.

Collingwood, R.G. and Myres, J.N.L. (1937) *Roman Britain and the English Settlements*, Oxford: Clarendon Press.

Davey, N. and Ling, R. (1981) *Wall-Painting in Roman Britain*, London: Britannia Monograph Ser., 3.

Dunbabin, K.M.D. (1999) *Mosaics of the Greek and Roman World*, Cambridge: Cambridge University Press.

Elsner, J. (1995) *Art and the Roman Viewer. The transformation of art from the pagan world to Christianity*, Cambridge: Cambridge University Press.

—— (1998) *Imperial Rome and Christian Triumph. The art of the Roman Empire* AD *100–450*, Oxford: Oxford University Press.

Freshwater, T., Draper, J., Henig, M. and Hinds, S. (2000) 'From stone to textile: the Bacchus mosaic at Stonesfield, Oxon., and the Stonesfield embroidery', *Journal of the British Archaeological Association*, 153: 1–29.

Haskell, F. and Penny, N. (1981) *Taste and the Antique*, New Haven, Conn. and London: Yale University Press.

Haverfield, F. (1915) *The Romanization of Roman Britain* (3rd edn), Oxford: Clarendon Press.

Henig, M. (1974) *A Corpus of Roman Engraved Gemstones from British Sites*, Oxford: BAR British Ser., 8.

—— (1993) *Roman Sculpture from the Cotswold Region*, Oxford: The British Academy, Corpus Signorum Imperii Romani. Great Britain, 1.7.

—— (1995) *The Art of Roman Britain*, London: B.T. Batsford.

—— (1999) 'A new star shining over Bath', *Oxford Journal of Archaeology*, 18: 419–25.

—— (2002) *The Heirs of King Verica*, Stroud: Tempus Publishing.

—— (forthcoming) *Roman Sculpture from the North West Midlands*, Oxford: The British Academy, Corpus Signorum Imperii Romani. Great Britain, 1.9.

Johns, C. (1996) *The Jewellery of Roman Britain*, London: UCL Press.

Lexicon Iconographicum Mythologiae Classicae (1981–99), Zürich and Munich: Artemis.

Ling, R. (1979) 'Review of Munby and Henig 1977', *Britannia*, 10: 381.

—— (1998) *Ancient Mosaics*, London: British Museum Press.

Liversidge, J. (1969) 'Furniture and interior decoration', in A.L.F. Rivet (ed.) *The Roman Villa in Britain*, London: Routledge and Kegan Paul, 127–72.

—— (1984) 'The painted wall-plaster', in S.S. Frere, *Verulamium Excavations III*, Oxford: Oxford University Committee for Archaeology Monograph, 1: 115–40.

Lysons, S. (1797) *An account of Roman antiquities discovered at Woodchester in the County of Gloucester*, London: Cadell and Davies.

—— (1813–17) *Reliquiae Britannico-Romanae: containing figures of Roman antiquities discovered in various parts of England* (3 volumes), London: Cadell and Davies.

Moret, J.-M. (1997) *Les pierres gravées antiques representant le rapt du Palladion*, Mainz: Philipp von Zabern.

Munby, J. (1977) 'Art, archaeology and antiquaries', in Munby and Henig (1977): 415–32.

Munby, J. and Henig, M. (eds) (1977) *Roman Life and Art in Britain*, Oxford: BAR British Ser., 41.

Neal, D. and Cosh, S. (2002–) *Roman Mosaics of Britain*. Vol. 1: *Northern Britain* (other vols forthcoming), London: Illuminata Publishers for the Society of Antiquaries of London.

Onians, J. (1999) *Classical Art and the Cultures of Greece and Rome*, New Haven, Conn. and London: Yale University Press.

Piggott, S. (1985) *William Stukeley. An eighteenth-century antiquary*, London and New York: Thames and Hudson.

—— (1989) *Ancient Britons and the Antiquarian Imagination*, London and New York: Thames and Hudson.

Plantzos, D. (1999) *Hellenistic Engraved Gems*, Oxford Monographs on Classical Archaeology, Oxford: Clarendon Press.

Robertson, M. (1977) 'Jocelyn Toynbee – an appreciation', in Munby and Henig (1977): 1–2.

Toynbee, J.M.C. (1934) *The Hadrianic School*, Cambridge: Cambridge University Press.

—— (1962) *Art in Roman Britain*, London: Phaidon Press.

—— (1964) *Art in Britain under the Romans*, Oxford: Clarendon Press.

Wright, C.J. (1997) *Sir Robert Cotton as Collector*, London: The British Library.

10

TACITUS, AGRICOLA AND THE ROLE OF LITERATURE IN THE ARCHAEOLOGY OF THE FIRST CENTURY AD

Birgitta Hoffmann[1]

The sources for the history of Roman Britain in the late first century AD are complex. In the absence of reliable archaeological data, nineteenth- and early twentieth-century classicists and ancient historians relied mostly on Tacitus' *Agricola* and, once archaeological evidence did begin to emerge, it was frequently grafted onto this pre-existing reconstruction as illustrative material, rather than as an independent form of evidence. With the ever-increasing gap between classics and archaeology over the last forty years, this originally text-based narrative is now perpetuated by archaeological professionals who are increasingly unable to assess the limitations of written sources, and thus their value, in comparison to their own archaeological evidence. This chapter will attempt to show that discussion of the late first century is progressing in both fields and that a renewed co-operation would be beneficial to both classics and Romano-British archaeology.

In 1425 Poggio, the Pope's secretary and book-collector in Rome, received a letter from the monastery of Hersfeld in Germany informing him that after checking his list of desiderata against the books preserved in their library, a volume of hitherto unknown works of Tacitus had been identified, namely the Dialogue on the *Orator*, the *Germania* and the *Agricola*. It took another thirty years for this manuscript to make its way from Germany to Italy where, from the 1470s onwards, a number of people made handwritten and printed copies. The original manuscript then vanished, only to partly resurface in the early twentieth century in Iesi in northern Italy (Petersen 1958: 149–51; Hunger *et al.* 1988: 413, 541). Given the problems that the *Germania* and *Agricola*, in particular, have caused, there must be Romanists who, at some point in their careers, have wished that the manuscripts had gone astray in the post to Rome; but instead the *Agricola* has risen to become one of the most read volumes on the history of Roman Britain.

151

The *Agricola* describes the career of one Roman senator, who rose from obscure beginnings to the governorship of Britain, where he had considerable military success, only to see his further career blighted by the jealousy of the Emperor Domitian. The story has much to commend it: a consistent story line, easily readable in an evening, with a well-developed plot and main character, some great tragic moments and a very entertaining style, punctuated with short sharp witticisms which burn themselves into the memory. As it is also the longest surviving literary source for Roman Britain, it has long been a focus of attention for archaeologists, historians and philologists alike.

While historians have been particularly interested in the text as a witness to the political climate in Rome at the time of the accession of Trajan, classicists often concentrate their research on obtaining a better understanding of the evolution of Latin away from the language of Cicero and Horace and the changing use of literary genres and style. Romano-British archaeologists, on the other hand, have looked to the text in search of a more detailed picture of the Roman presence in Britain at the end of the first century AD. Through most of the eighteenth and nineteenth centuries, views on the text differed markedly, but they all shared the same basis for argument: a thorough knowledge of the Latin text and an often more than basic understanding of the underlying demands of Latin literature and historical context. The later twentieth century saw a major change in this knowledge base, when the development of archaeology as an independent discipline and the consequent move of Romano-British studies away from history and classics resulted in a dramatic increase in the number of scholars who were no longer able to deal with the text in the original Latin and who also lacked the traditional 'underpinning' in the historical context of central Roman history in the first century AD. The outcome is that the majority of students today read the *Agricola* as Penguin or Oxford Classics (Mattingly and Handford 1948; Birley 1999) or even just paraphrased in the main introductory textbooks on Roman Britain (Frere 1967 or later editions; Salway 1981; Todd 1999). As convenient summaries, such introductions have had a major impact on our understanding of the *Agricola*. The prototype was the brainchild of R.G. Collingwood who sought to provide an easy way into the subject by drawing together data spread through numerous journals and publications, difficult to access even for the serious professional (Collingwood 1930: v). They have since, predictably, become the backbone of many university and further education courses on Roman Britain. Collingwood's *The Archaeology of Roman Britain* (1930) focused almost exclusively on archaeological features, but its better-known successors by, amongst others, Collingwood himself, along with the likes of Richmond, Frere, Salway and Todd, prefer a more historical approach and it is here that the *Agricola* finds itself included in a closely woven narrative of archaeological and literary material.

The initial examples – Collingwood and Myres's *Roman Britain and the English Settlements* ([1937] 1963) and Richmond's *Roman Britain* ([1955] 1963) – portray a period of Flavian expansion which sees Cerialis in Carlisle in *c.* AD 72 ([1955] 1963: 38), followed by Frontinus' activity in Wales and a comparatively vague account of the activities of Agricola up to AD 84 ([1955] 1963: 40–4). Indeed, Collingwood and Myres ([1937] 1963: 115–19) devote considerable space to analysing the historical problems associated with the text. By the first publication of Frere's *Britannia* in 1967, however, much had changed. While Cerialis is still credited with destroying the Brigantes, it is definitely Agricola who is given the most space (pp. 103–16), and we are presented with a year-by-year account with exact locations using archaeological sites (many at the time recently discovered by aerial archaeology and still undated). This narrative sets the tone for the later editions (1978 and 1987), as well as Salway's (1981) and Todd's (1981) accounts. What had happened? In 1967 a new commentary on the *Agricola* by I.A. Richmond and R.M. Ogilvie had been published, designed to update an earlier edition. This new commentary differed markedly from the earlier one as it not only contained a commentary on the Latin text (focusing on grammar, style and literary parallels), but also put forward ideas which were very much at variance with the prevalent thinking of the time on the reliability and context of the text (compare to Syme 1958 and references in Ogilvie and Richmond 1967). Indeed, some of its comments may have been designed by the authors as a challenge to 'the establishment view'. One of the biggest alterations was an attempt by Richmond to draw on the results of many years of excavations in northern Britain and integrate them with the Agricolan narrative to provide a coherent whole. The resulting text is problematic, as R.M. Ogilvie points out in the introduction (1967: vii). Richmond was only able to submit a first draft before his death in 1965 and, perhaps consequently, a number of footnotes, cross-references and comments on the extent of the archaeological evidence, as well as the legends to some of the maps, appear to be missing. Only Todd lists this book outright in his bibliography. Salway lists it in the sources section (where, as a commentary and edition, it has every right to be), rather than in the more frequently consulted main bibliography, and Frere's acknowledgement is even harder to find. The account itself, however, quickly found acceptance, and Richmond's interpretation (rather than the original text) quickly appears to have become the underlying origin for numerous maps and studies on Roman Britain – so much so that while few people today actually read the original, its influence continues to pervade our model of the late first century AD.

The following decades saw the publication of numerous studies which identified marching camps (e.g. St. Joseph 1958, 1969, 1970, 1973) and forts as Agricolan (Robertson 1977, 1983), thus increasingly driving more neutral terms, such as Flavian I and II, out of the discussion. The overuse of the adjective 'Agricolan' increasingly implied that the material culture of the period could be dated to within five years, while the date of construction of specific sites was often hypothesized on the basis of strategic ideas derived from the Richmond reconstruction (Frere 1981). Indeed, this often overrode any other method of dating as, for example, the case of Inchtuthil, which was dated, without any archaeological support, to Agricola's sixth season, i.e. AD 82/3 (St. Joseph, in Pitts and St. Joseph 1985: 272). A parallel process has been the detailed analysis of the text in search of further geographical clues to the siting of the major events of the text, especially the location of the battle of Mons Graupius. These exploits have received a detailed treatment by Maxwell (1990), who discusses the limitations of both archaeology and literary sources in some detail.

Disapproval of this mode of reconstruction exists, but seems initially to have been restricted largely to the field of classics, where not everybody favoured the positivism towards the text's historical reliability expressed by Ogilvie and Richmond. Nevertheless, there have been critics within the field of Romano-British archaeology, notably W.S. Hanson who, in a number of articles (e.g. Hanson 1980), culminating in his 1987 book *Agricola and the Conquest of the North*, points out numerous methodological problems with the then prevalent approach. In particular, he explicitly describes the acceptance of the account by Tacitus, where it cannot be verified, as an 'act of faith' (Hanson 1987: 20). In addition, archaeological results in England and Scotland since the 1960s have provided further evidence for problems with the reconstruction. For example, in the late 1980s, excavations in Annetwell Street, Carlisle produced timbers, which were dated by dendrochronology to AD 72/3. This corroborated older finds of early Flavian coins and samian from elsewhere in the city, and dated the establishment of the fort to well before Agricola's governorship. Having established an independent date and an associated archaeological assemblage for one site, further studies quickly showed that other supposedly 'Agricolan' bases such as Ribchester, Blennerhasset, Castleford, and even sites well into Scotland, had similarly early material and hence most likely pre-Agricolan dates (Caruana 1997). Moreover, David Shotter (2000) has singled out a number of forts even further north (including Castledykes, Newstead, Camelon and Strageath) that have produced disproportionately large bodies of early coinage which point towards activity in the early 70s. Nor is coinage the only group of finds to show unusually high levels of early material in the north. For example, the fort of Drumquhassle, near Loch Lomond, has yielded Terra Nigra, a pre-Flavian and very early Flavian pottery type that was imported from Gaul (G. Maxwell, pers. comm.), and sites such as Carlisle, Newstead, Inchtuthil and Castleford have all produced glass vessels which are markedly 'behind the times' in assemblages supposedly dating to the AD 80s. These have traditionally been dismissed as heirlooms or as traders dumping old-fashioned material with less discerning customers in the north, but they may equally well indicate an earlier start date for the sites.

In addition, the work of the Roman Gask Project, and others over the last few years, has revealed multiple structural phases on a number of Flavian military sites north of the Antonine Wall (Woolliscroft 2000: ch. 1). The phenomenon is best known from the series of fortlets and watchtowers on the Gask frontier between Doune and Bertha, but two distinct building phases have also now been recognized in the fort of Cardean and there are indications that Inchtuthil and Cargill may also have multiple phases. All of this suggests that the period of occupation in the north was substantially longer than the 'traditional' short chronology offered by Richmond and Ogilvie. Indeed, the archaeological evidence combines to suggest that a number of sites in the north, from Manchester to Strathmore, may already have been in occupation during the 70s, and this has led to a realization amongst scholars that the old 'Richmond reconstruction' stands much in need of revision, or as it was succinctly put at a recent conference 'nobody [of the experts there present] really believes this anymore'.

Little of these criticisms and new results seems to have filtered through to books for a larger audience, however (for a rare exception see Breeze 1996). In the general accounts, Hanson's *Agricola* (1987) is widely included in the recommended reading, but neither it nor the new excavations appear to have been able to change much. To give just one example: in Todd's account of Agricola's campaigns in the third edition of his *Roman Britain* (1999), the 'auld sang' seems to be writ in stone and every year another set of students and interested amateurs learns about the period from these so-called 'classics' of the reading list. On the other hand, with the rapid development of new archaeological techniques over the last forty years, many archaeology departments (increasingly science, rather than humanities based) unsurprisingly have more than enough approaches to teach apart from the combination of historical and archaeological data that dominated earlier times. As a result, any teaching of the use of historical sources, although vital to industrial, early modern and medieval as well as Roman archaeology, frequently has to be covered in the 'other half' of an archaeology and history degree. Apart from being a victim of timetabling, it also suffers from the fact that it is often seen as the aspect of archaeology with the longest proven track record of abuse. Coming as it does from a background in classics, classical archaeology has sometimes been seen as little more than 'the handmaiden of history', its main requirement being little more than to provide the location and lecture slides for major historical events, sometimes with the thinly veiled implication that should archaeology and history clash the history must be right. This widely publicized approach has often been found wanting when science-based archaeological dating techniques provided divergent dates or when archaeology moved away from historical inquiries into fields more closely associated with anthropology; consequently, there has been a growing tendency to deny written sources more than a peripheral role in archaeological research. Instead there has been an understandable, if often overstated view that they are either unreliable or of little relevance because they were written by authors who were marginal to the events or processes studied. If applied to the full, this negative approach would certainly make the archaeology of late first-century northern Britain easier to handle. For it would result in sites with archaeological material that can be dated to two or perhaps three different chronological horizons, identifiable through the material culture and datable by dendrochronology to, respectively, a period starting about AD 70/2 (Carlisle horizon) and another about the early 90s (Vindolanda horizon), possibly with an interim stage (Strageath interface) providing a *terminus post quem* of about AD 79/86, and characterized by a mixture of material from both horizons. The Carlisle horizon could be associated with a period of expansion, while the Vindolanda horizon appears to reflect a territorial contraction, although it also appears to be associated with a rise in civilian nucleated settlement types in the south and Midlands. Such a purely archaeological interpretation, while substantially correct, is, however, devoid of most of the features that make the Romans such an attractive culture for amateurs and archaeologists alike – i.e., the facts that make them seem so approachable as people just like us, with names, histories, personal foibles and so forth; in other words, the very features that set the Romans apart from the prehistoric cultures they superseded. This makes it unlikely that archaeology will abandon the 'historical undercurrent' in its treatment of the first century AD in any foreseeable future, raising instead the question of how the literary evidence might be brought to a methodologically sounder integration with the archaeological record.

This chapter started out by portraying a generation of scholars who may have disagreed on the role of Tacitus, but argued from the common starting point of a good understanding of his text. We have seen that archaeologists have given this a particular interpretation, which was then widely applied. What is lacking in archaeology is serious analysis of the text itself. This is hardly surprising since analysing Roman literary sources is traditionally the domain of Classics. Indeed, the success of Richmond and Ogilvie's reconstruction may be partly due to an acknowledgement that they, unlike most of their successors, were able to deal with Latin sources in the original and, more importantly, had been trained in the techniques associated with textual analysis in a philological and/or ancient historical framework.

Most Romano-British archaeologists have been attracted to the *Agricola* for two reasons: a belief, first, that the text provides an event history and, second, that it provides one of the clearest descriptions of 'Romanization', one of the core processes studied. Let us look at the first of these factors in more detail. In a perhaps somewhat old-fashioned approach to Roman history, archaeologists are primarily interested in three issues, which may be provided by the text: a date ('in the seventh summer of his governorship . . .'), a place ('at a place called Mons Graupius') and an event (a battle) and, hardly surprising, it is these that the 'Richmond reconstruction' addresses first and foremost. Modern Roman historians do not care very much for this simplistic approach and frequently counter the 'archaeology as handmaiden of history' slogan with the equally bitter 'history – the quarry of archaeologists', as it tends to mangle the source material equally effectively. The problem is that this approach is only permissible if the underlying limitations or biases of the source are clearly identified and understood. Interestingly, both Richmond's *Roman Britain* and Frere's early *Britannia* contain the caveat that the account may be partisan (Richmond [1955] 1963: 38; Frere 1967: 103), although only Collingwood and Myres ([1937] 1963: 115–19) address the problem at any length. Other accounts tend just to milk the story for every possible ounce of information. This raises the question of whether the text has been any more critically assessed by neighbouring disciplines. The immediate impression raises some doubts, given that modern biographies of the Flavian emperors frequently use Richmond and Ogilvie as their main source for the career of Agricola (e.g. Jones 1992). However, in imperial biographies Agricola's career is at best a sideshow and the use of a widespread and easily accessible treatment is hardly surprising. Tacitus' *Agricola* has, however, generated quite a serious discussion elsewhere, which appears to sit somewhere in the middle between historical and literary studies. As already stated, the text has caused heated debate for over 150 years but, for the sake of concision, I will focus on only a few studies, and use Syme (1958) as the point of reference for older research.

The first problem to be addressed is the question of the literary genre involved. This may not at first seem particularly important, but different literary genres have different requirements on the 'amount of truth and fact' they are expected to contain. In modern English literature historical novels are much more likely to be inexact than political biography, while historical studies should strive to be as accurate and objective as possible. To date, research on the *Agricola* has discussed whether it is a biography (with or without historical, laudatory or political overtones), a straight historical piece, a funerary oration, an apologia or a combination of all these elements (Streng 1970: 7 and 109 with further literature). These distinctions are important, for a funerary oration was meant to be purely laudatory and to show the deceased in the best possible light. A biography was meant to be slightly more truthful, but admittedly tends to focus on the contribution and character of the subject, which may create significant distortions, while a historical piece had the highest claim to historical realism (but for its limitations see below) (Syme 1958: 124–5).

A second major point of discussion, albeit closely linked to the first, is the role of Tacitus as a historian. Most archaeologists prefer to think of Roman historians as 'event recorders', but as Syme (1958) and many others have shown, that is exactly what Tacitus is worst at. Mellor (1993) defined him as one of the most important ancient political historians, more interested in processes within Roman society and the workings of power than pure events.

In fact Syme once identified Tacitus' greatest weakness as his disinterest in geography, in the military (1958: 170–2) and in preserving the chronological, rather than the logical order of events, especially for developments away from Rome (1958: 167). His greatest strength is in the careful selection of material to make a specific political point (Mellor 1993: 87–113) and, whilst many Roman archaeologists would certainly agree with the attraction of this approach over the older 'dates, battles and emperors' thinking, it means that archaeology has been looking for chronological and geographical detail in the most unlikely of places. Another point complicates matters further: Tacitus himself states that his theme (not the subject matter) for the *Agricola* is to prove '*that good men can prosper under bad emperors*' (*Agricola* 42.5). Under these circumstances he is unlikely to select material that would not suit his argument. Additionally, as many critics have mentioned (e.g. Breeze 1996: 20), Agricola and, more specifically, Tacitus were beneficiaries of the Flavian dynasty, to whom they owed their careers. The survivor, Tacitus, was in the unenviable position of having to defend his position after the fall of the dynasty, thus a treatise on the topic of 'good men under bad emperors' might have served to justify himself (and others, including the future emperor Trajan) and may thereby have encouraged a certain selectivity and weighting of the material covered. Ogilvie and Richmond mention this trend of interpretation, but refute it as unrealistic and unlikely (1967: 17); consequently little about these possible limitations resurfaces in later archaeological discussions. The possibility that the account is skewed unduly in favour of Agricola is, however, also borne out by an examination of who is and who is not mentioned. For, although Tacitus is at pains to point out all of Agricola's superiors, next to none of his subordinates is mentioned. Much is made, throughout the text, of Agricola's personal interest in provincial administration but, for example, the fact that most of the legal side of this work was carried out by a deputy (*iuridicus*) is ignored. This sits well with Tacitus' idea of *obsequium*, or intelligent obedience, and *moderatio*, in which a man's achievements were counted as those of his superior, but even so that superior was meant to encourage his subordinates and give credit where it was due. In this case, however, Tacitus seems to have felt no obligation to include any deputy's name as part of the team. Indeed, although we know Agricola's *iuridicus*, L. Salvius Liberalis Nonius Bassus, as one of the leading senators of the later Flavian and Trajanic period and a member of Pliny's and Tacitus' circle of friends, we are reliant on an inscription (Dessau, ILS 1011) for knowledge of his presence in Britain, demonstrating, if such proof was needed, that the *Agricola* is not a complete record of British events. Studies on the *Agricola* have also stressed how much of the content is derived from ideas already expressed by late Republican writers, foremost amongst them the ideal of the provincial governor. Margot Streng (1970) was able to show that this is, to a large extent, the late

Republican image of a militarily successful governor expanding the Empire whilst, at the same time, providing stable conditions in the hinterland of his province. The only major change is the stress Tacitus again puts on the importance of *obsequium* (similarly Syme 1958: 28), which a governor and senator should show to his superiors at all points in his career. Streng also stresses how closely Agricola is portrayed to match this ideal, while other governors are not. Noticing the difference in depiction, Syme (1958: 122) drew attention to the fact that by being slightly vague and disparaging to his predecessors, Tacitus was able to portray Agricola in a better light.

Detailed studies of Tacitus' style and language abound. A full survey would go far beyond the limits of this chapter, and most of them concentrate on the later and larger writings of the Histories and the Annals. There are, however, a number of recurrent features that are of particular interest to the reliability of the *Agricola*. All of Tacitus' writings are carefully structured. In particular they have framing chapters and plots separated by small excursions, to create the effect of chapters and sections. Tacitus is hardly original in this. Most literature operates within some form of framework, be it stanzas, chapters or acts, all of which fulfil specific functions. The *Agricola* takes this further, however. There is recognition, for example, that the structure of the text is substantially symmetrical, with a double frame (the introduction and ending, as well as Agricola's career before and after his stay in Britain). At the same time, Wille (1983) and Giancotti (1971) have shown that within the main British section, the text is split into three blocks of roughly equal length – namely, the earlier history and geography of Britain, the first six years of campaigning and the final season with the battle at Mons Graupius. The first and third of these parts have been carefully designed to parallel each other in language and content in several places (the demands for freedom during the Boudicca rising and in the Calgacus speech being the most obvious example), whilst other sections are designed to contrast each other. Even the description of Agricola's early career has been structured in such a way that it seems to repeat itself or at least cover the same topics both before and after AD 69.

The question could now quite understandably be raised as to why archaeologists should be interested in the structural details of a text; but the problem is that such careful composition is almost bound to affect the content. To achieve this level of parallelism one can hardly avoid compressing some data or rearranging them to achieve the desired stylistic effect. But that means that what we would consider 'historical accuracy', i.e. the correct rendering of a sequence of events, or the evaluation of its importance, may well have been compromised in the process, something that can certainly be demonstrated in the text in one small detail. Agricola's career before and after AD 69 is of a very different calibre. His career under Nero is an uneventful plodding through the *cursus honorum*, while from AD 69 onwards he suddenly finds himself promoted to patrician and runs quickly through the stages of legionary commander, provincial governor and consul, thereby showing that at least Vespasian thought well of him. The beginning of this change appears to be the 'Year of the Four Emperors', when we find Agricola raising troops for Vespasian in Italy. According to Tacitus' account, Agricola was doing nothing more than his duty. But put into its historical context it suddenly becomes apparent that these troops were being raised in Italy while Vitellius controlled Rome and most of the western provinces, whilst the Vespasianic faction in Rome was being decimated on the Capitoline, and while Vespasian's army under Mucianus was still far away on the Danube. Agricola was not, then, a quiet civil servant doing his job; his actions betray him as one of the earliest Flavian supporters in Italy and it is, therefore, small wonder that Vespasian favoured him with appointments after his victory. The structure of the text at this point, however, demanded the reduction of all this into a very brief mention, while Tacitus' theme of 'good men can prosper under bad emperors' makes this little adventure look thematically misplaced. So, as irrelevant and disruptive to the structure of the argument, it is compressed into half a sentence and easily overlooked, unless the reader has sufficient historical background knowledge. If events like this can be buried in such a way, what else may have been altered?

Closely linked with all this is the question of literary imitation. Unlike modern literature, where writers are encouraged to find their own voice, imitation of style and language were encouraged in Latin literature. Far from being just a competitive 'quote–unquote' game, these close adaptations were usually seen as a way for an author to demonstrate his erudition and place himself within the literary tradition, while documenting that he was able to use and improve on his models' writing (Albrecht 1965a, 1965b). This has led to a tradition among classicists to trace allusions or 'verbal echoes', and thereby the influences in classical authors. Tacitus is no exception and uses phrases and words that are adapted from several authors. Ogilvie and Richmond's commentary is full of references to Livy, Sallust and Cicero, but the text also includes a rather nice echo from Statius (Ogilvie and Richmond 1967: 218). Indeed Tacitus' famous description of Agricola's ability to explore in advance of the army and select excellent sites for forts (*Agricola* 20) was originally used by Statius to describe Vettius Bolanus' activities in Armenia (Statius, *Silvae* 5.2.41–5). Interestingly, this is the same man that Tacitus apparently disparages earlier in the text as well liked, but otherwise barely up to his job (*Agricola* 16).

Beyond these literary quotes, there are other forms of imitation: Woodman (1979: 149, 152) refers to them as 'significant' and 'substantive' imitation. The first consists of comparing particular features, but inviting readers to go further in their comparisons. Woodman (1979: 152) defines 'substantive imitation' as 'the technique of giving substance to a poorly documented incident by the imitation of one which is much better documented'. This could mean that while the bare fact of a battle at the site of Mons Graupius may be undeniable, the remaining material (speeches, number of enemies, exact battle lines, etc.) may well have been borrowed from a better recorded event, thereby providing a more exciting description. Woodman is able to point to several instances in the Annals and Histories where this happened, and one poignant case in the *Agricola* (37.6) is the death of Aulus Atticus, which is described in very similar terms to Catiline's as given by Sallust (Cat. 61). This treatment is symptomatic of a very different view of history, where truth and reality did not have quite the same role as in modern society. The reason for this imitation can be important; it invites comparisons between characters or situations, thereby implying that history can repeat itself, but, as Woodman suggests, it may sometimes reflect nothing more than a wish to entertain the audience (Woodman 1979: 154–5). However, given what was said earlier about the structure of the text influencing the length at which material is portrayed, some of this 'substantive imitation' could have been added to expand an otherwise 'thin' passage to the necessary length.[2]

A final point concerns Tacitus' careful control of the way events are portrayed. It has long been recognized by archaeologists and classicists alike that he can be annoyingly vague and suggestive (Crawford 1947: 128–9; Syme 1958: 315). Through careful use of phrases like 'it was said' or 'it could have been', or just by a particular way of presenting an event, Tacitus suggests motifs, actions or associations that create a particular atmosphere, without the ability or will to provide proof for the statement. The obvious example in this case is Domitian's reaction to Agricola's victory (*Agricola* 39). Short of reading a (nonexistent) diary of Domitian, there is no way that Tacitus could know about his thoughts and feelings but, by suggesting them, he gives the account a negative flavour. This is a form of reporting at which Tacitus excels (Mellor 1993: 68–87) but, unfortunately, it tends to make him very difficult to translate objectively because, while the undercurrents are easily enough recognized in the Latin, they are impossible to reproduce in English, leading to some interesting choices in wording. An example is the award of honours to Agricola after his return (*Agricola* 40). Mattingly and Handford (1948) choose to translate the implied subject (Domitian giving the award), thereby translating the insinuation, while Birley (1999: 29) stays close to the exact grammatical structure, which does not name Domitian at all, and leaves it open as to who awarded the triumphal ornaments (Dio Cass. 66.20.3 says Titus). Leading statements such as these are impossible to assess for their veracity and most classicists are careful in how they deal with them, often suggesting more than one possible interpretation. Ogilvie and Richmond (1967: 18), however, once again differ in their approach by accepting most of them as straightforward facts.

161

Comparing the picture painted by these few examples with the Richmond and Ogilvie reconstruction, a very different picture of Tacitus' *Agricola* emerges. Instead of a straightforward story, the classicists confront us with a complex work of art, where language, structure and content are closely interlinked, and this would suggest that Tacitus should be verified against other writers whenever possible. Other sources do exist for the last third of the first century AD in Britain, and these do combine to give a rather different picture. But Ogilvie and Richmond, who mention them only briefly, discard them outright as propaganda or as garbled (1967: 18), something that seems to have led to their omission from many archaeological accounts of Britain. These other literary sources are a poem by Statius, an epic by Silius Italicus, a geographical treatise by Pliny the Elder, a religious treatise by Plutarch, and a short excerpt from Cassius Dio, which survives in a fourth-century epitome. With the exception of the last (which is incidentally our best evidence that Tacitus' account may have problems with its sequence of events), the other sources are usually regarded as marginal and less reliable than straightforward historiography. Western European historians are notoriously suspicious of the use of poetry, mainly because we generally classify it as fiction. It is thus salutary to be reminded that Latin literature defined historiography as the closest literary art form to poetry, thereby demonstrating that these sources are actually less diverse than we think. But these sources all need textual criticism and stylistic analysis, to a similar depth as that lavished on Tacitus, before their reliability can be judged.

In today's circumstances we cannot hope that many Roman archaeologists will have the opportunity, ability or inclination to master the skills needed for an in-depth study of Latin and the finer points of Latin literary theory/analysis. But, in the same way that a large number of specialists exist within archaeology, to be consulted by colleagues, it would be useful to draw on the expertise of neighbouring fields like classics to achieve a better understanding of relevant material. The historical development that created a methodological rift between archaeologists and the rest of classics resulted in the archaeological world using a commentary that in many ways did not reflect, and even challenged, the views of the established Tacitean scholars of the time, whose reactions are only rarely reflected in the archaeological discourse. Nevertheless, as it created a very readable historical narrative it has become a 'classic', so integrated into the study of the period that its impact is often no longer realized. But Tacitean studies have moved on, as has archaeology, and both fields have added question marks to a number of points that were taken as reliable evidence by Richmond and Ogilvie. In acknowledging the progress achieved, and reintegrating the advances in both fields, we may have to revise one of our dearest chronological frameworks, but in doing so we would be gaining a more reliable chronology, as well as a better understanding of the role Rome wanted her provinces to play within the Empire. Romanization/acculturation/creolization is primarily a mental process; its documentation in certain forms of material culture is often only secondary. There are, however, only limited amounts of evidence for the underlying mental processes on both sides. One of the major contributions of Tacitean studies is to isolate the ideas that underlay both the *Agricola* and the *Germania*, and thus add substantially to our understanding of the Roman aristocracy's view of the outlying, exotic Roman provinces and the role a Roman senator was able to play in that context. This addition to one of the core interests of Romano-British studies should be well worth sacrificing the misplaced reliance on a hyper-exact chronological framework. We might have to restrict the adjective 'Agricolan' to the inscribed water-pipes in Chester, and return to the concept of early and late Flavian material, but we might in the process gain a better understanding of the long-term processes affecting Britain and Rome.

Notes

1 The author would like to thank a number of people who discussed aspects of this chapter with her in advance of publication, especially Dr Anna Chahoud, Profs Jim Crow, Bill Hanson and Lawrence Keppie. My thanks are also due to Dr David Woolliscroft for reading earlier drafts. Any remaining errors remain of course the author's.
2 The extent to which Tacitus was able to access eyewitness accounts, and how he integrated these within his account, is a closely related problem which needs addressing in more detail than this chapter allows. It will be reserved by the writer for a later publication.

Bibliography

Translations, editions and commentaries of Tacitus' Agricola

Birley, A.R. (trans.) (1999) *Tacitus, Agricola, Germany*, Oxford: World's Classics. Oxford and New York: Oxford University Press.
Mattingly, H. and Handford, S.A. (trans.) (1948) *Tacitus: The* Agricola *and the* Germania, Harmondsworth: Penguin Classics.
Ogilvie, R.M. and Richmond, I.A. (ed. and comm.) (1967) *Tacitus. De Vita Agricolae*, Oxford: Clarendon Press.
Petersen W. (ed. and trans.) (1958) *Tacitus, Dialogus, Agricola, Germania*, Cambridge, Mass. and London: Heinemann and Harvard University Press.

Secondary literature

Albrecht, M. von (1965a) 'Plagiat', in *Lexikon der Alten Welt*, Zürich and München: Artemis, 2335–6.
—— (1965b) 'Imitation', in *Lexikon der Alten Welt*, Zürich and München: Artemis, 1376.

Breeze, D. (1996) *Roman Scotland*, London: Batsford.

Caruana, I.D. (1997) 'Maryport and the Flavian conquest of North Britain', in R.J.A. Wilson (ed.) *Roman Maryport and Its Setting. Essays in memory of Michael G. Jarrett*, Kendal: Cumberland and Westmorland Archaeological and Architectural Society, 40–52.

Collingwood, R.G. (1930) *The Archaeology of Roman Britain*, London: Methuen & Co.

Collingwood, R.G. and Myres, J.N.L. ([1937] 1963) *Roman Britain and the English Settlements*, Oxford History of England (2nd edn), Oxford: Clarendon Press.

Crawford, O.G.S. (1947) *The Topography of Roman Scotland North of the Antonine Wall*, Cambridge: Cambridge University Press.

Frere, S.S. (1967) *Britannia. A history of Roman Britain* (1st edn), London: Routledge.

—— (1981) 'The Flavian frontier in Scotland', *Scottish Archaeological Forum*, 12: 89–97.

Giancotti, F. (1971) 'Strutture delle monografie di Sallustio e di Tacito', *Biblioteca di cultura contemporanea*, 108, Messina and Firenze: 231–341.

Hanson, W.S. (1980) 'The first Roman occupation of Scotland', in W.S. Hanson and L.J.F. Keppie (eds) *Roman Frontier Studies 12, 1979*, Oxford: BAR Int. Ser., 71, 15–44.

—— (1987) *Agricola and the Conquest of the North*, London: Batsford.

Hunger, H. *et al.* (1988) *Die Textüberlieferung der antiken Literatur*, München: dtv

Hunger, H., Stegmüller, O., Erbse, H., Imhof, M., Büchner, K., Beck, H.-G., Rüdiger, H. and Bodmer, M. (1961) *Geschichte der Textüberlieferung der antiken und mittelalterlichen Literatur*, 1, Zürich: Atlantis.

Jones, B.W. (1992) *The Emperor Domitian*, London: Routledge.

Maxwell, G. (1990) *A Battle Lost. Romans and Caledonians at Mons Graupius*, Edinburgh: Edinburgh University Press.

Mellor, R. (1993) *Tacitus*, London and New York: Routledge.

Pitts, L.F. and St. Joseph, J.K. (1985) *Inchtuthil: The Roman legionary fortress*, Britannia Monograph Ser., 6, London: Society for the Promotion of Roman Studies.

Richmond, I.A. ([1955] 1963) *Roman Britain,* Pelican History of England (2nd edn), Harmondsworth: Penguin.

Robertson, A.S. (1977) 'Excavations at Cardean and Stracathro, Angus', in D. Haupt and H.G. Horn (eds) *Studien zu den Militärgrenzen Roms, 2*, Köln: Rheinland-Verlag: 65–74.

—— (1983) 'Roman coins found in Scotland, 1971–1982', *Proceedings of the Society of Antiquaries of Scotland*, 113: 405–48.

Salway, P. (1981) *Roman Britain* (Oxford History of England), Oxford: Clarendon Press.

Shotter, D.C.A. (2000) 'Petillius Cerialis in northern Britain', *Northern History*, 36.2: 189–98.

St. Joseph, J.K. (1958) 'Air reconnaissance in Britain, 1955–7', *Journal of Roman Studies*, 48: 86–101.

—— (1969) 'Air reconnaissance in Britain, 1965–68', *Journal of Roman Studies*, 59: 104–28.

—— (1970) 'The camps at Ardoch, Stracathro and Ythan Wells: recent excavations', *Britannia*, 1: 163–78.

—— (1973) 'Air reconnaissance in Britain, 1969–72', *Journal of Roman Studies*, 63: 214–46.

Streng, M. (1970) *Agricola. Das Vorbild römischer Statthalterschaft nach dem Urteil des Tacitus*, Habelts Dissertationsdrucke, Reihe Alte Geschichte Heft, 9, Bonn: Habelt.

Syme, R. (1958) *Tacitus*, Volumes 1 and 2, Oxford: Clarendon Press.

Todd, M. (1981) *Roman Britain. 55 BC–AD 400* (Fontana History of England), London: Fontana.

—— (1999) *Roman Britain* (3rd edn), Blackwell Classic Histories of England, Oxford: Blackwell.

Wille, G. (1983) *Der Aufbau der Werke des Tacitus,* Heuremata, 9, Amsterdam: Grüner.

Woodman, T. (1979) 'Self-imitation and the substance of history: Tacitus, Annals 1.61–5 and Histories 2.70, 5.14–15', in D. West and T. Woodman (eds) *Creative Imitation and Latin Literature,* Cambridge: Cambridge University Press, 143–57.

Woolliscroft, D.J. (2002) *The Roman Frontier on the Gask Ridge, Perth & Kinross,* Oxford: BAR British Ser., 335.

Part IV

NEIGHBOURING CULTURES

11

HERODOTUS AND THE AMAZONS MEET THE CYCLOPS

Philology, osteoarchaeology and the Eurasian Iron Age[1]

Eileen M. Murphy

'Father of History' or 'Father of Lies', love him or loathe him, the works of Herodotus are universally recognized as being one of the foremost sources of written information concerning the societies of the classical world and beyond. Much has been written regarding the interpretation of his writings, but the supporting evidence for these conclusions has invariably been drawn through a comparison of his work with that of his contemporaries. In some cases, however, the findings of archaeological excavations have been found to shed light on his texts, particularly when these have involved the excavation of burial sites and cemeteries. The objective of this chapter is to focus on one aspect of scientific archaeology – osteoarchaeology – to highlight the valuable contribution that osteology and palaeopathology can bring to the interpretation of Herodotus' writings.

Herodotus and the study of his writings

Little is known about the life of Herodotus – the man credited by some as being the 'Father of History'. He was born between 490 and 480 BC at Halikarnassos, modern Bodrum, on the south-west coast of Asia Minor (Sélincourt 1962: 28). In his youth he travelled widely and it is considered highly probable that he had visited Upper Egypt, Thrace and parts of Scythia (the south of the former USSR), and that he was also familiar with parts of Greece and southern Italy (ibid.: 30). The precise limits of his travels are, however, uncertain. In addition to implying that he had visited the places he had written about he stated that he had spoken with the inhabitants of over forty Greek cities and districts, and of more than thirty other countries. In some cases he classified his sources as 'eyewitness' or 'hearsay' (Myers 1953:

9). In later life he became a citizen of Thurii in southern Italy, where he expanded and revised his *Histories*. He died in the period between 430 and 425 BC (Sélincourt 1962: 31–2).

The writings of Herodotus have been subject to scrutiny, in the form of translation, commentary and criticism, over the past twenty-five centuries (Hartog 1988: xvi). While his texts received much criticism from early classical writers, including Thucydides, Ctesias and Plutarch (Myers 1953: 17–19), it was not until the nineteenth century that there was a renewed interest in his work and the first attempts were made, particularly by German scholars, to analyse his writings. Niebuhr attempted to separate Herodotus from his sources (ibid.: 20); Nitzsch suggested Herodotus was little more than an industrious but unintelligent compiler (ibid.: 22); and Wecklein belittled his writings, believing that they represented little more than a Greek tendency to moralize traditional anecdotes, accredit Greek successes to the gods and invent causes for historical occurrences (ibid.). The first real attempt at constructive criticism, however, would appear to have been made in 1878 by Bauer, who believed that defects of the work had arisen as a consequence of the text having been compiled from drafts. He recognized that such an elaborate history would have taken time to write and that a degree of revision would have been inevitable (ibid.: 22–3). Nevertheless, Bauer's work was followed by further 'violent attack on the competence and honesty of Herodotus, and of reckless speculation about his authorities' (ibid.: 23).

The balance was redressed by historians and military historians writing in the final years of the nineteenth century and the first decades of the twentieth century. They appreciated that there were problems with the writings of Herodotus, but that these were inevitable due to his lack of military experience and his reliance on other sources; Herodotus' status as an observer and historian, however, had been restored (ibid.: 24–5). A fresh examination of the sources was made in 1913 by Jacoby, who rejected many of the reconstructions of previous historians and showed that there was an earlier ethnographical and a later historical phase in Herodotus' development as a historian (ibid.: 27, 29). More recent historians have also turned to the interpretation of Herodotus' writings (e.g. Hartog 1988; Fehling 1989) and the context in which he compiled them (e.g. Thomas 2000). Such approaches have enabled a greater understanding to be gained as to the reasons why Herodotus undertook his travels and wrote the *Histories*.

To summarize, during the nineteenth century historians concluded, on the basis of omissions and mistakes, that Herodotus had compiled his record from unreliable sources. His general silence regarding his sources was considered to be an indication of deliberate plagiarism; he had neither visited the places nor seen the objects which he described. This phase of criticism was then followed by a revision which saw historians gain respect for Herodotus' honesty and industry. In addition, the latter historians tended to be more appreciative of the difficulties which he had faced, and his problems of differentiating between good and bad sources. Writing in the 1950s Sir John Myers (1953: 31) concluded that 'his information is now seen to be such as an intelligent and observant man, of his age and upbringing, might reasonably accept, on eyewitness and hearsay, as true'.

From this brief overview of the historical background to research on the writings of Herodotus it is clearly apparent that this work was undertaken largely by classical and military historians. It is only on the rare occasion that such scholars would appear to have turned to the archaeological record to glean further insight into his texts (e.g. Sélincourt 1962: 239). Archaeologists, however, have displayed a willingness to draw on the information contained in the *Histories* for inspiration to aid with the interpretation of their findings (e.g. Rudenko 1970; Murphy and Mallory 2000; Davis-Kimball 2002). The objective of the following discussion is to demonstrate how the use of the writings of Herodotus as a research tool has clearly benefited the interpretation of archaeological findings from the Eurasian Iron Age.

Herodotus and Scythia

Herodotus devoted a large proportion of Book 4 of his *Histories* to writing about ancient Scythia, an enormous area which stretched over a distance of approximately 3,000 miles from the Podolia district of the Ukraine to the borders of China (Sélincourt 1962: 238). He described the tribes that inhabited the area as pastoral nomads, who were brave, warlike and knew nothing of urban civilization (ibid.). Herodotus wrote this section of his *Histories* in Olbia, a Greek town located on the mouths of the Bug and Dnieper rivers that was friendly with the Scythians and largely dependent on trade with the Scythian world. This settlement is considered to be the farthest point in Scythia that Herodotus visited, and it is probable that he was stationed there when he gathered much of his information about Scythia as a whole (Wheeler 1854: 141). Archaeological research in this region has verified the authenticity of a number of the accounts of Scythian life that are contained in the *Histories*, of which the following are but two examples.

The Pazyryk burials

Excavation of high-status frozen kurgans (burial mounds) at Pazyryk in the Altai of south Siberia by Sergei Rudenko in the 1940s produced some spectacular remains dating to the Iron Age. In addition to mummified humans and horses an array of organic material had been preserved beneath the permafrost. As he attempted to explain his discoveries Rudenko made use of the writings of Herodotus and discovered a number of startling correlations between the historical text and the archaeological record. A number of the mummies had shaved heads, for example, which did not solely appear to be related to the fact that they had been trepanned during the post-mortem period. Herodotus (4.23), however, had recorded of the Argippaei, who would have been close neighbours of the Altaian tribes, 'that all of them, men and women, are bald-headed from birth' (Rudenko 1970: 105). In addition, a male mummy recovered from Kurgan 2 displayed clear evidence of having been scalped (ibid.: 221; Murphy *et al.* 2002). Herodotus (4.64) discussed the practice of scalping among the tribes of the Scythian world in great detail, and his description is generally accepted as the earliest historical reference for the practice (Reese 1940: 7). He recorded that the heads of vanquished enemies were carefully processed, with the skin being stripped from the head by making a circular cut around the ears; the skull was then shaken out. He went on to relate how the flesh was scraped from the skin using an ox rib, cleaned and worked by the warrior until supple, and then used as a form of handkerchief. The handkerchiefs were hung on the bridle of the warrior's horse as symbols of battle prowess.

The Pazyryk mummies also displayed evidence of having been deliberately embalmed. A number of the crania had been trepanned to enable the extraction of the brain, and once this had been removed the endocranium was filled with soil, pine needles and larch cones (Rudenko 1970: 280–2). Removal of the intestines of the Pazyryk individuals had been undertaken by means of a slit which extended from the inferior aspect of the thorax to the navel. Once disembowelling had been completed the slit was sewn with sinews or horsehair. In addition to the extraction of the brain and disembowelling, the embalming procedures employed at Pazyryk displayed a number of variations. In Kurgan 2, for example, cuts on the arms and legs of the male mummy appear to have facilitated the introduction of a preservative fluid. In the female mummy from this tomb, however, cuts on the buttocks, thighs and calves had been used to enable the removal of body tissue from these areas. Once the flesh had been detached from the corpse it was replaced with a sedge-like grass and the slits were sewn with horsehair (ibid.: 280–1). Again, Herodotus (4.71.1) provides a valuable insight into the treatment of dead royals among the tribes of the Scythian world when he recorded that a royal corpse was prepared for burial by having its stomach slit open, the various organs removed and the resulting cavity filled with a variety of aromatic substances, including crushed galingale, parsley seeds and anise. Following this procedure it was then sewn up and covered in wax.

Female warriors

Herodotus (4.110–16) related a story which involved the union of Scythian male warriors with Sauromatae female warriors, more commonly known as Amazons. The Scythian warriors had fought against a group of Amazons (whom they had presumed were males) in defence of their property. Once they discovered that the Amazons were female, however, they were eager to join with them, and the two camps were united. The Scythians wanted to bring the Amazons back to their families, but the Amazons replied that they were too different to the Scythian females in that they were riders and warriors, whereas the Scythian women 'stayed at home in their wagons occupied with feminine tasks' and never hunted. Eventually the two groups compromised and settled together in a different part of the country. Here the Amazons were said to have maintained their traditional lifestyle – hunting on horseback, participating in warfare, and wearing the same clothes as males (Hdt. 4.116.2). Herodotus (1.205–14) also recounted that in the Massagetae tribe Queen Tomyris ruled following the death of her husband. He indicated that she was responsible for co-ordinating the battle against the aggressor King Cyrus of the Medes and Persians (Gera 1997: 187–204).

The archaeological evidence has again been found to corroborate Herodotus' accounts of the existence of female warriors among Eurasian nomadic tribes. The remains of female warriors have been identified on the basis of their association with weaponry as grave goods and, in a number of cemeteries, they have been found to represent as many as 37 per cent of the burials (Melyukova 1990: 106). Most recently Jeannine Davis-Kimball has identified the burials of at least seven female warriors at the Pokrovka cemetery in southern Russia (Davis-Kimball 1997: 47; 2002).

The cemetery of Aymyrlyg

From the examples provided above it is evident that archaeologists are more than willing to call upon the writings of Herodotus to help explain their findings. It is possible, however, to take such multidisciplinary research a step further by employing a biocultural approach. This methodology involves a strong emphasis being placed on the role that health plays in the interaction between a population and its social organization, material culture and physical environment, and it involves a synthesis of palaeopathological, documentary and archaeological evidence. The current author used a biocultural approach for her analysis of the cemetery complex of Aymyrlyg in south Siberia (Murphy 1998). This study also represented one of the first detailed palaeopathological analyses to have been undertaken on a substantial corpus of Iron Age human skeletons from Eurasia.

The cemetery was excavated in the period between 1968 and 1984 by Drs Mandelshtam and Stambulnik from the Institute for the History of Material Culture of St Petersburg. Approximately 800 individuals of the Scythian period were recovered, most of whom were considered to date to the third and second centuries BC (Mandelshtam 1992: 185). The majority of the 200 burials recovered during the later years of the programme, under the direction of Stambulnik, were found to date to the Hunno-Sarmatian period of the third century BC to the second century AD (Stambulnik 1983: 34).

A number of the osteological and palaeopathological features apparent in the remains of these population groups find clear parallels in the accounts of Herodotus. There was irrefutable evidence of the warfaring nature of these peoples, including, for example, the occurrence of a number of scalped individuals and possible female warriors (Murphy et al. 2002; Murphy 2003).

A proportion of the bodies from Aymyrlyg displayed cutmarks which were indicative that they had been disarticulated, and in some cases defleshed, after death. This finding was interpreted as evidence for secondary burial practices related to the seasonal migrations between the mountains and valleys that these semi-nomadic peoples would have undertaken (Murphy 2000a). The writings of Herodotus provide a number of accounts which imply that the tribes of the Scythian world practised cannibalism (Murphy and Mallory 2000, 2001). Indeed, Rudenko (1970: 283) had suggested that flesh may have been removed from some of the Pazyryk mummies for this reason. Murphy and Mallory (2000, 2001), however, have put forward the theory that Herodotus' source or sources had miscomprehended the secondary burial practices of these peoples which, if observed by a foreigner, could quite easily have been misinterpreted as the butchering and consumption of one's deceased.

Developmental defects at Aymyrlyg

Another particularly interesting finding from the analysis of the human remains from Aymyrlyg was the occurrence of a high proportion of individuals among both populations with evidence of developmental defects (Murphy 1998, 2000b). Although the majority of the defects may be regarded as occult, since they would not have had obvious detrimental effects on the affected individuals, a number of individuals displayed severe congenital malformations which would have resulted in these people displaying physical disabilities and abnormal appearances. Many societies – both past and present – deliberately eliminate infants with obvious physical abnormalities at birth. The infants are frequently not afforded burial in the societies' cemeteries and, as a consequence, their remains are rarely present among archaeological skeletal populations (Gregg et al. 1981: 220). This does not seem to have been the case at Aymyrlyg. Evidently individuals with physical abnormalities were considered to be members of the society and were allowed to live their lives among the 'normal' population. In addition, some individuals were so severely afflicted by developmental defects that their existence into adulthood must have been facilitated to at least some degree by other members of society, as the following examples illustrate.

Two Scythian period individuals were affected by developmental dysplasia and congenital dislocation of the hip. Both of these individuals would have had abnormal gaits and poor locomotory powers. Three Scythian period and two Hunno-Sarmatian period individuals displayed possible slipped femoral capital epiphyses. A further Scythian period individual had a malformed proximal femur. These individuals may also have had gait disturbances and less powerful locomotory capabilities relative to the unaffected members of society.

Three Scythian period individuals were also identified as having suffered from possible syndromes, or congenital conditions, which result in multiple physical defects. As Turkel (1989: 76) has pointed out, 'skeletons collected for study from individuals with rare syndromes are more rare than the syndromes', making these three cases extremely important palaeopathological discoveries. These three individuals would definitely have displayed abnormal facial characteristics. A female with possible neurofibromatosis would have had a notably enlarged and probably protruding eyeball (Murphy *et al.* 1998) (Figure 11.1). In addition, she would probably have had reduced vision in the affected eye. Other physical characteristics of neurofibromatosis include the occurrence of '*café au lait* spots', skin tumours, spinal curvature and joint disease, as well as a large range of other abnormalities (Gorlin *et al.* 1976: 536–8). Since only the skull was preserved, however, the full extent of the lesions apparent in this individual remain unknown. A child displayed one side of his/her skull to be smaller than the other (hemifacial microsomia), indicating that this individual possibly suffered from Goldenhar syndrome. He or she may also have displayed abnormalities of the external ear and may

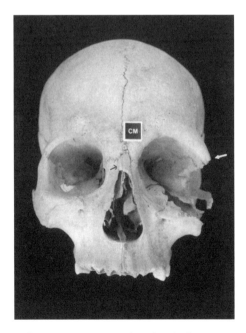

Figure 11.1 Cranium of a Scythian period adult female from Aymyrlyg with a grossly enlarged left orbit possibly indicative of neurofibromatosis (photo E. Murphy)

have been deaf. The child may also have had eye defects, possibly including an absent or reduced eye, and could have suffered from mental retardation and have had vertebral anomalies (ibid.: 548–50). Since only the skull of the individual was available for analysis, however, it is not possible to ascertain the full extent of skeletal involvement. An adult male with possible fronto-metaphyseal dysplasia would also have displayed abnormal facial character-istics. His facial features would have been coarse, with large brow-ridges, widely spaced eyes and an asymmetrical face and chin. He may also have been deaf, had poor vision, a short trunk with long extremities, elongated fingers and relatively immobile joints (McAlister and Herman 1995: 4207). Again, unfortunately, only the skull was preserved and it is therefore impos-sible to determine the full extent of skeletal involvement.

The Hunno-Sarmatian period population also included a number of indi-viduals who displayed developmental defects. A male individual with a half vertebra and two fused vertebrae may have had slight lateral curvature of the spine. A female individual displayed severe lateral spinal curvature, whereby the upper thoracic spine was angulated to the right and the lower thoracic spine displayed lateral curvature of approximately ninety degrees to the left (Figure 11.2). A child with a possible meningocele and hydrocephalus would have had an abnormally large head, possibly with an extra nubbin of tissue situated on the superior aspect of the forehead. A female individual with a possible clubfoot would definitely have displayed an abnormal gait and would have had problems with locomotion.

We will explore in the following sections whether such osteoarchaeolog-ical findings are of any relevance for a critical analysis of Herodotus.

Developmental defects and Herodotus

People hold a morbid fascination for humans and animals with malforma-tions, as the story of John Merrick, the 'Elephant Man', testifies (Montagu 1971). This fascination stretches back into prehistory. Depictions of humans displaying developmental defects are present on prehistoric rock art from Australia (Warkany 1959: 84). At some time between the ninth and seventh centuries BC the Chaldean priests of Babylon recorded details of congenital malformations, which they believed had prophetic meanings, in the stone tablets of the Royal Library of Nineveh (Ballantyne 1894: 129–30). A detailed list of defects and prophecies are inscribed on these tablets and this may suggest that the Chaldeans were familiar with a wide range of congen-ital malformations. References to individuals with developmental defects are also found in the writings of the Greek philosopher Empedocles, who lived in the fifth century BC, in the texts of Aristotle, and in the first century AD writings of Pliny the Elder (Warkany 1959: 93). In addition, references to 'deformed children' arise in the *Hippocratic Writings* (Lonie 1978: 323). An anencephalic infant Egyptian mummy was discovered in the catacombs of

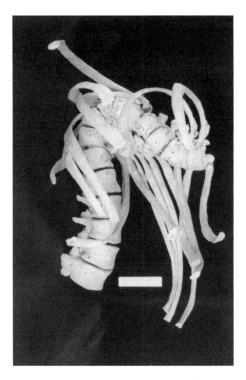

Figure 11.2 Reconstruction of the spine and rib cage of a Hunno-Sarmatian period
adult female from Aymyrlyg with congenital scoliosis. This condition
would have caused the woman to have had severe lateral curvature of the
spine. Scale bar represents 6 cm (photo E. Murphy)

Hermopolis where the sacred ape and ibis were normally interred (Brothwell
and Powers 1968: 182). This finding has been interpreted in two ways: either
the population regarded the infant as sub-human and buried the child with
animals, or they revered it and consequently buried it in a sacred catacomb
(Turkel 1989: 122). Writing in the fifteenth century Hartmann Schedel
included a series of woodcuts depicting twenty-one 'monsters and mythical
creatures' in his *Chronicle of the World*. These depictions were inspired by
descriptions provided by classical writers, and some, almost certainly, derive
from Herodotus (Füssel 2001: 636; Schedel 1493: XII; Figure 11.3).

People with unusual appearances from the Scythian world are reported in
Herodotus' Book 4. These descriptions are, however, generally dismissed by
historians as being nothing more than tall stories. Hartog (1988: 14), for
example, regards these descriptions of 'men with the hooves of goats' to be
hearsay. Indeed, it would even seem that Herodotus (4.25) himself may
have considered them as such (Sélincourt 1962: 239). Waters (1985: 88)
states that Herodotus (3.116.1, 4.13, 4.27) did not believe the account of

177

Figure 11.3 Hartmann Schedel, on the authority of classical authors including Pliny (*HN* 7.II = 7.9–32), who in turn used Herodotus, reported on and depicted a range of 'monstrous' human beings in his world chronicle of 1493: notably a one-eyed cyclops thought to live in India (left, second from top), a person with horse hooves from Scythia (right, sixth from top), a person with huge ears also from Scythia (right, third from top), and a satyr with hooked nose and goat horns and hooves, here placed in the Egyptian desert (right, fourth from top)

Source: Schedel (1493: XII), reproduced with the kind permission of the Bodleian Library, University of Oxford [Douce 304] 'one-eyed Arimaspians', and he is of the opinion that in this instance 'reason certainly predominates over fantasy here!' It is generally considered to be the case that Herodotus knew progressively less about the populations he describes the further one travels in a north-easterly direction from Scythia. It is possible, however, that these 'stories' should not be dismissed quite so readily and that their genesis may have been based on fact. Given the discovery of people with severe developmental defects at Aymyrlyg, it is possible that palaeopathology can perhaps help to explain what Herodotus' witnesses had seen.

Cyclops

Herodotus (4.13) recounted details of a poem written by Aristeas in which he related how he had journeyed to the country of the Issedones, beyond which lived the one-eyed Arimaspians, and beyond them the gold-guarding griffins. It is possible that the story of the 'one-eyed' Arimaspians had in some way developed from the existence of a congenitally malformed individual or individuals (see Figure 11.3). As stated above, a Scythian period female from Aymyrlyg displayed a grossly enlarged orbit as a result of neurofibromatosis (Murphy et al. 1998). Although admittedly the woman would not have been one-eyed she would have had quite a remarkable appearance, with a notably enlarged and probably protruding eyeball. In addition, the Scythian period child from the cemetery with possible Goldenhar syndrome may have had a reduced or absent eye.

There are also a variety of developmental defects which do result in individuals being born with a single eye. These include the cyclops malformation, which is associated with D trisomy and results in the development of a single orbit, although this defect is not compatible with life. There is, however, another condition called cebocephalus that is closely related to the cyclops deformity and is compatible with life (Potter and Craig 1975: 525–30). Such a condition would have had a dramatic effect on the appearance of the affected individual. It is therefore possible that the birth of even a single baby with the cyclops condition, or the occurrence of a single individual with cebocephalus may have been enough to trigger tales describing a strange one-eyed people.

Goat-footed race

Herodotus (4.25) also makes reference to a 'goat-footed' race (cf. Figure 11.3). In this case it is possible that the account had originated as a result of the observation of an individual or individuals with clubfoot. Clubfoot deformity (*equinovarus congenita*) arises as a result of an abnormal relationship of the tarsal bones, in which the navicular and calcaneus are positioned medially around the talus. The typical clubfoot abnormality involves three main elements – equinus (in which the foot is fixed in the plantar-flexed position), varus (in which there is an inward rotation of the hindfoot) and adduction (in which the foot is generally rotated inward) (Turco 1981: 44–5). The equine part of the name is derived from the fact that the foot is fixed in a plantar-flexed position similar in morphology to a horse hoof. A possible example of clubfoot was evident in a Hunno-Sarmatian period individual from Aymyrlyg. Palaeopathological cases of clubfoot are relatively rare, perhaps because of the difficulty of accurately identifying the defect in the archaeological record (Roberts and Manchester 1995: 38). Brothwell (1967: 424–8), however, does mention three possible cases of the defect, while Ortner and Putschar (1981: 364) make reference to a further possible example. It is quite possible that an individual with this malformation could be interpreted as being 'goat-footed'. Again, it is feasible that the occurrence of one or two individuals with this defect in a group would have been enough for tales to be disseminated of a tribe of goat-footed humans.

Enarees

Herodotus (1.105) makes reference to the effeminity of the Scythians and states that the Scythians who robbed the temple of Aphrodite at Ascalon in Syria were punished by the goddess and inflicted with what is known as the 'female disease'. He related that the disease was still present in the Scythian population during his time, and that those affected were known as 'Enarees'.

The developmental defect of slipped capital femoral epiphysis, which was present in several Scythian and Hunno-Sarmatian period individuals from Aymyrlyg, may shed light on these individuals. Slipped femoral capital epiphysis is common in adolescent males with delayed sexual characteristics. Such individuals may have the adiposogenital syndrome which is characterized by obesity, increased height, and deficient gonadal development. In addition, there is a childlike pattern of hair without secondary sexual characteristics, the limbs are longer than normal and a feminine pattern of fat deposition may be evident (Gruebel Lee 1983: 177). Perhaps the effeminate males Herodotus refers to as 'Enarees' were suffering from such a testosterone deficiency.

It is now known that abnormalities of the sex chromosome can also occur. In some cases individuals are classed as 'sex-reversed' since their sex chromosomes are at odds with their physical appearance (Brown 1998: 39). It is also possible that such abnormalities of the sex chromosomes may have been responsible for the Scythian 'Enarees'. Descriptions of Siberian tribes of the early twentieth century describe how male shamans took on the characteristics of female shamans and, although more rare, vice versa. The phenomenon was also recorded by travellers in the eighteenth and nineteenth centuries (Czaplicka 1914: 248). In some cases the male shamans simply began to dress like women and undertake female tasks. In more extreme cases, however, the 'male' shaman began to 'feel himself a woman', sought a male lover and occasionally got married (ibid.: 249).

Conclusions

The reliability of Herodotus' writings concerning Scythia would appear to have been vindicated on the basis of a variety of archaeological findings from Eurasia. In general, however, ancient historians have tended not to use archaeologically derived information in their work to the extent that archaeologists have employed information from ancient historical sources, although there are notable exceptions such as Aubrey de Sélincourt (1962: 39) who went so far as to state that 'future archaeological research will prove many a statement of Herodotus, which scholars have hitherto taken as guesswork or fairy-tale, to be substantially true'. It can further be suggested that osteoarchaeological and palaeopathological evidence has the potential to provide additional insights into the world that Herodotus endeavoured to describe.

The adoption of a biocultural approach for the study of the Iron Age populations from Aymyrlyg revealed a range of skeletons displaying a variety of developmental defects. This analysis was the first major palaeopathological study to have been undertaken on an Iron Age Eurasian population, but its results have been of great importance and provided new information on the lives of these semi-nomadic peoples. A number of individuals had developmental defects that would have caused them to have had unusual physical appearances, but it is clear that these people were afforded a place in the Scythian and Hunno-Sarmatian period societies. It is worth noting at this point that the Greek world would seem to have displayed an aversion to physical defects; many deformed infants were the victims of infanticide. The Spartans, for example, were known to carefully examine newborn babies for defects and faults and any who were found to be imperfect were killed (Scott 1999: 69–70). In addition, individuals with deformities were demonized in contemporary literature since they were thought to have extraordinary powers which enabled them to rule and dominate their societies (ibid.: 70; Papadopoulous 2000: 97–102). To a visitor from the Greek world, these Scythian individuals with abnormalities would probably have seemed abhorrent and incredible, particularly if such people were eliminated at birth or ostracized by Greek society. It can be argued, therefore, that the fabulous accounts of unusual individuals and peoples in Scythia that are related by Herodotus in his writings may have had their origin in real people with abnormal physical appearances who lived freely among these populations.

As stated previously, the biocultural study of ancient peoples in the region is in its infancy. As such, it can be argued that the increased use of palaeopathology when studying the archaeological populations of Iron Age

Eurasia might elucidate further examples of individuals suffering from developmental defects, and that these individuals may have been the source for the strange peoples reported by Herodotus.

Note

1   I would like to thank Professors Yuri Chistov and Ilyia Gokhman, Department of Physical Anthropology, Peter the Great Museum of Anthropology and Ethnography, St Petersburg, for granting me permission to examine the Aymyrlyg human remains. I am also grateful to Dr Colm Donnelly, School of Archaeology and Palaeoecology, Queen's University Belfast for his comments on the text.

Bibliography

Ballantyne, J.W. (1894) 'The teratological records of Chaldea', *Teratologia*, 1: 127–43.

Brothwell, D. (1967) 'Major congenital anomalies of the skeleton: evidence from earlier populations', in D. Brothwell and A.T. Sandison (eds) *Diseases in Antiquity*, Springfield, Ohio.: Charles C. Thomas.

Brothwell, D.R. and Powers, R. (1968) 'Congenital malformations of the skeleton in earlier man', in D.R. Brothwell (ed.) *The Skeletal Biology of Earlier Human Populations*, London: Pergamon Press.

Brown, K.A. (1998) 'Gender and sex: distinguishing the difference with ancient DNA', in R.D. Whitehouse (ed.) *Gender and Italian Archaeology: Challenging the stereotypes*, Accordia Specialist Studies on Italy, 7, London: Institute of Archaeology, University College London.

Czaplicka, M.A. (1914) *Aboriginal Siberia: A study in social anthropology*, Oxford: Clarendon Press.

Davis-Kimball, J. (1997) 'Warrior women of the Eurasian steppes', *Archaeology*, Jan./Feb.: 44–8.

—— (2002) *Warrior Women*, New York: Warner Books.

Fehling, D. (1989) *Herodotus and His 'Sources'* (first English translation), Leeds: Francis Cairns.

Füssel, S. (2001) 'Appendix', in H. Schedel, *Chronicle of the World, 1493. The complete and annotated Nuremberg Chronicle*, London: Taschen, 634–67.

Gera, D. (1997) *Warrior Women: The anonymous Tractatus de Mulieribus*, New York: E.J. Brill.

Gorlin, R.J., Pindborg, J.J. and Cohen, M.M. (1976) *Syndromes of the Head and Neck* (2nd edn), London: McGraw-Hill.

Gregg, J.B., Zimmerman, L., Clifford, S. and Gregg, P.S. (1981) 'Craniofacial anomalies in the upper Missouri river basin over a millennium: archaeological and clinical evidence', *Cleft Palate Journal*, 18: 210–22.

Gruebel Lee, D.M. (1983) *Disorders of the Hip*, London: J.B. Lippincott.

Hartog, F. (1988) *The Mirror of Herodotus*, London: University of California Press.

Lonie, I.M. (1978) 'Embryology and anatomy', in G.E.R. Lloyd (ed.) *Hippocratic Writings* (revised edn), London: Penguin Classics.

McAlister, W.H. and Herman, T.E. (1995) 'Osteochondrodysplasias, dysostoses, chromosomal aberrations, mucopolysaccharidoses, and mucolipidoses', in D. Resnick (ed.) *Diagnosis of Bone and Joint Disorders*, 6 (3rd edn), London: W.B. Saunders.

Mandelshtam, A.M. (1992) 'Ranniye kochevniki Skifskova perioda na territorii Tuvi', in M.G. Moshkova (ed.) *Stepnaya Polosa Aziatskoi Chasti SSSR v Skifo-Sarmatskoye Vremya*, Archeologiya SSSR, Moscow: Nauka. (Early nomads of the Scythian period in the territory of Tuva.)

Melyukova, A.I. (1990) 'The Scythians and Sarmatians', in D. Sinor (ed.) *The Cambridge History of Early Inner Asia*, Cambridge: Cambridge University Press.

Montagu, A. (1971) *The Elephant Man: A study in human dignity*, New York: E.P. Dutton.

Murphy, E.M. (1998) 'An osteological and palaeopathological study of the Scythian and Hunno-Sarmatian period populations from the cemetery complex of Aymyrlyg, Tuva, South Siberia', Unpublished Ph.D. thesis, Queen's University Belfast.

—— (2000a) 'Mummification and body processing – evidence from the Iron Age in southern Siberia', in J. Davis-Kimball, E. Murphy, L. Koryakova and L. Yablonsky (eds) *Kurgans, Ritual Sites, and Settlements: The Eurasian Bronze and Iron Age*, Papers from the European Association of Archaeologists 4th and 5th Annual Meetings, BAR Int. Ser., 890, Oxford: Archaeopress.

—— (2000b) 'Developmental defects and disability: the evidence from the Iron Age semi-nomadic peoples of Aymyrlyg, south Siberia', in J. Hubert (ed.) *Madness, Disability and Social Exclusion*, One World Archaeology, 40, London: Routledge.

—— (2003) *Iron Age Archaeology and Trauma from Aymyrlyg, South Siberia*, Oxford: BAR Int. Ser. 1152, Oxford: Archaeopress.

Murphy, E.M. and Mallory, J.P. (2000) 'Herodotus and the cannibals', *Antiquity*, 74: 388–94.

—— (2001) 'Herodotus and the "Cannibals"', *Discovering Archaeology*, 3: 16.

Murphy, E.M., Donnelly, U.M. and Rose, G.E. (1998) 'Possible neurofibromatosis in an individual of the Scythian period from Tuva, south Siberia', *International Journal of Osteoarchaeology*, 8: 424–30.

Murphy, E.M., Gokhman, I.I., Chistov, Y.K. and Barkova, L.L. (2002) 'A review of the evidence for Old World scalping: new cases from the cemetery of Aymyrlyg, south Siberia', *American Journal of Archaeology*, 106: 1–10.

Myers, J.L. (1953) *Herodotus: Father of history*, Oxford: Clarendon Press.

Ortner, D.J. and Putschar, W.G.J. (1981) *Identification of Pathological Conditions in Human Skeletal Remains*, Smithsonian Contributions to Anthropology, 28, London: Smithsonian Institution Press.

Papadopoulos, J.K. (2000) 'Skeletons in wells: towards an archaeology of exclusion in the ancient Greek world', in J. Hubert (ed.) *Madness, Disability and Social Exclusion*, One World Archaeology, 40, London: Routledge.

Potter, E.L. and Craig, J.M. (1975) *Pathology of the Fetus and the Infant* (3rd edn), London: Year Book Medical Publishers.

Reese, H.H. (1940) 'The history of scalping and its clinical aspects', *Yearbook of Neurology, Psychiatry and Endocriminology*: 3–19.

Roberts, C. and Manchester, K. (1995) *The Archaeology of Disease* (2nd edn), Stroud: Alan Sutton Publishing.

Rudenko, S.I. (1970) *Frozen Tombs of Siberia: The Pazyryk burials of Iron Age horsemen*, London: J.M. Dent & Sons.

Schedel, H. (1493) *Registrum huius operis libri cronicarum cu figuris et ijmagibus ab inicio mudi* [sic], Nuremberg: A. Koberger.

Scott, E. (1999) *The Archaeology of Infancy and Infant Death*, Oxford: BAR Int. Ser., 819.

Sélincourt, A. de (1962) *The World of Herodotus*, London: Secker and Warburg.

Sélincourt, A. de and Burn, A.R. (1972) *Herodotus: The Histories* (revised edn), Harmondsworth: Penguin Books.

Stambulnik, E.U. (1983) 'Noviye pamyatniki Gunno-Sarmatskova vremeni b Tyvye: Nekotoriye itogi rabot', in *Drevniye Kulturi Euraziiskih Stepei*, Leningrad: Institute for the History of Material Culture. (New monuments of the Hunno-Sarmatian period in Tuva: some results of the work.)

Thomas, R. (2000) *Herodotus in Context*, Cambridge: Cambridge University Press.

Turco, V.J. (1981) *Clubfoot*, London: Churchill Livingstone.

Turkel, S.J. (1989) 'Congenital abnormalities in skeletal populations', in M.Y. Iscan and K.A.R. Kennedy (eds) *Reconstruction of Life from the Skeleton*, New York: Alan R. Liss.

Warkany, J. (1959) 'Congenital malformation in the past', *Journal of Chronic Diseases*, 10: 84–96.

Waters, K.H. (1985) *Herodotos the Historian*, London: Croom Helm.

Wheeler, J.T. (1854) *The Geography of Herodotus*, London: Longman, Brown, Green and Longmans.

184

12

CELTOSCEPTICISM

A convenient excuse for ignoring non-archaeological evidence?

Raimund Karl

Ten years ago, what were formerly known as the Celts suddenly became nothing but a myth. It became fashionable to deconstruct the Celts. No more than knocking down a straw person, many have said since. An absolute necessity, long overdue, others stated. Even the word 'Celt' itself has, in some circles, become a dirty word, politically incorrect, a no-say.

Some lone voices have expressed some doubt about whether anyone in that debate was really looking at any evidence at all, rather than jumping onto the fashionable bandwagon of Celtoscepticism or trying to defend old Celtomaniac dreams of a heroic age 'when the grass was greener, the light brighter, more flashy and shiny than we would ever dare imagine'. Today, thanks to Celtoscepticism, it seems as if Celtomania has almost been overcome. The Celts, as one people, as one culture, as one essential group, are dead.

But did we benefit from Celtoscepticism? Have our explanations of Iron Age peoples in Britain, Ireland or anywhere else in Europe become any better? Or is it rather that we killed an idea that none but a few had ever really believed anyway, and while doing so threw out the baby with the bathwater? Should we not better be sceptic about Celtoscepticism as well?

While Malcolm Chapman's (1992) and Simon James's (1999) deconstructions of the 'Celtic Myth' have probably received the greatest public attention, the direct relevancy of their studies for what might have been called 'Celtic archaeology' is limited. Rather, it is in the wake of the renewed interest in the creation of identity, and especially 'ethnic' identity (Graves-Brown et al. 1996; Jones 1997), that a number of scholars, spearheaded by John Collis (1994, 1996, 1997a, 1997b, 1999a, 1999b), have expressed Celtosceptic views in a direct archaeological context. John Collis (1999b) gives a summary of the main Celtosceptic arguments:

1   The classical sources are ambiguous; it is impossible to locate the origin of the Celts.

2   The idea of Celts in Great Britain is a modern invention.

3   The use of the term 'Celts' . . . by linguistic criteria is erroneous.

4   The use of the term 'Celts' for a people speaking a Celtic language cannot be extended back into antiquity.

5   The interpretation of La Tène artwork as 'Celtic' depends on a modern definition of the Celts and thus is unacceptable.

6   The correlation of La Tène culture with Celts is based on a questionable interpretation of classical sources.

7   The methodology of the paradigm that 'La Tène culture' equals 'Celtic language' equals 'the Celts' is based on the unacceptable method of the German archaeologist Kossinna (1911).

8   This methodology is a medium for a political and racist interpretation of archaeology and therefore has to be refuted.

(Collis 1999b: 16; my translation)

Many of the above points are doubtless correct and require no further discussion. Problematic are Collis's points 2, 3 and 5, which can only be explained by a belief that we can directly access a past reality via our interpretation of the archaeological sources. This, however, is an epistemological impossibility: all definitions, any term, every model we might ever use to describe a past always remain modern constructs (Karl 2002a). Thus, contrasting 'invented' or 'constructed', 'modern' definitions or ideas with an unspecified and unexplained opposite, implying a (miraculously arrived at) knowledge of how 'the past really was' by Celtosceptics, can only be understood as a tool to discredit any opposition by pretending that the Celtosceptic views would be less 'constructed', more 'real', less 'modern', more truly representing 'ancient' reality 'as it was'.

Reconstructing Iron Age societies

John Collis (1994) most clearly points out what the ground rules for reconstructing Iron Age societies should be from a Celtosceptic's point of view. It is one of the main criticisms of Celtosceptics on reconstructions of Iron Age societies that non-archaeological sources, either from classical or Irish literature, are used to reconstruct social aspects of Iron Age societies by scholars like Barry Cunliffe (1984). Collis, in laying out his creed, writes:

> 'Celtic Society' is still very much with us, using either the classical sources, or the Irish literature. The first ground rule must be that detailed descriptions of societies are only directly applicable to the place and time they describe. I suspect there is nothing in the written European sources which remotely resembles the Iron Age societies of central southern England in the Middle Iron Age which Cunliffe

was trying to interpret, and African analogies may well be as relevant, perhaps more relevant, than the Irish sources of a millennium later. The ethnographic record encompasses a wider and better described range of choices than the two or three 'Celtic' societies handed down to us by ancient sources . . .

The second ground rule is that ancient descriptions of social structure are simply a model of how ancient people viewed their own, or other ethnic groups' social structure. This is obvious where Caesar talks of the 'senate' of the Aedui, perhaps less obvious in the tripartite division of Gallic society into warrior élite, bards and the common people. The societies described with this simple social division vary from developed urbanised societies to ones in which settlement patterns at least are decentralised. Though it is interesting to consider the ancient author's understanding of how societies functioned, their knowledge is limited in comparison to our own, and cannot be used as a basis from which we can work . . .

When considering the various sorts of society which have been termed 'Celtic', it is clear from the archaeology that there is an enormous range, from the urbanised societies of Gaul in the 1st century BC to the decentralised societies of the English Pennines; from the highly stratified societies represented in the burials of Vix and Hochdorf, to societies where it is difficult to pick out any prestige material goods . . . One of our first principles must therefore be to work from the archaeological evidence, and only use documentary evidence as we would use any other ethnographic material (the exception being when the written sources relate directly to the society being studied), and then to compare and contrast with the archaeology rather than using the written sources to form the basis for the archaeological interpretation.

(Collis 1994: 31–2)

Collis has one valuable point here. Non-archaeological sources have to be used with caution, like any ethnographic material. But otherwise, these paragraphs are quite characteristic of the general dislike of non-archaeological evidence amongst Celtosceptics. Blatant errors, like misquoting Caesar as mentioning bards where he actually speaks of *druides*, clearly show that Collis did not bother to consult Caesar's excursus on society in Gaul to look up the three short paragraphs in *De Bello Gallico* (6.13–15), let alone read the whole text, which contains a lot more information on Gaulish social structures than Collis would have us believe. Similarly, his knowledge of Irish sources obviously does not extend beyond the suspicion that there is nothing in them that might even remotely resemble anything in Iron Age societies in the southern English Middle Iron Age – a suspicion obviously not even worth minimal scrutiny.

But it is not only the dislike of non-archaeological sources that makes this approach highly suspicious, it is also its total conviction in the 'truth' of archaeological results that is highly questionable, given the epistemological and practical problems associated with the analysis of social structures in the archaeological record (see Burmeister 2000: 95–128). To argue, for instance, with the insurmountable differences between the allegedly highly stratified communities represented in the burial of Hochdorf, and societies where it is difficult to pick out any prestige material goods (as, for instance, the communities of early medieval Ireland that produced the literature usually used to interpret Iron Age societies), becomes an almost laughable overestimation of the possibilities of archaeological social analysis when one compares the results arrived at by Eggert (1988, 1991, 1999, and 2001: 329–38) or Burmeister (2000: 169–211) for the allegedly highly stratified communities of Hallstatt D in Württemberg and the results arrived at by analysing the Irish literature (seventh to tenth century AD) for the contemporary communities of early medieval Ireland (Charles-Edwards 1993, 2000; Jaski 2000; Kelly 1995; Patterson 1994). In such a comparison, the Irish society decidedly shows the much higher social complexity.

Even worse, as a logical consequence of the negation of any application of results beyond the strict confinements of any 'particular society' (Collis 1994: 32), however such a society might be defined and with evermore regional studies of local differences, which doubtless exist even between single neighbouring settlements, it follows that any explanatory possibilities for wide-ranging similarities other than in an *ad hoc* manner are lost. True, the old paradigm of a uniform, monolithic, genetically related, essential 'Celtic' culture is dead, and it is rightfully dead (see also Karl 2002b, 2003). But, as Andrew P. Fitzpatrick has put it:

> The importance of the correlation between an archaeological culture and a people in the interpretation of the 'Celts', and the weaknesses of it are evident. Consequently, it can be tempting to dismiss the correlation out of hand, but it should be clear: the ancient evidence *remains to be explained* rather than *explained away*. That evidence poses a fundamental question; 'why did peoples widely distributed across central and western Europe make material cultures which were different in some respects but essentially similar in others?'.
>
> (Fitzpatrick 1996: 246)

And, in fact, similarities that remain to be explained are not limited to the material culture but appear in many other kinds of sources that tell us about communities that, if we would take only the archaeological evidence into account, would seem fundamentally different from each other.

Are the Celts back?

So, what about these similarities? Are the Celts back? Yes and no, to a certain extent. I will try to show in two short case studies, based on the Viennese approach to Celtic studies (Karl 2002b), that, and why, it is necessary to use the full amount of available sources to gain a better understanding of Iron Age and early medieval 'Celtic' societies.

To start with, however, it has to be stated explicitly that the 'Celts' I will be talking about are neither uniform nor monolithic, nor unchanging nor essentially 'Celtic', and not at all one unified, common entity, related by one racial, genetic, religious, political, ethnic or any other genetic relationship and/or identity (Karl 2002b). They are doubtlessly considerably different from each other in many aspects, not least in material culture in numerous cases; but all the while they are also similar in many aspects, enough to necessitate the use of all sources to gain a better understanding of them (for a discussion of how such similarities develop, see Karl 2002a; 2003: 3–28). Thus, readers who dislike the term 'Celt' and its derivations are free to replace it by any other of their liking – for instance by a tongue-twister like *Cwehabimas* (central and western European Hallstatt to British and Irish Middle Ages societies) – it would not affect the interpretation.

'Testosterone-driven young men in fast vehicles'

A lot has been written on Iron Age chariots, and more than once have these vehicles been related to the chariots described in Irish literature – for instance in the arguments of Kenneth H. Jackson (1964), who thought of the earliest Irish tradition as a 'Window on the Iron Age' – a position that, in Irish literature studies, has long been discredited, and a biblical or classical origin of the chariots as described in Irish literature has been proposed (McCone 1990). Raftery (1994: 104–7) has cast doubt on the existence of chariots in Iron Age Ireland bearing any similarity to those of the European Iron Age, a position fitting well with the reconstruction of very basic 'carts' put forward by the linguist David Greene (1972) based on Irish texts. The existence of such chariots in the Irish early medieval period has not even remotely been considered. As such, the conclusion arrived at as yet by disciplinary separatism has been that no connection can be drawn between the high-status burials with chariots in Iron Age Europe and the vehicles described in Irish literature.

Yet, the term for the two-wheeled, high-status vehicle that was used by Celtic-speaking populations in almost all of ancient Europe and beyond (though it was put in the graves only in some regions), Latin *carpentum*, also attested in Gaulish as *carbanto*, is a clear cognate to *carpat*, the term for the vehicle used in the early Irish sources, with cognates in Welsh and Breton as well, derived from a Celtic **karbænto-* (Karl and Stifter 2002). That term

189

is not the only term for vehicles in the Irish texts; the term used consistently throughout the Old Irish literature for the 'ordinary' cart or wagon, i.e. the non-high-status transport, is OIr. *fén*, finding a cognate in Gaulish *benna*. As such, if the Irish never, neither in the Iron Age nor at any time later, had any of these high-status vehicles used at least by some of the continental and British peoples, and if they had another term that they consistently used for non-high-status transports, how come that the term they used in their medieval literature for the high-status transports is a cognate of the one used for the high-status transports in Iron Age Europe and Britain?

As I have explained elsewhere in greater detail (Karl and Stifter 2002; Karl forthcoming b), the different uses of chariots in the European Iron Age, as they can be reconstructed from archaeological, historical, numismatic and iconographic evidence, are as civil and military transports, with the warrior getting off the vehicle to join close combat afoot, for status representation, for sport and as death biers. That these vehicles are open to the front and the rear, and that both driver and passenger usually sit on them, are two additional characteristic features. An analysis of the Irish evidence, including not only the literature but also the archaeological record, the pseudo-historical annals, the Old Irish law texts and the iconographic record on Irish High Crosses, allows us to develop a similar model of attested uses of high-status chariots as they were depicted in early medieval Ireland. Perhaps surprisingly the two models thus developed are perfect matches, while neither of the proposed 'alternative' origins of the chariots in the Irish literature, the Greek epics or the Bible, allow us to create models that, even though partially overlapping with the above models, fit as well. As far as the evidence thus allows, not only are the Iron Age chariots and the chariots described in early Irish literature called by a similar name in the respective local languages, they are also used in very similar ways, by similarly high-status individuals. It thus is likely that the chariots described in the early Irish literature were vehicles closely related to those of the European Iron Age of the same name, still used in a similar fashion, by a group of people of relatively similar social status in Ireland in, or at least shortly before, the time when the texts were written – even though we have virtually no archaeological evidence for their existence (some wooden pieces from the seventh to tenth centuries AD Lough Faughan crannog could be chariot parts; see Collins 1956: 65–7, 70).

With this connection established it not only becomes possible to explain why the Old Irish used the same word for a very similar vehicle, but we can, by using the Iron Age archaeological record, also gain a better understanding of what the vehicles described in these texts actually looked like and how they functioned, thus allowing us to explain 'heroic feats' like jumping across fallen trees; this might actually be possible with a vehicle that has its platform set in a spring suspension (Furger-Gunti 1991, 1993; see also the 2002 Wetwang chariot reconstruction in the British Museum). On the other hand, the Irish texts allow us to gain many more insights into the terminology that might already have been used for Iron Age chariots. Even more importantly, there are quite a number of additional insights on chariot-related aspects of material and immaterial culture that can be gained by comparing Irish textual evidence with archaeological and historical sources for the European Iron Age, like the road network, road construction and upkeep, as I have discussed in greater detail in another study (Karl forthcoming c).

Touta, contrebia, druid, rix, or a short story of social similarities

One of the central arguments of Celtosceptics is that archaeology tells us that the different societies of the European Iron Age lived in many fundamentally different forms of social organization, ranging from almost completely unstratified groups living in decentralized local communities to highly stratified, urbanized societies (Collis 1994: 32; less specifically James 1999: 78–9). It is, however, a most questionable assumption that archaeology is at all able to provide us with a comprehensive picture of social organization based on this with sufficient certainty to exclude all other possible lines of inquiry out of hand; it is not even clear how any such 'society' is defined. (This is nowhere clearly expressed, and it is implicitly assumed that material culture allows us unquestionably to define different societies and to distinguish between them.) Is this assumption justified at all? Were social organizations in the west and central European Iron Age really that fundamentally different from one another as we are expected to believe?

Again, it is worth while examining a few similarities in non-archaeological sources. Strabo (*Geographika* 4.4.4) informs us that 'the Celts' held some men in special honour, the bards, the vates and the druids ('. . . Βάρδοι τε καὶ Οὐάτεις καὶ Δρυΐδαι . . .'). Of course, it is well known that the cognates to the above terms, OIr. *druïd*, *fáithi* and *báird* (Birkhan 1997: 896) are widely used in the early Irish sources, and that the roles of *dryw* and *bardd* appear in the early Welsh sources as well, cognate terms yet again being known from many Celtic languages (Holder 1896: 347–8, 1321–30). It will hardly come as a surprise that the druids in all cases are depicted as some sort of priest/magician/prophet, and that they are seen as having been held in especially high regard in descriptions of both Gaulish and early Irish society, even though it is clear from the Irish law texts that they had been reduced to mere wizards in the times the texts were actually written. Nonetheless, in the monks' paintings of the Irish past, the druids feature in a role that is very close to that described for the same class of people in the ancient sources. Similar observations apply to the bards, described as singers of praise by Strabo, which fulfil precisely the same function in both Irish and Welsh literature as ascribed to them in classical sources. Of course, this could, theoretically, have been knowledge imported by educated Christian monks, who knew Caesar and the other classical authors and simply applied what these had written to an Irish and Welsh context. But, on the other hand, this does not solve the question as to why they used indigenous terms, rather than loanwords from Latin or Greek, to describe these functions, terms specific enough that they should not have existed had these societies no such social functions; nor does it explain why these monks should have done so in the first place, if, as Celtosceptics have correctly observed (e.g. Collis 1994: 32; James 1999: 43–66), no one living in the British Isles ever self-identified as a Celt before the seventeenth century AD. If we do not want to resort to simple *ad hoc* explanations and believe in an almost incredible coincidence, the best explanation is that these functions existed in both societies in roughly similar form.

The Celts, obviously, were anything but a monolithic bloc existing in isolation: while some elements of social organization are not attested outside what is traditionally considered to be part of the Celtic world (e.g. the bards and druids), they shared other elements and the terminology to describe them with neighbouring societies in central Europe and even central Italy, as I will show in the following paragraphs. It might be unnecessary, but nonetheless worth while, to mention that the term for 'king', as in Gaulish *rix*, as well as their 'female counterpart', *rigani*, yet again finds cognates in other Celtic languages, as in OIr. *rí* and *rígan*, Welsh *rhî* and *rhiain*, MCorn. *ruy*, *ruif*, and well beyond them, the most prominent probably being Latin *rex* and *regina* (Holder 1904: 1185, 1197–8). Germanic **rikos* (as in Gothic *reiks*, Old Norse *ríkr*, OHGerm. *rîh*, *rîch* and Frankish *-ricus*) is an early loan from Celtic, before the first German sound shift, probably in or before the fourth century BC (Holder 1904: 1197). All these terms refer to the ruler of a socio-political unit, or to a unit led by such a ruler. I assume we can basically agree that the terms mentioned as yet are those for social roles, for some kind of professional specialization on the one hand and social hierarchy on the other.

Given that social structures develop through individual interaction, starting (for the individual) in his immediate individual social environment (Karl 2003: 3–23, 54), and that individual behaviour is structured by the habitus (Bourdieu 1977: 78–87) resulting in self-similar social expressions, it might also seem relevant that quite a number of terms that relate to this immediate social environment exist – as for instance in Gaulish *cenetl*, which has its cognates in OCymr. *cenedl*, OIr. *cenél*, OCorn. *kinethel*, OBret. *chenetdl* (Vendryes 1987: C 64) – for the biological descendants of a common ancestor. These terms describe more or less the same kind of group (even though the terms in non-Celtic languages are not cognates of the Celtic terms) as Greek γένος, Latin *gens* and OGerm. *kindi-* (Pokorny 1994: 374). Similarly, the terms for the settlement unit are quite similar, Gaulish *trebâ* (Holder 1904: 1908–9) having cognates in OCymr. *tref*, OIr. *treb*, Corn. *tre*, OBret. *treb*, also found in OGerm. *þorpa-*, Old Norse *þorp*, 'small farm', OEngl. *þorp*, 'small village' and OHGerm. *dorf*, 'village' (Holder 1904: 1909), as well as

Latin *tribus*, 'settlement community, extended descent group' (Benveniste 1969: 293–319). Similar is true for the terminology for larger communities consisting of several such settlement units, as attested in Celtiberian *Contrebia* 'dwelling together, community' (Holder 1896: 1109–11), with cognates in Ir. *coitreb*, 'community', and Corn. *kentrevak*, 'neighbour' (Holder 1896: 1109–11; Vendryes 1978: T 126–8), and maybe also OCymr., *cantref*, usually explained as 'hundred settlements'; to the latter also OIr. *cét treb*, 'hundred settlements'. Similar forms can be found in *Atrebates* (from Gaul. *ad-treba*, 'dwelling together') and *Ambitrebius* (Holder 1896: 1109). Hardly surprisingly any more, the land inhabited by the Boii in the Gallia Cisalpina was subdivided into 112 *tribus* according to Pliny (*HN* 3.116), which might well have been either such *trebia* or *contrebia*, small districts similar to the Welsh *cantrefydd* (Birkhan 1997: 95).

Even more widely distributed is the term for the (independent) socio-political group, Gaulish *toutâ*, which has cognates in OIr. *túath*, OCymr. *tut*, MBret. *tut, tud* (Holder 1904: 1804–19, 1896–1900), which also appears in Sabinian *touta, tôta*, Umbrian *tûtu*, Oskian *tauta*, OGerm. *þeuðo*, Gothic *þiuda*, Old Norse *þíoð*, OEngl. *ðéod,* Old Saxon *thiod, thioda*, OHGerm. *diot, diota* and Old Prussian *tauta*, all of them meaning 'people', still present in the modern German ethnonym '*Deutsche*' (from OHGerm. *diutisc*, 'belonging to the people'; Holder 1904: 1804–5). This term is closely similar in meaning to Greek *ethnos* or *poleîs*, and Latin *civitas* – the latter term the one used consequently by Caesar to describe the socio-political groups in which his enemies in Gaul were organized. There even seems to have been a widely used term for 'rulers' of such a *toutâ,* being *toutiorix* (Holder 1904: 1897), mirrored in such terms as OIr. *ri túaithe* and *rí túath*, and OCymr. *tudri*, OBret. *tuder*, but also in Welsh *Tudor*, like the royal dynasty, and OGerm. **þiuðarîk-*, as in the name of the famous king of the Goths, Teodericus. Given all this, it is hardly surprising that the probably first-century BC Celtiberian inscription of Botorrita IV (= Contrebia Belaisca) starts with the words: *} tam : tirikantam : entorkue : toutam {|} : sua kombal{ke}z : . . .* (Villar *et al.* 2001: 75, 83), which has lately been argued as being an equivalent formation to a Greek and Roman phrase that could be translated as 'The senate and the people have decided . . .' (Stifter 1996: 100–4).

One might explain all of this as pure coincidence, because people spoke similar – even though mutually unintelligible – languages, and that all those different peoples living across half of Europe just happened to call totally unrelated, fundamentally different social structures and forms of social organizations by very similar names for no apparent reason at all. But given James's (1999: 67) claim that 'other people's own views of their identity and affiliations should be given prominence' rather than speaking about them in outsider's terms, one should at least consider if it would not be worth taking a look at the linguistic evidence and, rather than talking about the various 'ethnic groups' in Iron Age Britain and Ireland, take the term the Iron Age

British and Irish would most likely have used for their own societies – *toutâ*. As all necessary information to do so is easily available, James's own unwillingness to find this easily recoverable terminology makes his claims rather seem as a hypocritical lip-service to a fashionable paradigm, in an attempt to sell us a very specific way of looking at archaeological sources, than as real interest in the peoples concerned.

But let us stay with the *toutâ*. The Irish early medieval archaeological record shows us a society approximately as decentralized as that of the Middle Iron Age in the British Pennines. What do the Irish sources tell us about such a *túath*? Well, first and foremost it might be worth mentioning that throughout the seventh to tenth centuries AD Ireland was inhabited by about a hundred of them at any time, and each of them was expected to have, besides its king, poets, justices and priests. Each *túath* had what the Irish called *nemed* people ('privileged, holy', also found in *nemeton*, the Gaulish term for sanctuary), to which the said persons, the 'secular' nobility (OIr. *flaith*, 'lord, noble') and several expert craftsmen like the master wright (OIr. *ollam suad saírsi*) belonged, and ordinary freemen (OIr. *grád féne* or *aithech*), ordinary farmers, less respected craftsmen as well as simple musicians, and various grades of half-free and unfree persons (Kelly 1995: 3–98). Current estimates assign an average of about 3,000 persons to each such *túath* (Kelly 1995: 4); estimations for contemporary ruling kings based on the Irish annals range from 80 (MacNeill 1935: 96) to about 150 (Byrne 2001: 7) at any given time between the fifth and twelfth centuries AD. But what about those famous Irish High Kings? While social organization of up to *túath* level was relatively localized and stable, beyond that political organization included at least two more 'levels' of kings (at least at theoretical level), the *rí túath* or *ruiri*, king of several *túatha*, and above that the *rí cóicid* or *rí ruirech*, the 'king over great kings' (Kelly 1995: 16). It is only at this level of organization that military power, diplomatic ability and thus overall political success led to larger political units, that were, for the greater part, much less stable than the localized *túatha* but could become as large as to consist of half or more of the island of Ireland, and were under the control of a single king like Brían Bóruma or at least a single royal dynasty like the Uí Néill or the Eóganacht (Byrne 2001; Charles-Edwards 2000; Jaski 2000).

Of course, this does not necessarily explain quite similar shifting patterns in, for instance, Gaulish societies of the Late Iron Age, but it definitely fits well with such 'confederations' as the *Regnum Noricum* obviously was with its at least twelve main 'subgroups' (Dobesch 1980: 177–280), and easily explains such phenomena as the independent actions of parts of greater *civitates*, like Caesar describes for the Tigurini, one of the four *pagi* of the Helvetii (*B. Gall.* 1.12.4–6), deployment of military units based on to which *pagus* they belong (*B. Gall.* 7.19.2), kings of parts of *civitates* as Catuvolcus of the Eburones (*B. Gall.* 6.31.5), the frequent exchange of hostages as sureties for treaties (numerous examples in *B. Gall.*; compare Kelly 1995: 167–76), combined military actions at levels above the *civitates* under the rule of a single leader, like that of the Belgae (*B. Gall.* 2.4) or of all Gaul under the leadership of Vercingetorix (*B. Gall.* 7), and the penultimate struggle between various Gaulish nobles for what seemingly was one of the highest goals a Gaulish noble could dream of, the *principatus totius Galliae* (again numerous references in Caes., *B. Gall.*), the latter struggle almost perfectly mirroring the constant and almost never successful struggles of Irish early medieval kings for the High Kingship of Ireland (Byrne 2001; Charles-Edwards 2000; Jaski 2000).

That all of these examples are mere coincidences seems hardly likely, especially given that it is only a small fraction of the total evidence (for a more extensive treatment, see Karl 2003). People living across most of northwestern Europe used similar terms for several specialized social professions, for a ruling elite, for their kin, the community in which they actually lived, for larger communities at organizational level, and for the ruler of the sociopolitical unit and the unit in which they lived, terms in Celtic languages partially overlapping with terms used by other peoples speaking related, but less similar languages further abroad. Of course, all the societies that used these terms might still have had fundamentally different social systems. But, given all these similarities, how likely is that?

It is rather more likely that all, or at least almost all, of these societies were actually using very similar building blocks to create their social systems, blocks like *bardd*, *druid* and *rix* as social functions, and *cenetl*, *trebâ*, *contrebâ* and *toutâ* as social groups, and thus their social systems ended up as relatively similar. Of course, these systems still may have differed considerably in their size, number of members and level of complexity, hierarchy and heterarchy, depending on differing necessities arising from population numbers and settlement density, on resource availability, the location of main routes for travel and trade and whether they went close by or were far off, political and military success of individual leaders or influence groups, and plenty of other factors. But that they were so totally and fundamentally different that looking at the much wider but hardly better described ethnographic record, a record telling us of totally unrelated societies to those in question, should seem to be more promising than to look at the 'two or three "Celtic" societies handed down to us', that 'African analogies may well be as relevant, perhaps more relevant, than the Irish sources of a millennium later', as Collis (1994: 31) suspects, can only be attributed to total ignorance of the available evidence and an even greater unwillingness to enter into any serious debate with disciplines other than archaeology.

Conclusions

The Celts, as a uniform, monolithic, unchanging people, as a '*Volk*' in the sense that Kossinna (1911) or the Nazis would have used it, are dead.

Whether this is thanks to Celtoscepticism or not, the Celtosceptics at least can claim the credit that they made this very evident in British archaeology. But beyond that point, the paradigm that underlies most Celtosceptic arguments is highly questionable. Especially problematic is the disregard with which Celtosceptics treat non-archaeological sources. The utter conviction that we archaeologists know, better than anyone else, how things really were back then, that 'the ancient author's understanding of how societies functioned, their knowledge is limited in comparison to our own, and cannot be used as a basis from which we can work' (Collis 1994: 32), that 'linguistics . . . still clings to established ideas . . . which are actually based on earlier cultural assumptions embedded in scholarship' (James 1999: 82) is ridiculous and demonstrates almost incredible disciplinary arrogance due to ignorance, not to our much better knowledge or understanding.

In fact, if I had to choose between Caesar's (*B. Gall.* 6.11–20) description of the developed urbanized societies of Gaul, James's (1999: 78–9; 87–100) description of the decentralized societies of the British and Irish Iron Age or the general theoretical models that Collis (1994: 32) would have us use, I would opt for Caesar, as his description is not only much more detailed than those of James and Collis but also incredibly more accurate – even though Caesar did not intend to write a sociological study.

As yet, Celtosceptics have provided us with little if any advances in our understanding of societies in the European past, and their ignorance of, and dislike of the use of, any sources other than those that comply with their very limited paradigm make it unlikely that they will ever be able to do so. As Olivier Büchsenschütz has argued:

> The use of broad-brush models, such as 'central place' or 'chiefdom' or 'archaic state' . . . is inappropriate for the delineation of European societies between 500 BC and 1000 AD. To apply the latest sociological theory to societies which are known not only from archaeology, but also from textual sources, their coinage and so on, may in the end allow that theory to be evaluated; but it does not help us in our knowledge of the period. The solution will rather be provided by juxtaposing the evidence obtained from different kinds of sources (archaeological, literary, and numismatic) . . . More ambitious questions need to be tailored to take account of the nature and quantity of the data available, and of the complexity of the problems that require to be dealt with.
>
> (Büchsenschütz 1995: 63)

To knock down the 'common ancient Celt' may have been valuable from a political point of view as an attack at modern nationalist self-identities, on identities that have been modelled upon the old idea of one language, one culture, one nation, one people, unchanging in time and with an age-old claim to land, world-domination or whatever else (given the time at which Celtoscepticism emerged in force, it might even have been nothing more than devolution), that have carried the most horrible atrocities in their wake in the past, and might well do so in the future again, and as such, we should be thankful to the Celtosceptics for trying to educate us and our society about its dangers. But for improving our understanding of societies of central and western Europe between the Iron Age and the early medieval period it is a complete failure. As such, it seems little more than a convenient excuse to ignore non-archaeological evidence.

Abbreviations

Corn.	=	Cornish
Gaul.	=	Gaulish
Ir.	=	Irish
MBret.	=	Middle Breton
MCorn.	=	Middle Cornish
OBret.	=	Old Breton
OCorn.	=	Old Cornish
OCymr.	=	Old Cymric (Welsh)
OEngl.	=	Old English
OGerm.	=	Old German
OHGerm.	=	Old High German
OIr.	=	Old Irish

Bibliography

Benveniste, É. (1969) *Le vocabulaire des institutions indo-européennes. 1. économie, parenté, société, 2, pouvoir, droit, religion*, Paris: Editions Errance.

Birkhan, H. (1997) *Kelten. Versuch einer Gesamtdarstellung ihrer Kultur*, Vienna: Verlag der österreichischen Akademie der Wissenschaften.

Bourdieu, P. (1977) *Outline of a Theory of Practice*, Cambridge Studies in Social Anthropology, 16, Cambridge: Cambridge University Press.

Büchsenschütz, O. (1995) 'The significance of major settlements in European Iron Age society', in B. Arnold and D.B. Gibson (eds) *Celtic Chiefdom, Celtic State. The evolution of complex social systems in prehistoric Europe*, Cambridge: Cambridge University Press, 53–63.

Burmeister, S. (2000) *Geschlecht, Alter und Herrschaft in der Späthallstattzeit Württembergs*, Tübinger Schriften zur ur- und frühgeschichtlichen Archäologie, 4, Münster: Waxmann Verlag.

Byrne, F.J. (2001) *Irish Kings and High-Kings* (2nd edn), London: Four Courts Press.

Chapman, M. (1992) *The Celts. The construction of a myth*, London and New York: Macmillan.

Charles-Edwards, T. (1993) *Early Irish and Welsh Kinship*, Oxford: Oxford University Press.

—— (2000) *Early Christian Ireland*, Cambridge: Cambridge University Press.

Collins, A.E.P. (1956) 'Excavations in Lough Faughan Crannog, Co. Down, 1951–52', *Ulster Journal of Archaeology*, 3rd Ser., 18: 45–73.

Collis, J.R. (1994) 'Reconstructing Iron Age society', in K. Kristiansen and J. Jensen (eds) *Europe in the First Millennium B.C.*, Sheffield Archaeological Monographs, 6, Sheffield: Collis, 31–9.

—— (1996) 'Celts and politics', in P. Graves-Brown, S. Jones and C. Gamble (eds) *Cultural Identity and Archaeology. The construction of European communities*, London and New York: Routledge, 167–78.

—— (1997a) 'The origin and spread of the Celts', *Studia Celtica*, 30: 17–34.

—— (1997b) 'Celtic myths', *Antiquity*, 71: 195–201.

—— (1999a) 'George Buchanan and the Celts of Britain', in R. Black, W. Gillies and R.Ó. Maolalaigh (eds) *Celtic Connections*, Vol. 1. *Proceedings of the Tenth International Congress of Celtic Studies*, East Lindon: Tuckwell, 91–107.

—— (1999b) 'Los Celtas Antiguos y Modernos', in J.A. Arenas Esteban and V. Palacios Tamayo (eds) *El Origen del Mundo Celtibérico. Actas de los encuentros sobre el origen del mundo Celtibérico* (Molina de Aragón, 1–3 de Octubre de 1998), Molina de Aragón: Gráficas Minaya, S.A., 13–17.

Cunliffe, B. (1984) *Danebury: An Iron Age hillfort in Hampshire, 2: The finds*, London: CBA Research Report, 52.

Dobesch, G. (1980) *Die Kelten in Österreich nach den ältesten Berichten der Antike. Das norische Königreich und seine Beziehungen zu Rom im 2. Jahrhundert v. Chr.*, Vienna: Böhlau Verlag.

Eggert, M.K.H. (1988) 'Riesentumuli und Sozialorganisation: Vergleichende Betrachtungen zu den sogenannten "Fürstengrabhügeln" der Späten Hallstattzeit', *Archäologisches Korrespondenzblatt*, 18: 263–74.

—— (1991) 'Prestigegüter und Sozialstruktur in der Späthallstattzeit: Eine kulturanthropologische Perspektive', *Saeculum*, 42(1) (= *Urgeschichte als Kulturanthropologie. Beiträge zum 70. Geburtstag von Karl J. Narr*, Teil, 2): 1–28.

—— (1999) 'Der Tote von Hochdorf: Bemerkungen zum Modus archäologischer Interpretation', *Archäologisches Korrespondenzblatt*, 29: 211–22.

—— (2001) *Prähistorische Archäologie. Konzepte und Methoden*, Tübingen and Basle: Francke Verlag.

Fitzpatrick, A.P. (1996) '"Celtic" Iron Age Europe: the theoretical basis', in P. Graves-Brown, S. Jones and C. Gamble (eds) *Cultural Identity and Archaeology. The construction of European communities*, London and New York: Routledge, 238–55.

Furger-Gunti, A. (1991) 'The Celtic war chariot', in S. Moscati, O.H. Frey, V. Kruta, B. Raftery and M. Szabó (eds) *The Celts*, Milan: Bompiniani, 356–9.

—— (1993) 'Der keltische Streitwagen im Experiment. Nachbau eines essedum im Schweizerischen Landesmuseum', *Zeitschrift schweizerische Archäologie und Kunstgeschichte*, 50/3: 213–22.

Graves-Brown, P., Jones, S. and Gamble, C. (eds) (1996) *Cultural Identity and Archaeology. The construction of European communities*, London and New York: Routledge.

Greene, D. (1972) 'The chariot as described in Irish literature', in C. Thomas (ed.) *The Iron Age in the Irish Sea Province*, London: CBA Research Report, 9: 59–73.

Holder, A. (1896) *Alt-celtischer Sprachschatz*, I. Band A–H, Leipzig: Teubner Verlag.

—— (1904) *Alt-celtischer Sprachschatz*, II. Band I–T, Leipzig: Teubner Verlag.

Jackson, K.H. (1964) *The Oldest Irish Tradition: A window on the Iron Age*, Cambridge: Cambridge University Press.

James, S. (1999) *The Atlantic Celts. Ancient people or modern invention?*, London: British Museum Press.

Jaski, B. (2000) *Early Irish Kingship and Succession*, Dublin: Four Courts Press.

Jones, S. (1997) *The Archaeology of Ethnicity. Constructing identities in the past and present*, London and New York: Routledge.

Karl, R. (2002a) 'Cognitive constructs, self-similarity and the problem of archaeological multiculturalism', in C. Witt (ed.) *Archaeological Multiculturalism. Papers presented to the EAA 2001 in Esslingen, Germany*, Oxford: BAR Int. Ser.

—— (2002b) 'Erwachen aus dem langen Schlaf der Theorie? Ansätze zu einer keltologischen Wissenschaftstheorie', in E. Poppe (ed.) *Keltologie heute. Themen und Fragestellungen. Akten des 3. Deutschen Keltologensymposiums – Marburg, März 2001*, Studien und Texte zur Keltologie 5, Münster: Nodus Verlag, 291–303, 2003.

—— (2002c) *Altkeltische Sozialstrukturen anhand archäologischer, historischer und literarischer Quellen*, ÖAB-Verlag, Vienna.

—— (forthcoming a) 'Die Kelten gab es nie! Sinn und Unsinn des Kulturbegriffs in Archäologie und Keltologie', in R. Karl (ed.) *Archäologische Theorie in Österreich – eine Standortbestimmung*, ÖAB-Verlag, Vienna.

—— (forthcoming b) 'Iron Age chariots and medieval texts. The necessity to break down disciplinary boundaries', in *eKeltoi*, http://www.uwm.edu/Dept/celtic/ekeltoi (online journal of the University of Minnesota Centre for Celtic Studies).

—— (forthcoming c) 'Achtung Gegenverkehr! Straßenbau, Straßenerhaltung, Straßenverkehrsordnung und Straßenstationen in der eisenzeitlichen Keltiké', in J.K. Koch, R. Rolle, U. Küster (eds) *Reiten und Fahren in der Vor- und Frühgeschichte*, Hamburger Werkstattreihe zur Archäologie, 7.

Karl, R. and Stifter, D. (2002) 'Carpat – carpentum. Die keltischen Grundlagen des "Streit"wagens der irischen Sagentradition', in A. Eibner, R. Karl, J. Leskovar, K. Löcker and C. Zingerle (eds) *Pferd und Wagen in der Eisenzeit*, Wiener keltologische Schriften, 2, Vienna.

Kelly, F. (1995) *A Guide to Early Irish Law. Early Irish Law Series*, 3 (3rd edn), Dublin: Dublin Institute for Advanced Studies.

Kossinna, G. (1911) *Die Herkunft der Germanen. Zur Methode der Siedlungsarchäologie*, Mannus-Bibliothek, 6, Leipzig: Mannus Verlag.

McCone, K.R. (1990) *Pagan Past and Christian Present in Early Irish Literature*, Maynooth Monographs, 3, Maynooth.

MacNeill, E. (1935) *Early Irish Laws and Institutions*, London.

Patterson, N. (1994) *Cattle-lords and Clansmen. The social structure of early Ireland* (2nd edn), Notre Dame and London: University of Notre Dame Press.

Pokorny, J. (1994) *Indogermanisches etymologisches Wörterbuch* (3rd edn), Tübingen and Basle: Francke Verlag.

Raftery, B. (1994) *Pagan Celtic Ireland. The enigma of the Irish Iron Age*, London: Thames and Hudson.

Stifter, D. (1996) 'Neues vom Keltiberischen: Notizen zu Botorrita IV', *Die Sprache*, 38/3 [2001] = *Chronicalia Indoeuropaea*, 38: 91–112.

Vendryes, J. (1978) *Lexique étymologique de l'irlandais ancien*, T U, par les soins de E. Bachellery et P.-Y. Lambert, Dublin and Paris: Dublin Institute for Advanced Studies.

—— (1987) *Lexique étymologique de l'irlandais ancien*, C par les soins de E. Bachellery et P.-Y. Lambert, Dublin and Paris: Dublin Institute for Advanced Studies.

Villar, F., Díaz Sanz, M.A., Medrano Margués, M.M. and Jordán Cólera, C. (2001) *El IV Bronce de Botorrita (Contrebia Belaisca)*: Arqueología y Lingüística, Acta salmanticensia, Estudios filológicos, 286.

INDEX

Page numbers in *italics* refer to illustrations